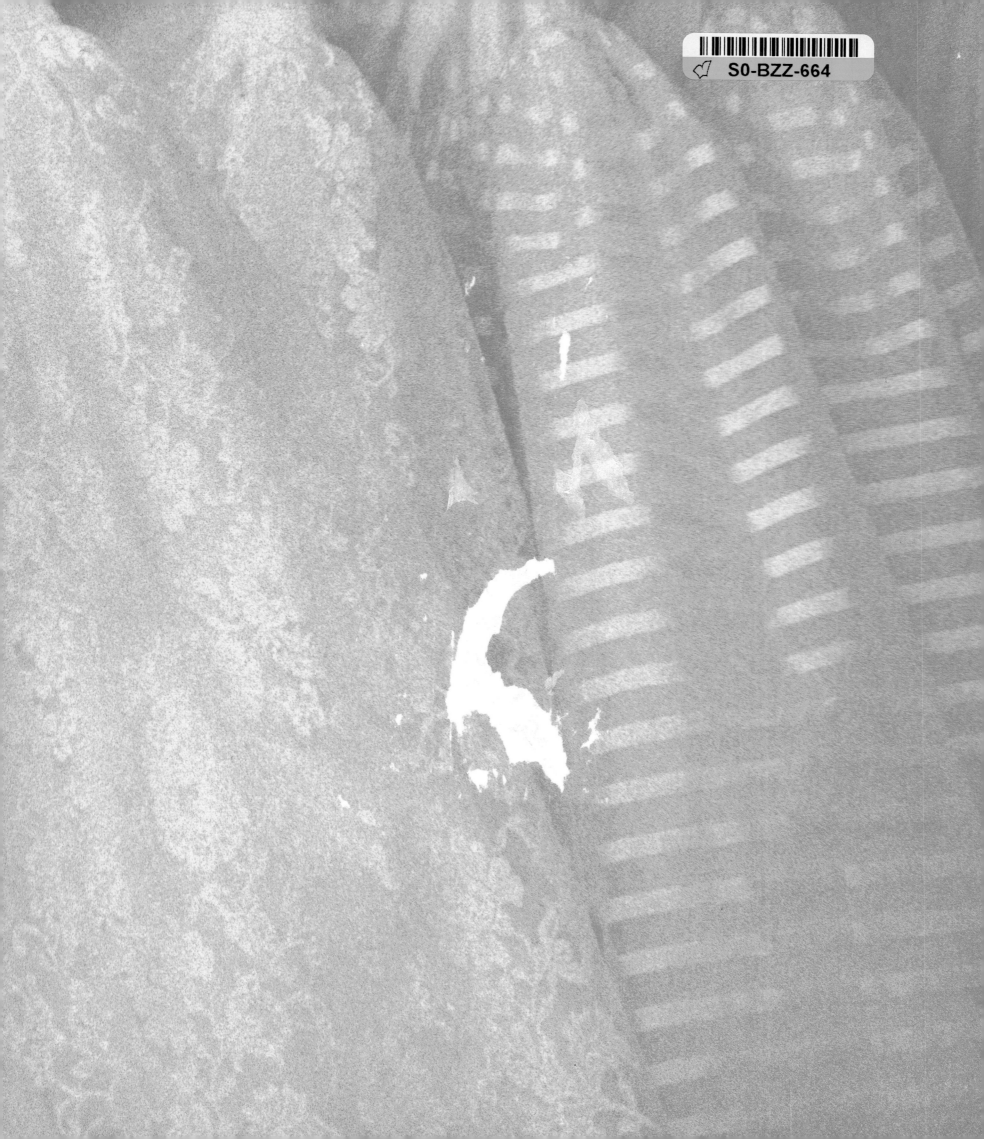

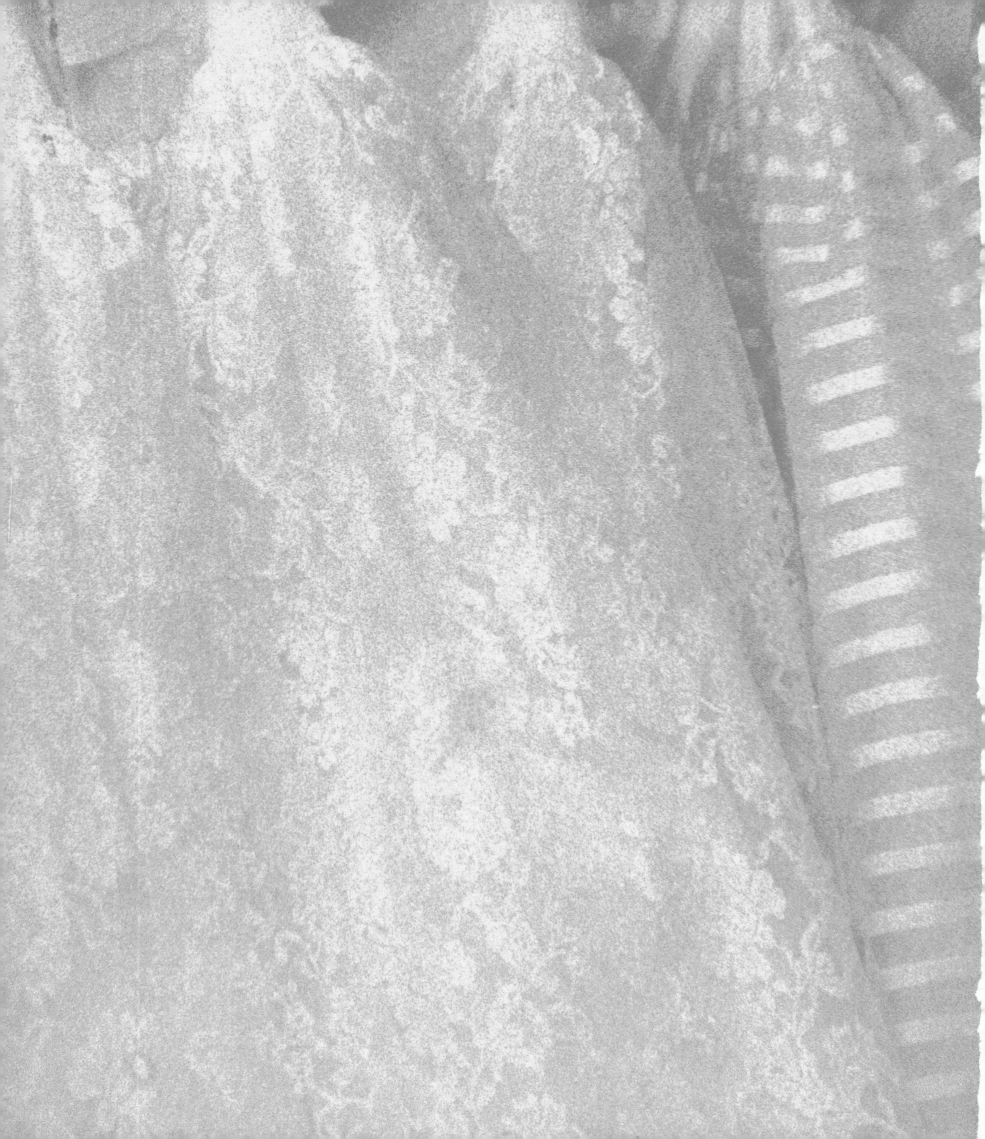

THE

WEDDING

DRESS

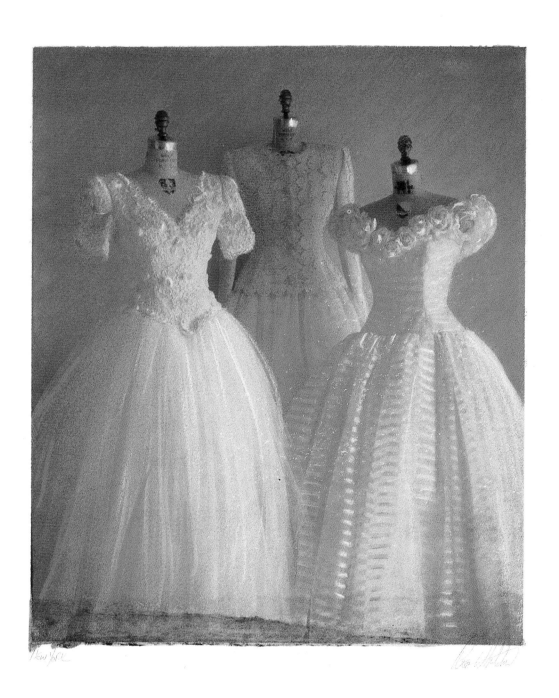

New York

THE

WEDDING

DRESS

Maria McBride-Mellinger

Foreword by Barbara Tober, Editor-in-Chief, *Brides & Your New Home*

Random House, New York

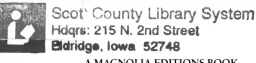
A MAGNOLIA EDITIONS BOOK

Library of Congress Cataloging-in-Publication Data

McBride-Mellinger, Maria.
    The wedding dress / Maria McBride Mellinger.
      p.   cm.
    Includes bibliographical references and index.
    ISBN 0-679-41884-9
    1. Wedding costume.   I. Title.
    GT1752.M33 1993
    392'.54--dc20   93-17435

THE WEDDING DRESS
was prepared and produced by
Magnolia Editions, Ltd.
15 West 26 Street
New York, New York 10010

Editor: Sharyn Rosart
Art Director: Jeff Batzli
Designer: Tanya Ross-Hughes
Photography Editors: Jennifer Crowe McMichael, Anne K. Price, Amla Sanghui
Production Director: Karen Matsu Greenberg

ADDITIONAL PHOTOGRAPHY CREDITS

Typeset by Classic Type, Inc.
Manufactured in Italy.

98765432   24689753   23456789

First Edition

The author and publisher would like to thank the following suppliers for generously providing the gowns and accessories featured in the photography listed below:

Cover: gown, Richard Glasgow; veil, Debora Jackson; gloves, Fownes Brothers. **Back cover**: gown, Richard Glasgow; veiling, La Sposa Veils. **Title page**: gowns, Richard Glasgow. **P. 6**: gown, Ronald Mann for Victoria Royal; gloves, Carolina Amato; shoes, Peter Fox; jewelry, Roxanne Assoulin; hair and makeup, Mel Rau; location, State Suite at The Plaza Hotel, New York City. **P. 7**: Left photo, shawl, Jean Hoffman/Jana Starr Antiques; jewelry, Roxanne Assoulin; shoes, Stuart Weitzman; hair and makeup, Betsy Lyn; location, The Plaza Hotel, New York City. Right photo, gloves, Carolina Amato; hair and makeup, Patricia Bowden; location, The Pierre Hotel, New York City. **P. 8**: gown, Bob Mackie; earrings, Kenneth Jay Lane; gloves, Shalimar; hair and makeup, Patricia Bowden; veiling, La Sposa Veils. **P. 13**: headpiece, La Sposa Veils; necklace, Kenneth Jay Lane; earrings, Cultured Pearl Association of America; hair and makeup, Betsy Lyn; location, State Suite at The Plaza Hotel, New York City. **P. 19**: shawl, Jean Hoffman/Jana Starr Antiques; jewelry, Roxanne Assoulin; location, The Plaza Hotel, New York City; hair and makeup, Betsy Lyn. **P. 43**: Earrings, Roxanne Assoulin; location, The State Suite at The Plaza Hotel, New York City; jewelry, Kenneth Jay Lane; gloves, Shalimar; veiling, La Sposa Veils; hair and makeup, Patricia Bowden. **P. 46**: her shoes, Stuart Weitzman; his tuxedo, Lord West; his shoes, Johnston & Murphy; hair and makeup, Betsy Lyn. **P. 52**: Earrings, Cultured Pearl Association of America; hair and makeup, Mara Schiavetti. **P. 54**: Handbag, Paloma Picasso; headband, La Sposa Veils; gloves, Shalimar; location, The Plaza Hotel, New York City; hair and makeup, Mel Rau. **P. 57**: Cashmere sweaters, Cashmere-Cashmere; porcelain bouquet, Miho Kofuda;

jewelry, Cultured Pearl Association of America; hair and makeup, Mel Rau; location, The Plaza Hotel, New York City. **P. 58**: Fabrics, B & J Fabrics; antique buckle, Jean Hoffman/Jana Starr Antiques. **P. 60**: Straw beret, Patricia Underwood; earrings, Roxanne Assoulin; hair and makeup, Betsy Lyn. **P. 62**: Pincushion, Suzanne Spellan; antique hat pins, Jean Hoffman/Jana Starr Antiques; fabric, B & J Fabrics. **P. 63**: Right, fabrics, B & J Fabrics; buttons, La Sposa Veils; antique tongs, Jean Hoffman/Jana Starr Antiques. **P. 67**: Fabrics, B & J Fabrics; antique rhinestone buttons and ivory earrings, Jean Hoffman/Jana Starr Antiques; gilt napkin rings, Colette Malouf. **P. 74**: Earrings, Carolina Herrera; shoes, Peter Fox; hair and makeup, Patricia Bowden. **P. 79**: Headpiece, La Sposa Veils; necklace, Kenneth Jay Lane; earrings, Cultured Pearl Association of America; hair and makeup, Betsy Lyn. **P. 84**: Tophat, Patricia Underwood; luggage, Jean Hoffman/Jana Starr Antiques; shoes, Peter Fox; location, The Plaza Hotel, New York City. **P. 93**: Miniature bouquet, Blue Meadow Flowers; earrings, Kenneth Jay Lane; fabric, B & J Fabrics; ribbon, Midori. **P. 95**: Jewelry, Roxanne Assoulin; shawl, Jean Hoffman/Jana Starr Antiques; location, The Plaza Hotel, New York City; hair and makeup, Betsy Lyn. **P. 103**: Beret, Patricia Underwood; jewelry, Roxanne Assoulin; location, The Plaza Hotel, New York City. **P. 105**: Location and hats, Lola's Millinery; jewelry, Kenneth Jay Lane; shoes, Dyeables; gloves, Carolina Amato; hair and makeup, Mel Rau. **P. 106**: Jewelry, Mish; veil, Debora Jackson; location, State Suite at The Plaza Hotel, New York City; hair and makeup, Betsy Lyn. **P. 109**: Jewelry, Cultured Pearl Association of America; flowers, Valorie Hart; hair and makeup, Mara Schiavetti. **P. 112**: Mongolian fur hat, Patricia Underwood; gloves, Shalimar; location, Nick and Eddie Restaurant, New York City; hair and makeup, Mel Rau. **P. 116**: Location, The Pierre Hotel; gloves, Carolina Amato; hair and makeup, Patricia Bowden. **P. 125**: Both photos, location, Kleinfeld;

hair and makeup, Clentera English. **P. 130, 131**: Location, Kleinfeld; hair and makeup, Clentera English. **P. 136**: hair and makeup, Betsy Lyn. **P. 137**: Flowers, Leslie Ferrar. **P. 138**: Veil, La Sposa Veils; necklace, Lisa Marinucci; bra, Jezebel; hair and makeup, Mel Rau. **P. 140**: Top, location, The Pierre Hotel, New York City; hair and makeup, Mara Schiavetti. Bottom, shoes, Peter Fox; garter, Angel Threads; petticoat, Cross & Spellan. **P. 141**: Jewelry, Karl Lagerfeld Bijoux, Kenneth Jay Lane, Carolina Herrera, and Gitano Fazio. **P. 142**: Top to bottom, glove, Shaneen Huxham at Showroom Seven; headband, La Sposa Veils; pearl circlet, La Sposa Veils; large pearl headband, Patricia Underwood; veil, La Sposa Veils; fabric, B & J Fabrics. **P. 143**: Location, State Suite at The Plaza Hotel, New York City; handbag, Paloma Picasso; necklace, Carolina Herrera; gloves, Andrea Jovine; sequin stole, Norma Kamali. **P. 144**: Bottom, pearl choker, Roxanne Assoulin; pearl-studded handbags, Judith Leiber; pearl and rhinestone shoe, Stuart Weitzman. Top, flowers, L. Becker; shoes, Stuart Weitzman; gown, Carolyne Roehm. **P. 147**: Necklace, Kenneth Jay Lane; location, The Pierre Hotel, New York City; earrings, Carolina Herrera; hosiery, Hanes; shoes, Peter Fox; hair and makeup, Mara Schiavetti. **P. 148**: top, ostrich plume hat, Robert Legere for The Diamond Collection; lingerie, Only Hearts; location, The Pierre Hotel, New York City; hair and makeup, Mara Schiavetti. **P. 148**, bottom, and **p. 149**: Location, The Pierre Hotel, New York City; earrings, Carolina Herrera; hosiery, Hanes; shoes, Peter Fox; hair and makeup, Mara Schiavetti. **P. 152**: Veil, Debbie Jackson; jewelry, Karl Lagerfeld Bijoux; shoes, Dyeables; hair and makeup, Mel Rau. **P. 154**: Sequin stole, Norma Kamali; her shoes, Dyeables; men's jackets, North Beach Leather; luggage, La Maison Moderne; wedding cake, Gail Watson Custom Cakes; tuxedo trousers and shirts, Lord West.

DEDICATION

To my mother and father, wed on a perfect June day. And to my own sweet groom, Brett.

ACKNOWLEDGEMENTS

Without the help of family, friends, and associates, I could never have completed this book with my sanity intact. This page is an acknowledgement and this wonderful book is a tribute to the talents of dozens. A wise mentor once clued me into a basic truth: you're only as good as the team that supports you. Today, as this last page of the book is composed, I am reminded of the sagacity of my mentor.

The conception of The Wedding Dress rests with Caryn Malitzky, who first recognized the merit and potential beauty of this book. I will always be grateful for her unflagging dedication to produce a handsome and authoritative tome.

My co-editors and associates at Brides & Your New Home were always enthusiastic and forthcoming with helpful and expert information. The foreword of this book was graciously penned by Barbara Tober. As editor-in-chief, she originally hired me as an assistant in the fashion department many years ago. She nurtured my career and inspired me, as she does everyone, with her exuberant, enduring romantic philosophy. Important background information for the text of The Wedding Dress was generously offered by Millie Martini Bratten, executive editor; Rachel Leonard, fashion editor; Denise O'Donoghue, beauty editor; and Andrea Feld, managing editor. I am thrilled to feature lavish photographs from the archives of Bride's magazine; these pictures represent the unquestionable talents of these editors and more, especially Phyllis Richmond Cox, art director; associate editors Elizabeth Rundlett and Renee Sheffey; and gone but not forgotten editors Joyce Cohen and Fiona Donnelly. I thank Belle Zimmer Hoffman and her reliable knack for facilitating results. And I thank Linda Peters and Naomi Charap for valuable information regarding the bridal market.

Forecasting fashion's best trends, documenting fashion's—and history's—vivid directions, Condé Nast magazines are the premier package in publishing, providing a coveted forum for the best photographers. I am hon-ored to feature many glorious images from Brides & Your New Home, American Vogue, British Brides & Setting Up Home, and Vogue Sposa. I thank all the photographers and their editors for producing inspired, important visual celebrations of the bride that will live on in The Wedding Dress. And I thank Cindy Cathcart and Diana Edkins for providing access to these incredible resources.

I thank my friends who were invaluable in the production of original art for The Wedding Dress. Through the eyes of photographers Marili Forastieri, Scott Hagendorf, Kam Hinatsu, Alan Richardson, and Ross Whitaker—all dedicated to capturing the essence of beauty within the square confines of a transparency— a woman and a dress become forever memorable. I thank my valued, trusted associates who never hesitated to work a little longer: Susan Keller, Cindy Zdzienicki, Cherri Crump O'Donoghue, Susan Holmes, and Vivian Rullo. I thank the talented hair and makeup artists: Patricia Bowden, Mel Rau, Betsy Lyn, Mara Schiavetti, and Clentera English for taking a beautiful woman and making her exquisite. I thank Jean Owen for her valuable contacts. I thank the wonderful models: Mireille Comstock, Dana Douglas, Susan Davidson, Rebecca Hobert, Kerry Hoefler, Rochelle Hunt, Carol Leska, Esteban Riviera, and Aleksandra Szulaczkowski, and their agents: Beth Anne, Company, Elite, and Wilhelmina Model Managements. I also thank two prestigious New York City landmarks, both elegant locales for weddings and photography: the glorious Plaza Hotel, coordinated by Rachel Doran and Dan Klores Associates and the exemplary Pierre Hotel, coordinated by Mary Jo McNally. I thank Lola Ehrlick and Phillip and Stephanie Hoffman for the chance to photograph their elegant emporiums. I thank the expert crew at Kleinfeld, especially Nancy Aucone, Susan Finale, Linda Pizzuto, and Grace Decker for opening their doors to fascinating, behind-the-scenes photography. I also am indebted to the talented, generous Richard Glasgow for the chance to spend a day photographing the meticulous creation of his remarkable, beautiful gowns. Many thanks also to Ondyn Herschelle and Ronald Mann for their wonderful, inspired illustrations and to Susan Salinger and Dana Schulman for bringing us together.

The collation of historical details, review of current fashion news and newsmakers, exposé of the sharp eyes that shape the best of design, unveiling of the artistic skill of dressmakers, and revelation of the practicalities and options for every bride are the results of hard labor. I thank my dedicated intern, Edina Sultanik, for every invaluable hour spent in dusty libraries. I thank my father, Russell McBride, for his enthusiastic approach to raw, ethereal research. I thank Amy M. Spindler and Sarah Greenberg for their couture contacts and contributions. I thank Hedda Schachter, Debora Jackson, Cathy Nixon, Mel Cohen, and Karen Metz and Marcy Blum for their authoritative information.

I thank every fashion designer, many of whom are represented in this book and the many more, because of space limitations, it was impossible to include, who ever brought to life a glorious fabrication from mere threads and imagination. This book would be impossible without their elegant handiwork.

And I thank the team at Magnolia Editions, especially Chris Bain, Jeff Batzli, Tanya Ross-Hughes, Jenny McMichael, Anne Price, Amla Sanghvi, and Karen Greenberg for coping with impossible deadlines and reams of material to somehow produce a book. Special thanks are in order for Sharyn Rosart and Olga Seham for smoothly editing page after page with finesse. And I thank Ann Rittenberg for her counsel and support.

And finally and importantly, I thank my family and friends for just being there, even if I wasn't.

Many people provided invaluable assistance in the creation of this book. I have attempted to include each one, but for any inadvertent omissions, I apologize.

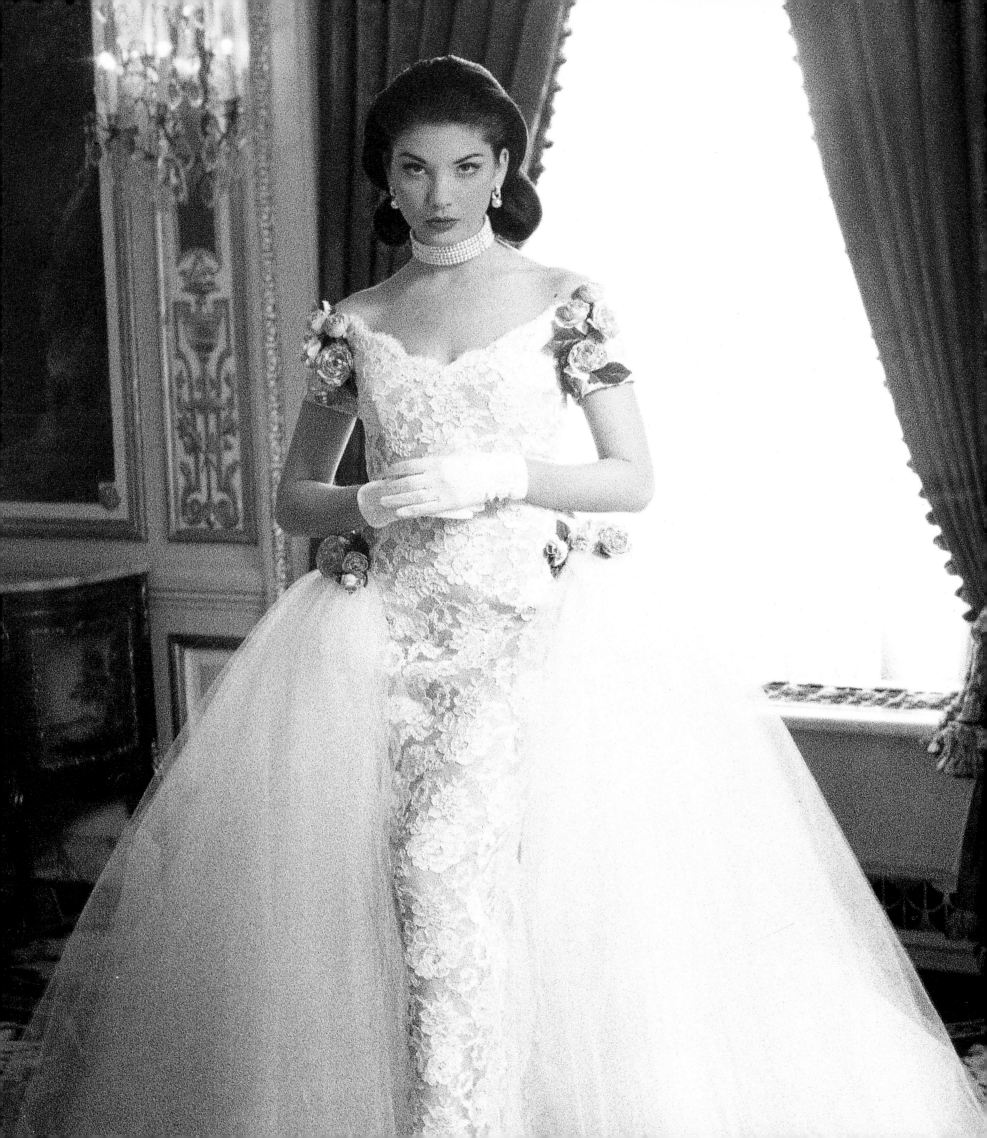

CONTENTS

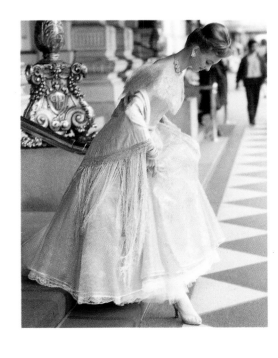 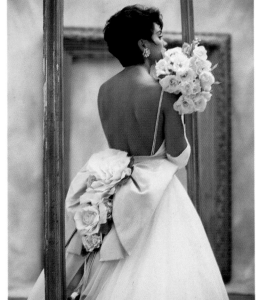 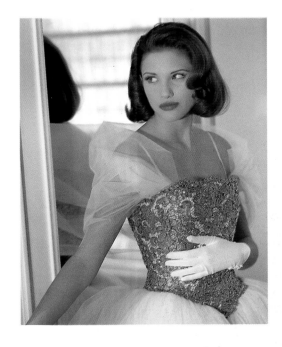

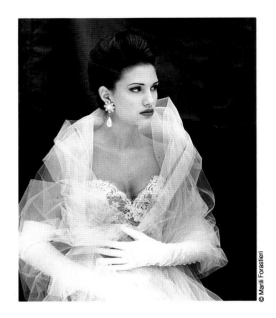

© Marili Forastieri

FOREWORD

The Wedding Dress. No other raiment speaks so symbolically of promise, of the mysteries of good luck and, conversely, the daunting challenges of the future. As she celebrates the rite of passage that takes her from single to married, the bride is transformed. This stunningly photographed book, *The Wedding Dress*, is about that transformation—as it exists now and as it has influenced civilization throughout history. *The Wedding Dress* is not only about being costumed for a unique occasion; it is about the image of the bride as she is perceived by friends, family, and even total strangers and about the folklore that has kept her in the forefront of art and culture throughout these many centuries.

As editor-in-chief of *Bride's* Magazine for three decades, I have been either personally or peripherally involved with hundreds of thousands of weddings. In every case, the bride, often her family, and certainly her groom feel a catch in their collective throat, a moment of exultation—in the mirror or before the congregation—when they see the bride in her wedding dress.

Maria McBride-Mellinger has traced the custom of dressing for the wedding from its earliest beginnings to the present day. The myths, customs, and legends of the veil, the accessories, the various colors (after all, why *do* we marry in white?), and even the fashions of the times and who dictated them are explored here. There are elements of poetry and practicality, facts and fantasies to explore as one plans the creation of this once and only drama that is the wedding day.

Enjoy this book for its full range of possibilities. Give it time to impact upon your subconscious, time to do its magic so that you can make decisions, *knowledgeable* decisions that make your wedding day so unique, so memorable, and unequivocally *you* that it becomes a personal statement about a very special individual.

Barbara Tober, Editor-in-Chief

Bride's & Your New Home Magazine

INTRODUCTION

Silk, tulle, satin and lace—mere yards of fabric to some, but to every bride these threads are at the heart of a romantic dream—her wedding dress. The wedding dress, in all its frothy fabrications, is a gown symbolic not only of the rewards of romance but also of the importance of marriage throughout history.

The significance of "I do," two very simple words, is reflected in the elaborate celebrations that are universally associated with weddings and the exalted position of the bride in every culture. From Tokyo to Buenos Aires, from Saskatchewan to Zimbabwe, from Jerusalem to London, and from Paris to Detroit, brides wear white. The traditional white wedding gown connotes so powerful an image that it is universally acknowledged as the "proper" bridal hue. Although the white wedding gown has been widely worn for only the last hundred years, it has always been traditional to dress the bride in special vestments. Today, virtually every bride will exchange her nuptial vows attired in a special dress meant to be worn only once, as a hallmark of the significance of the event.

Unlike any other element of fashion, the wedding dress has a unique history. No other dress can match the poetic heritage of the wedding dress or rival the sentimental attachment each bride has for her gown. The enduring beauty of the wedding dress lies beyond its brilliance of design, sumptuous fabrication, or fineness of construction; the wedding gown's magic rests in its distinction as a symbol of romance throughout the ages. Yet the wedding dress represents more than the timelessness of romance; it also reflects the history of the world. Brides have always worn the most luxurious fabrics, and the demand for opulent textiles helped to spur exploration of the world and fueled the economy of nations. The status of a nation was apparent in the fashions of its citizens, and the wedding dress has always reflected the fashion of each era.

Until 1960 the silhouette of the wedding gown followed the current vogue of everyday dressing. As feminine fashions evolved from purely decorative to at least partly utilitarian, the wedding gown became an opportunity to revel in the pageantry of the past. As changing values strengthened the sentimental aspect of the wedding dress, it became an important symbol of continuity, a link to tradition. The ball gown, today's most popular wedding style, borrows its shape from bygone fashions in a tribute to the romance of the past and a celebration of the female form. And even the most avant-garde gown has a strongly traditional character if it is white—the color alone says it all.

In the context of pure fashion, the wedding dress is a representation of the highest standards of the couturier: a hand-sewn, made-to-measure gown designed according to the classic principle that a dress should enhance the true beauty of the wearer's body. The decision to wear a made-to-measure wedding gown provides the bride with an opportunity that is rare in the modern world —to indulge in a garment made according to the standards of design, workmanship, and service of the past.

Whether marrying for the first or third time, most women will opt to wear a traditional, white wedding gown. Yet describing the gown of choice as traditional and white does not begin to illuminate the wide range of choices available to the modern woman. A bride's gown may be frankly feminine, undeniably sophisticated, stark white, splashed with color, elaborately embellished, or deliberately streamlined. It may feature a bared back or bared legs, have cascades of tulle or lace, or be edged with black or trimmed with lush roses. This diversity of choice may seem confusing but it allows each bride the luxury of expressing her personal style through her wedding dress.

This book is a tribute to the wedding dress, an exquisite, stylish, glamorous, sentimental, purely feminine gown, the romance of its evolution, the artistry of its creation, and the splendor of its design. After months of strategic planning, the carefully orchestrated drama lasts only a day, but the memories last a lifetime. Ultimately, each wedding dress takes its place in history as a testament to the enduring history of the human heart.

THE WEDDING DRESS IN HISTORY

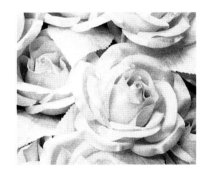

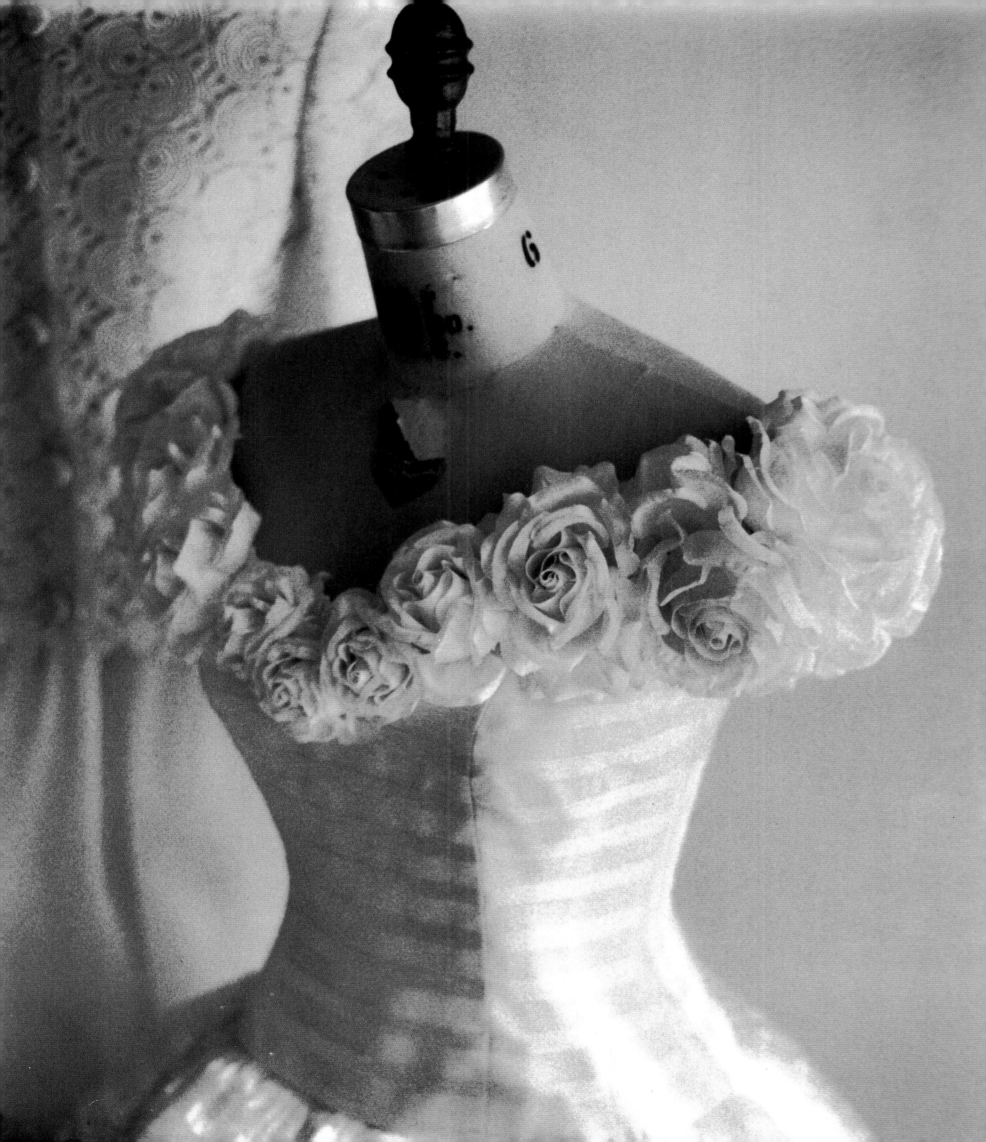

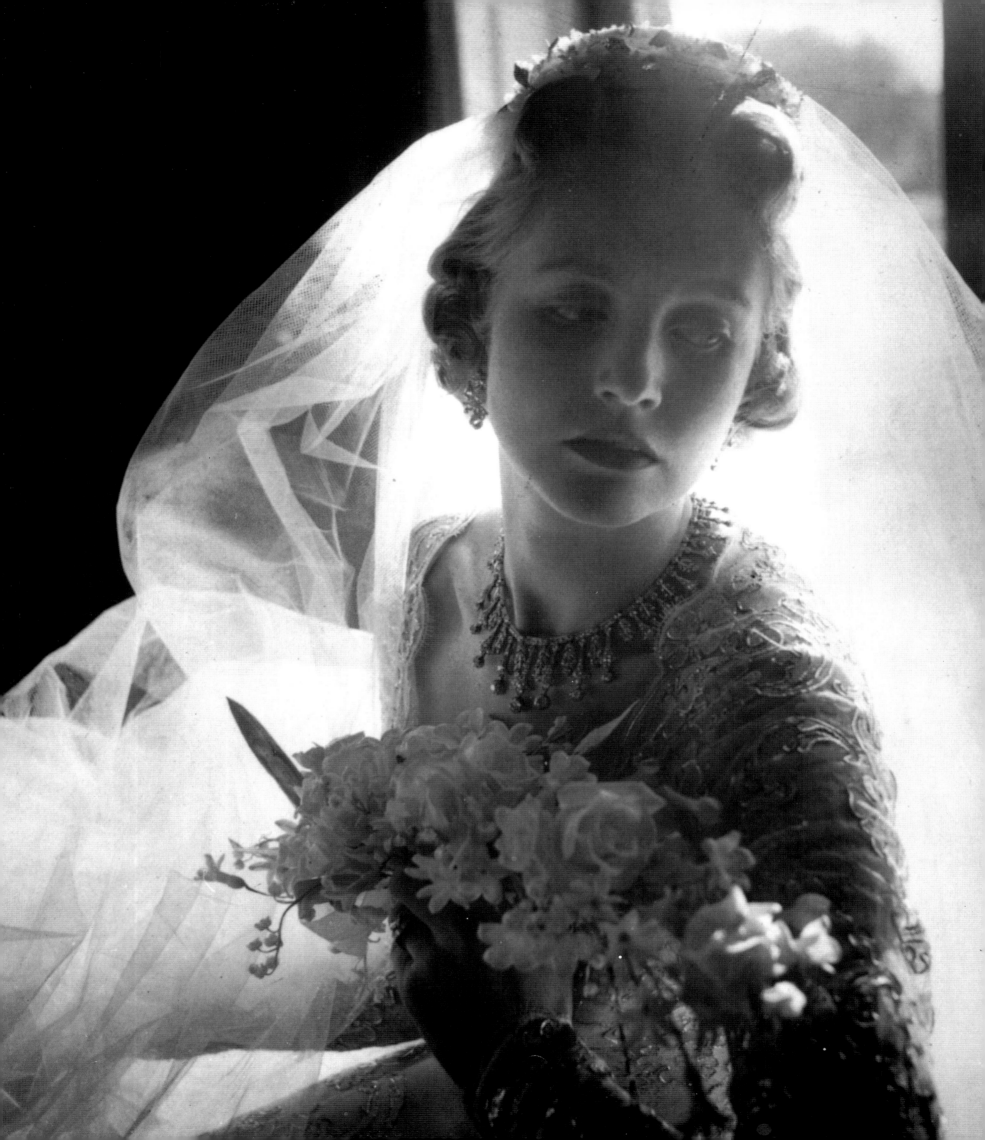

Much more than just a dress, the wedding gown has always been a highly symbolic garment, its color, details, and accessories resonant with meaning. For today's bride, the wedding dress symbolizes pure romance, all the magic and beauty of the union of bride and groom. Yet the wedding dress, and indeed the wedding itself, have not always been associated with love. Until the last few centuries—and even more recently—it was typical for the bride and groom to be virtual strangers on their wedding day. Marriage was an institution based not on love and shared values but on the improvement of family circumstances. Love was inconsequential. It's quite likely that in the earliest marriages a great emphasis was placed on how the bride appeared precisely because she represented her family in a public contract. Thus, the legacy of the bride's dress is a reflection both of the historical significance of marriage and of the importance of a beautifully clothed bride for the family's reputation. In many ways the survival of a family—and more broadly, a culture—depended on the success of the marital union. Naturally, communities endowed such pivotal events with all the superstitions and glamour of their society. Indeed, the celebration of the wedding itself is among the most ancient tradition we follow today.

History, often seen through art and literature, has shaped our perceptions of how the modern bride appears. Of course, she wears a white dress and a veil, and looks beautiful. But why? Many of the most popular and entrenched traditions associated with today's bride and the modern wedding originated as recently as the Victorian era. Yet even the most ancient cultures celebrated matrimony with rituals that influenced later generations. Each society molded its inherited traditions to fit the community's evolving value system, adding ethnic or folkloric twists to the universal celebration of marriage through specific customs of dress and ceremony. A ritual celebration in almost every society throughout history is the adornment of the bride, who, for one exciting day in her life, is pampered, preened, and exquisitely dressed to take her place at the center of attention. Her appearance is a reflection of everything her culture finds beautiful. Over the centuries recurring elements of the bridal outfit—the bridal veil, for example—have refined a look, a style, a sentimental incarnation that is universally recognized and manages to inspire teary-eyed reflections in even the most stoic observer.

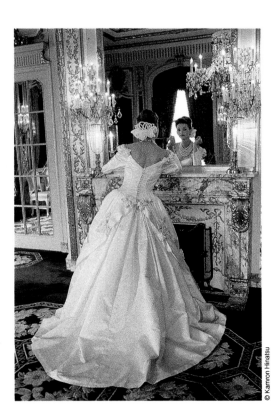

The bridal gown endures. **PAGE 11:** *Ethereal organza edged with lush silk roses by Richard Glasgow.* **OPPOSITE PAGE:** *Bridal gowns have a naturally majestic presence. The ancient pageantry that is at the root of today's wedding dresses is evoked by a grand dress of heirloom lace.* **ABOVE:** *A ball gown of duchesse satin by Catherine Rayner.*

THE ANCIENT ERA

Archaeological records of ancient Egyptian civilization date back as far as 4000 B.C., and the hieroglyphic records left by the ancient Egyptians provide us with many of the details of their lives, including matrimonial customs. The people of this highly sophisticated society were dedicated to elaborate, pleasurable rituals of bathing, makeup, and adornment. Their keen attention to personal grooming bears a striking similarity to our modern fascination with cleanliness and appealing presentation. Egyptian nobles rarely groomed and dressed themselves; instead, they yielded themselves to the ministrations of serving maidens in an early version of our modern ritual of bridesmaids dressing the bride. An Egyptian bride was traditionally draped in gossamer layers of accordion-pleated white linen.

The religion of our ancient Greek and Roman ancestors featured a complex pantheon of gods and goddesses, each representative of a different aspect of life. The bridal ceremony typifies the classical tendency to imbue every event and even articles of clothing with symbolism. The color white, symbolic of joy, was often worn on festive occasions, including weddings. The bride wore a new tunic, a gift from her parents, its pristine condition symbolic of virginity. The tunic was secured with a Herculean knot, to be loosened only by the groom. The most important element of the Roman bride's dress was her veil. In fact, *nubere*, the term for veiling, was synonymous with marriage, and the day after the consummation was known as the unveiling. The veil, saffron-hued, symbolized the flame of Vesta, the goddess of the home and provider of life. The bride's hair was elaborately braided to emulate the six braids of the Vestal Virgins who served the goddess. Under her veil, the bride wore a wreath of lilies for purity, wheat for fertility, rosemary for male virility, and myrtle for long life.

After the fall of the Roman Empire and its withdrawal from Brittany in the fourth century, the Anglo-Saxons in Gaul, intent on consolidating their power and reducing tribal conflicts, eliminated their primitive practice of marriage by capture and instituted the more stable arrangement of marriage by purchase. The groom's pledge to pay the bride's father a fee was known as a *wedd*. These early marriages were arranged for unromantic, practical considerations: the bride was a valued laborer and procreator, worthy of high compensation. Despite, or perhaps because of the utilitarian aspect of marriage, the wedding tended to be a raucous celebration and a purely secular event. To shield the shy bride from leers and curious stares, the nuptials were exchanged under a care cloth or veil, similar to the Hebrew *huppah*. Brides wore their best and often only dress (fabric, homespun, was a laboriously achieved luxury) and their hair curled, loose, and flowing. Once married, the couple would proceed to the local church for a blessing, after which both the bride and groom were crowned with a wreath for luck.

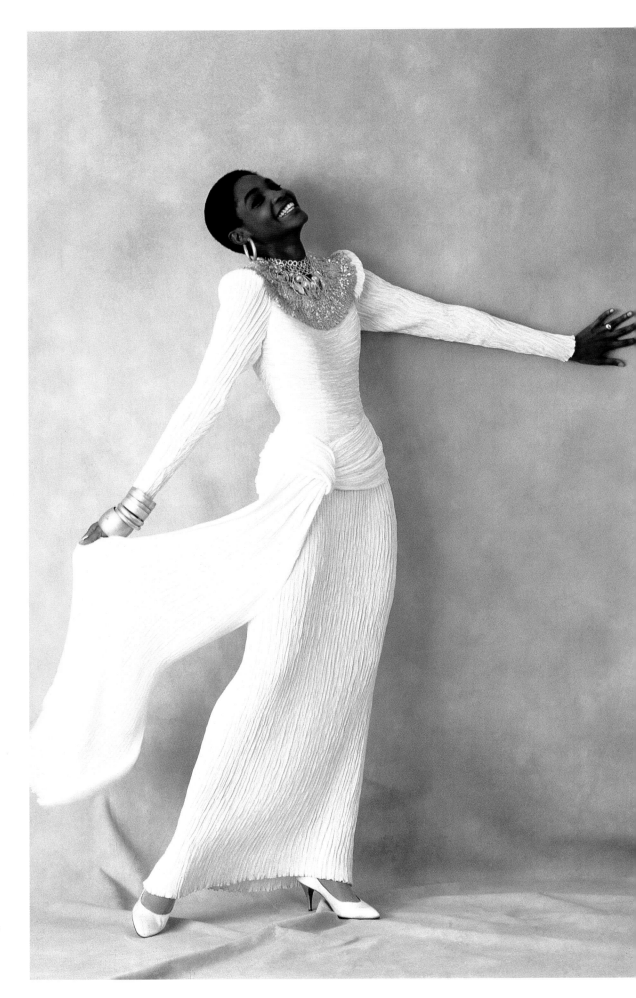

THE MIDDLE AGES AND RENAISSANCE

During the Middle Ages, war and marriage were the most common methods of consolidating empires. The desirability of peacefully protecting family wealth, lands, and relationships made marriage a powerful tool. The church, recognizing the significance of weddings, made marriage a religious ceremony and by the tenth and eleventh centuries it had issued edicts against civil weddings, thereby consolidating its power over this institution.

The heady, historic unions of powerful and wealthy families called for major wedding celebrations that included glorious tournaments at which knights in shining armor jousted, followed by enormous banquets featuring sumptuous dishes of wild game and fowl. The festivities often lasted for days, even weeks. As early as the end of the twelfth century, royal weddings were celebrated with almost overwhelming pageantry. Phillip III of France, for example, insisted that his entire wedding party, including guests, dress according to his picturesque color scheme: the men wore scarlet, the ladies gold with silver lace. Today's brides share this penchant for elaborately color-coordinated weddings.

The growing wealth of royalty and nobles was readily apparent in their elaborate dress and jewels. Since the tenth-century explorers had opened trade routes to the East, silks,

satins, velvets, and brocades had been available to the upper classes. Sumptuary laws were instituted to strictly enforce the divisions between classes. A law established in England in 1350 made it a crime for non-royalty to wear the clothes of gold, furs of miniver and ermine, or jewel-encrusted gowns and robes. The wearing of silk and silver cloth was limited to persons of high rank and a certain income level. Tradesmen and wives were limited to skins of lamb, rabbit, cat, and fox. Even shoes were regulated: a prince's slipper could sport a pointed toe up to two feet long, while commoners were

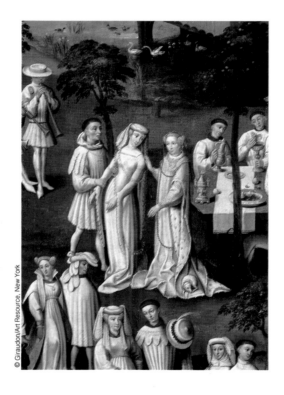

OPPOSITE PAGE: *A thoroughly modern sheath from Mary McFadden echoes the stunning silhouette worn by ancient Egyptian brides.* **ABOVE:** *This depiction of a royal wedding between Isabelle of Portugal and Philip the Good of France in 1430 illustrates the svelte styles that predated the invention of shape-constricting and enhancing undergarments, which were to conceal a woman's true form for hundreds of years.*

allowed no more than six inches. Bridal garb was not specifically legislated—it was assumed that a bride would wear the best her family could afford. A member of the nobility would commission a new gown, one that reflected her family's fortune, and could be worn again for other important events.

By the fourteenth century the cotehardie (literally, "bold coat"), a close-fitting dress-like garment with a train, was the traditional wedding gown. Laced up the back or front, the cotehardie had long, tight sleeves and a full skirt slit to show the underdress, which also sported a train. (The train, which remained an essential element of any fashionable dress until the twentieth century, continues to be a classic feature of most modern bridal gowns.) Women lucky enough to own cotehardies of precious fabrics such as silk brocades, usually in rich, deep colors, would pass these luxurious robes on to their daughters. Brides who did not inherit a dress usually rented one for their wedding. For weddings, the cotehardie was worn with a belt of gold, encrusted with as many jewels as the family could afford. The bride's trousseau included only three dresses: her cotehardie, which would be worn again for very special occasions; a good dress for Sundays; and another for every day. Regardless of the bride's fortune, she traditionally wore only three ornaments: a ring representing eternal vows and true love; a brooch, a token of chastity and a pure heart; and a crowning garland, symbolizing virtue, worn over loose, flowing hair.

During the Middle Ages veils waxed and waned in popularity. It was unusual—if not unlikely—for the bride to wear a veil on her wedding day if it wasn't the day-to-day fashion. However, veils were a common head adornment of various times from the tenth to the thirteenth centuries. In the fourteenth century, the jeweled cap and the linen coif—

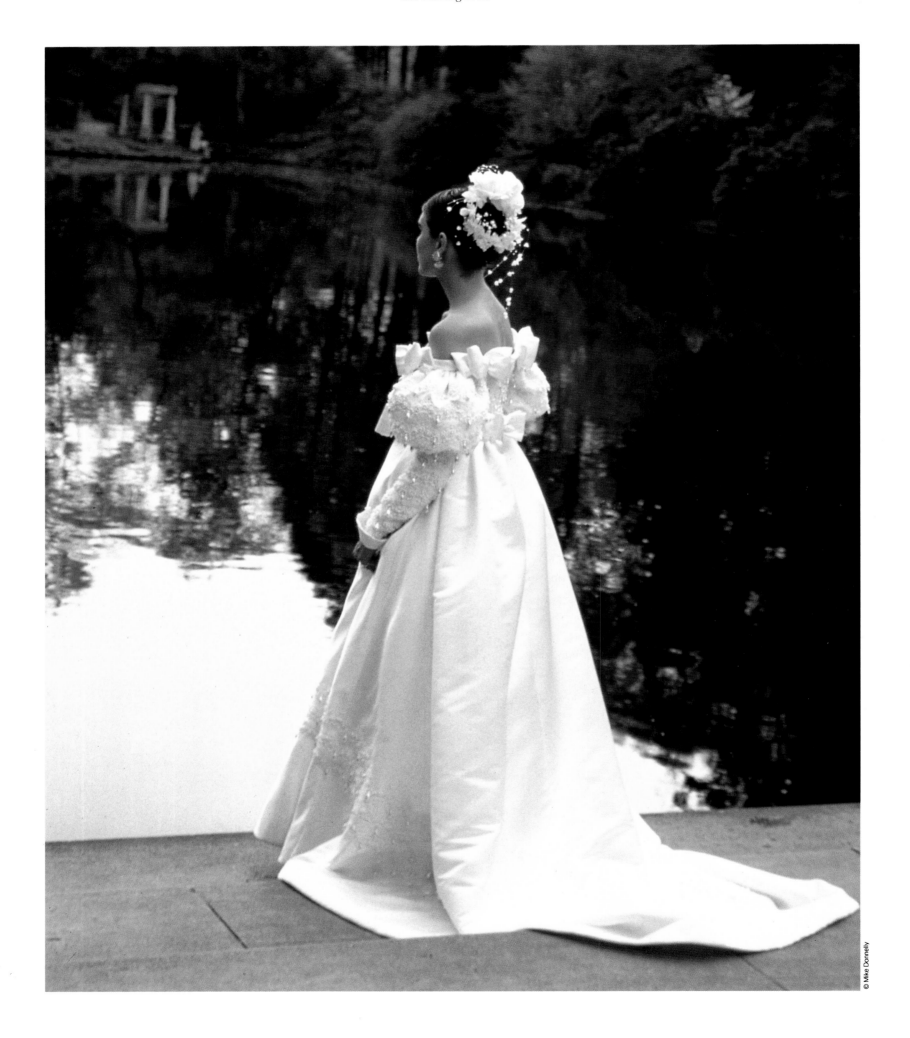

OPPOSITE PAGE: *Today's modern wedding designers mix fashionable details from past eras into their modern creations, as in this regal gown from Timothy Sampson.* **BELOW:** *An empire waist and a graceful train were featured in* The Arnolfini Marriage, *painted in 1434.* **RIGHT:** *Luxuriant in a jewel-encrusted gown, Queen Elizabeth I favored enduring bridal details—a collar of lace and the distinctive basque waist.*

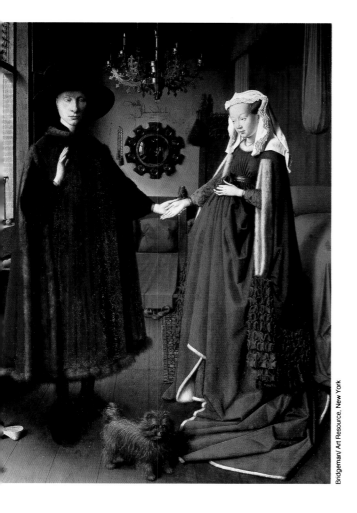

ground. During the sixteenth century, veils went out of fashion again and women sported small, brimmed hats instead. Veils did not make a reappearance on female brows until the nineteenth century.

Although medieval weddings were traditionally arranged for unromantic reasons, the notion of a love match was gaining favor: dutiful members of the nobility continued to marry according to family dictates while hoping that a noble alliance might also prove to be a true romance. In royal courts minstrels composed songs and tales of love and honor for entertainment. Poets glorified romance and chivalry. Finely tuned words celebrated the beauty of the maiden bride, the gallantry of her heroic suitor, and the virtue of true love. The romantic embellishments of poets fueled the enduring image of the maiden clad in white, her spirit embodied in every bride. As an Elizabethan poet declared in his "Rhapsody of Love":

> Maid. The moon doth borrow light;
> you borrow grace:
> When maids by their own virtue
> graced be
> White is my colour;
> and no hue but this it will receive,
> no tincture can it stain.

As a literary device, white represented qualities of true honor, blinding passion, immaculate innocence, and spiritual purity—all embodied in the bride's attire.

Vanity also was a force behind the popularity of white: white was the favorite color of Henry VIII's daughter, Queen Elizabeth. Her striking red hair and pale skin offset white robes to a great advantage, or so the court

poets and jesters, no fools they, insisted. Odes dedicated to the fair maiden with golden or red hair clad in virginal white abound, including the following, a bridal tribute by Edmund Spenser:

> Comes along with portly pace,
> Lyke Phoebe, from her chamber of
> the East,
> Ary sing forth to run her mighty race,
> Clad all in white, that seems a virgin
> best.
> So well it her beseemes, that ye would
> seeme
> Some angell she had beene.
> Her long loose yellow locks lyke
> golden wyre,
> Sprinkled with perle and perling
> flowers atweene,
> Doe lyke a golden mantle her attyre;
> And, being crowned with a garland
> greene,
> Seeme lyke some mayden Queene.
>
> —*Epithalamion*

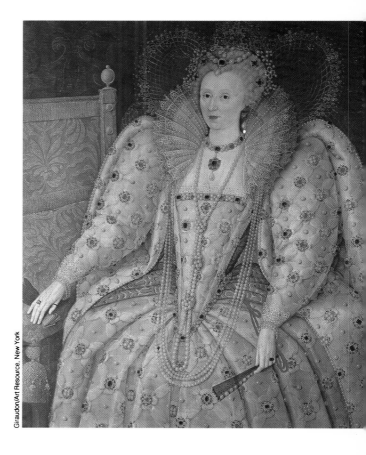

a short, opaque headdress worn over conical spirals of hair—were in vogue. Cowls, gold or silk mesh hoodlike caps derived from head armor worn by knights, were worn in the late fourteenth century. By the next century, a long conical headdress, known as a henin, was popular. Worn tilted back on the head, the henin featured a long, sheer veil cascading from the point of the henin to the

Possibly the earliest recorded example of an all-white bridal gown was that worn by Princess Philippa, daughter of Henry IV of England, in 1406. She married Eric of Denmark when she was twelve and wore a tunic and mantle of white satin trimmed with white miniver and ermine. When Mary Queen of Scots married into the French royal family in 1558, she wore a wedding gown "as white as lilies," defying and altering the French tradition that decreed white as the royal color of mourning. Not only were royal marriages politically expedient maneuvers, they were also important opportunities for

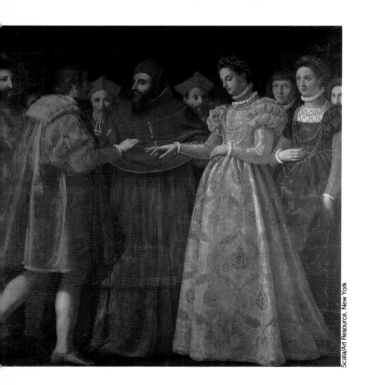

Most bridal gowns trace their roots to royalty.
ABOVE: *Monarchs, like Catherine de' Medici, who became Queen of France in the sixteenth century, typically wed wearing lavish gowns of gold or silver.* **OPPOSITE PAGE:** *A courtly wedding dress by Pat Kerr blends spun gold organza with gilt heirloom lace in one ethereal gown.*

cultural exchange as national mores, traditions, fashions, and skills crossed borders, too. Royal brides never expatriated alone, but were accompanied by massive entourages, and the influence of new ideas that they brought with them trickled down to every level. When Catherine de' Medici of Florence married into the French monarchy in 1533, she popularized lace, the heeled shoe, and underwear, plus the practice of dancing at the wedding, all important to future brides.

Early journals and letters written by nobles and clergy provide most of the surviving descriptive details of actual weddings. As is to be expected, royal weddings have been precisely recorded while those of commoners often went unremarked, ordinary folks at that time generally being illiterate and unable to document their lives. Yet, while it was the aristocratic weddings that gave shape to our modern image of the bride, it was the peasant and citizen who preserved and passed on the bridal festivities we cherish today. For example, Elizabethans at every level of society loved a lively wedding. Thomas Delancey in 1597 recounted the wedding of a middle-class bride:

The bride, being attired in a gown of sheep's russet and a kirtle of fine worsted…her hair as yellow as gold hanging down behind her, which was curiously combed and plaited, she was led to church between two sweet boys with bride laces and rosemary tied about their silken sleeves. There was fair bride cup of silver gilt carried before her, wherin was a goodly branch of rosemary, gilded very fair, hung about with silken ribands of all

colours. Musicians came next, then a groupe of maidens, some bearing great bride-cakes, others garlands of wheat finely gilded; and thus they passed into the church; and the bridegroom finely apparelled, with the young men followed close behind.

This ceremony ended in a riotous manner: the young men tore ribbons, garters, and bridal laces from the bride as souvenirs, later the crowd raucously escorted the bridal couple to their bedchambers.

The Elizabethan wedding featured many of the customs of today's weddings: vows and rings were exchanged, there was a bridal party procession, brides wore wreaths of blossoms and carried bouquets trimmed with love knots, wedding cake was eaten, and the garter presumably went to the next to be married. Four hundred years have passed and it all still sounds very familiar.

Unlike their subjects, princesses typically wore amazingly lavish gowns, and their weddings were dazzling spectacles, paid for, until the 1500s, by royal marriage taxes levied on landowners. When England's sixteen-year-old Princess Elizabeth married Frederick of Bohemia in 1613, she was attended by sixteen bridesmaids. All the maids and the princess were robed in ephemeral white and silver tissue trimmed with silver lace. Princess Elizabeth's train of silver and sleeves, solidly encrusted with diamonds, were truly worth a princess' ransom. The princess wore her hair loose, hanging to her waist, in the traditional maidenly fashion, with a crown of gold, in typical regal fashion. The wedding, its festivities, the

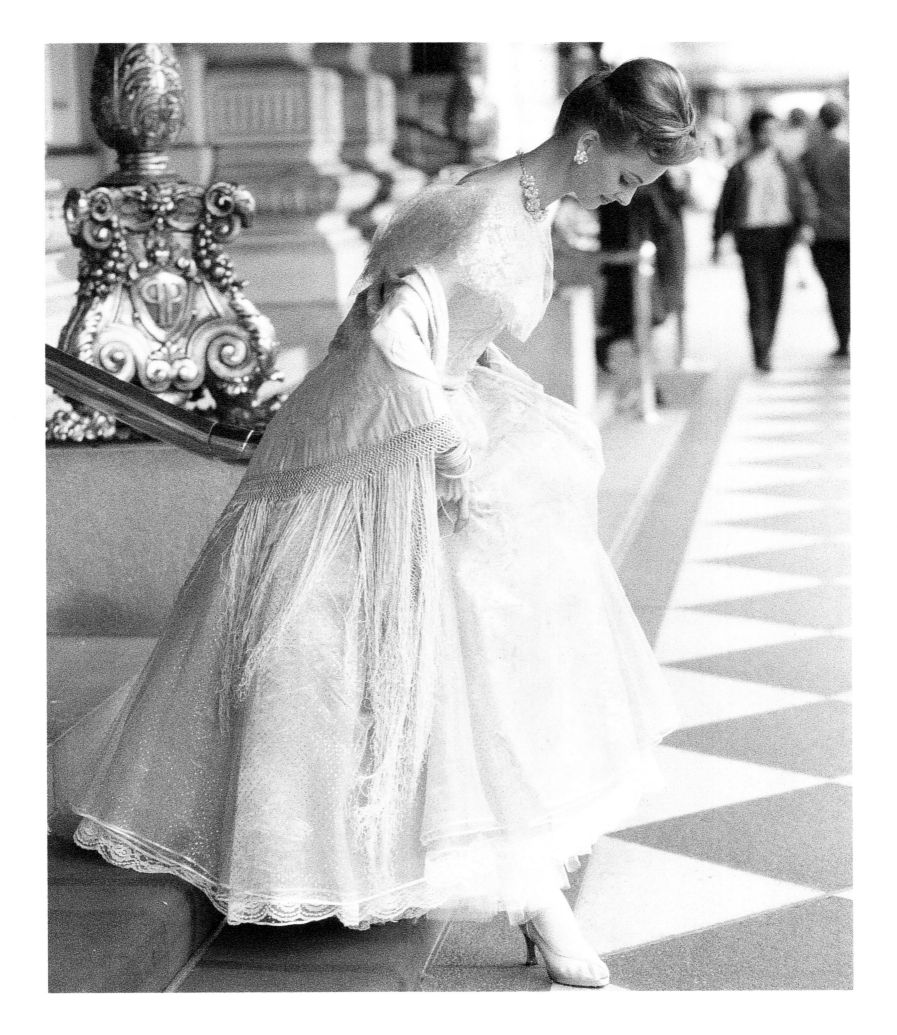

bridal party's gowns, and the princess' dowry cost her father about £95,000 sterling (over $5 million today).

Across the channel, Princess Henrietta Maria married on the porch of the cathedral of Notre Dame in 1625. The princess wore a velvet-and-gold train so heavy that a man had to assist her three ladies and support the train from underneath with his head and hands. Despite the weighty dilemmas of such regal excess, royal brides unanimously favored ornately jeweled gowns of silver until the Victorian era. Today's brides also appreciate the glamorous affect of a richly embroidered gown and a lengthy train—regardless of the tricky physical maneuvers.

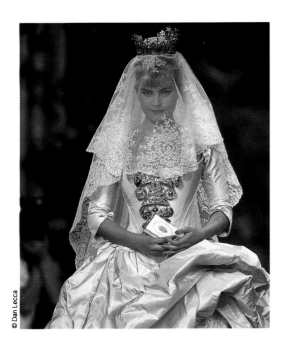

*A revealing decolletage, in vogue from the Elizabethan era until the Victorian era, provided an alluring glimpse of the otherwise well-concealed feminine form. Whether ornamented with gilt (**ABOVE**, by Christian Lacroix) or with antique lace and bows (**OPPOSITE PAGE**, by Christine & Company) this flattering neckline remains a favorite of brides.*

THE AGE OF REASON

Britain in the seventeenth century saw the brief rise and fall of Oliver Cromwell and the Puritan ethic. Although the Puritans did not remain in power long, many of their reforms had long-term impact. Wedding ceremonies were no longer boisterous affairs; instead they became low-key, private events. Popular traditions—like wearing an all-white wedding gown—went out of favor. Practically speaking, even if money was no object, it made sense to invest in a gown with the greatest potential for an afterlife in the bride's trousseau. For their wedding, most brides wore a fashionable gown—sometimes new, sometimes an old favorite—and then rewore it often.

Across the Atlantic, brides in the newly settled colonies generally wore their best dress to wed. If fortunate, they would order a stylish, new, best dress made for their wedding day. Despite brides' hunger for the latest fashions, styles originated in Europe and took plenty of time to cross the ocean, making fashions in the New World slightly behind the times. Whenever ships arrived with their precious cargo of information and fabric, dressmakers would be swamped with appointments. Colonial women anxiously awaited the arrival of miniature dolls known as fashion babies, tiny, perfect ladies dressed in the best fabrics according to the latest fashions, which were influential, international ambassadors of style.

Colonists lavished attention on newlyweds. A tradition known as "coming out bride" lasted four consecutive Sundays after the wedding. Interrupting the Sunday church service, the bride and groom would rise and turn two or three times in place, affording everyone in the congregation a good look at their wedding best. Not only was this a chance to celebrate the bridal couple, it also stimulated the inclination of brides to wear distinctive wedding clothes—a trend that would eventually become a hallmark of all weddings. However, not until the twentieth century did this distinctive gown become a garment to be worn only once.

In both the old and new worlds, improvements in trade, communications, and manufacturing contributed to the growth of a flourishing middle class, fueling a fashion revolution that ushered in a new era of opulence. The upwardly mobile members of eighteenth-century society eagerly subscribed to the self-indulgent recreation of personal adornment. Popular painters, especially Watteau and later Fragonard, captured the beauties of society in idyllic scenes and were, in a documentary sense, fashion illustrators. Exquisitely detailed paintings featured women, often at play, in luscious fashionable gowns. Watteau's paintings portrayed women whose regal deportment showed off flowing gowns with trains that cascaded from the back shoulder to the ground. Today this train is universally recognized as the Watteau train and is frequently used in bridal design.

As the middle class grew more powerful, clothing ceased to be purely utilitarian, instead becoming a form of wearable art. Gowns of feathery lace and resplendent

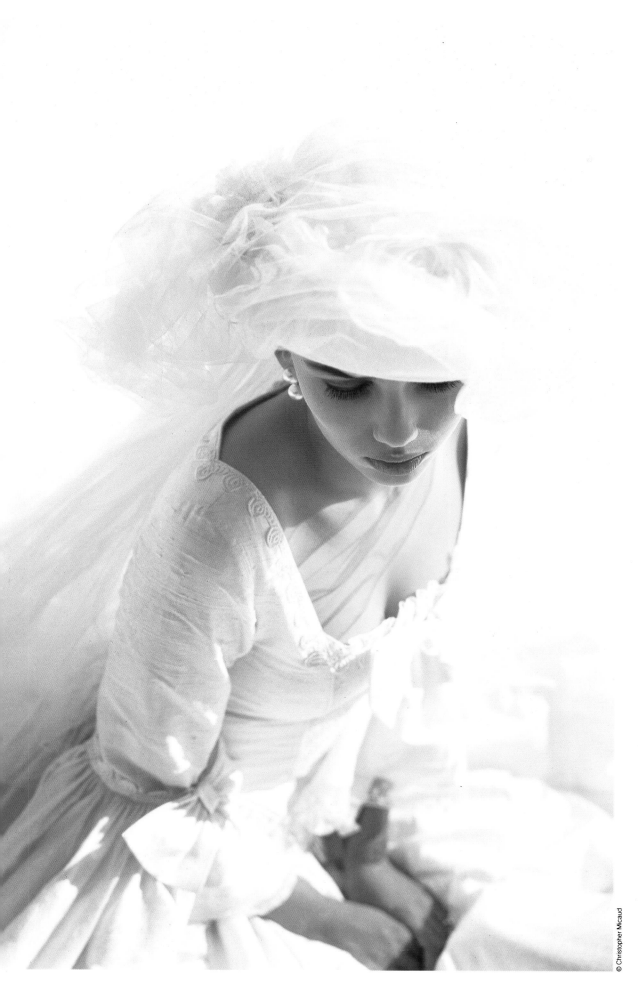

brocade, silk, and satin were lavishly embellished with embroideries, bows, flowers, ribbons, and jewels. Dresses featured extremely full, often dramatically hooped skirts, sweeping trains, and revealing off-the-shoulder necklines. For the eighteenth-century bride, these alluring designs were the fashion of the day, but their picturesque, romantic style is reinterpreted in many modern bridal collections.

By the end of the 1700s, magazines dedicated exclusively to fashion and style were published in London, Paris, and Philadelphia, featuring sketches of the latest fashions and offering sage advice for every woman. Fashion writers prescribed the best dress, most elegant grooming, and appropriate etiquette for every important moment in a woman's life—consequently, almost every issue featured a bridal dress. The earliest fashion reports were of royal events. A London journal in 1734 described Princess Anne's wedding gown made of silver tissue with an incredible six-yard train trimmed with lace. Columns and columns of type were dedicated to describing minute details of the costumes worn by the most fashionable members of society. The journals had a strong influence on their subscribers, who followed the written advice whenever possible. White was such a popular recommendation for special events, especially weddings, that not only the bride, but also the guests, would wear white.

The fascinating tangle of politics and fashion is clearly visible in the royal extravagance that characterized eighteenth-century France. Royalty had a history of excess—the indisputable evidence worn on their backs—that went unchecked until the French Revolution. The

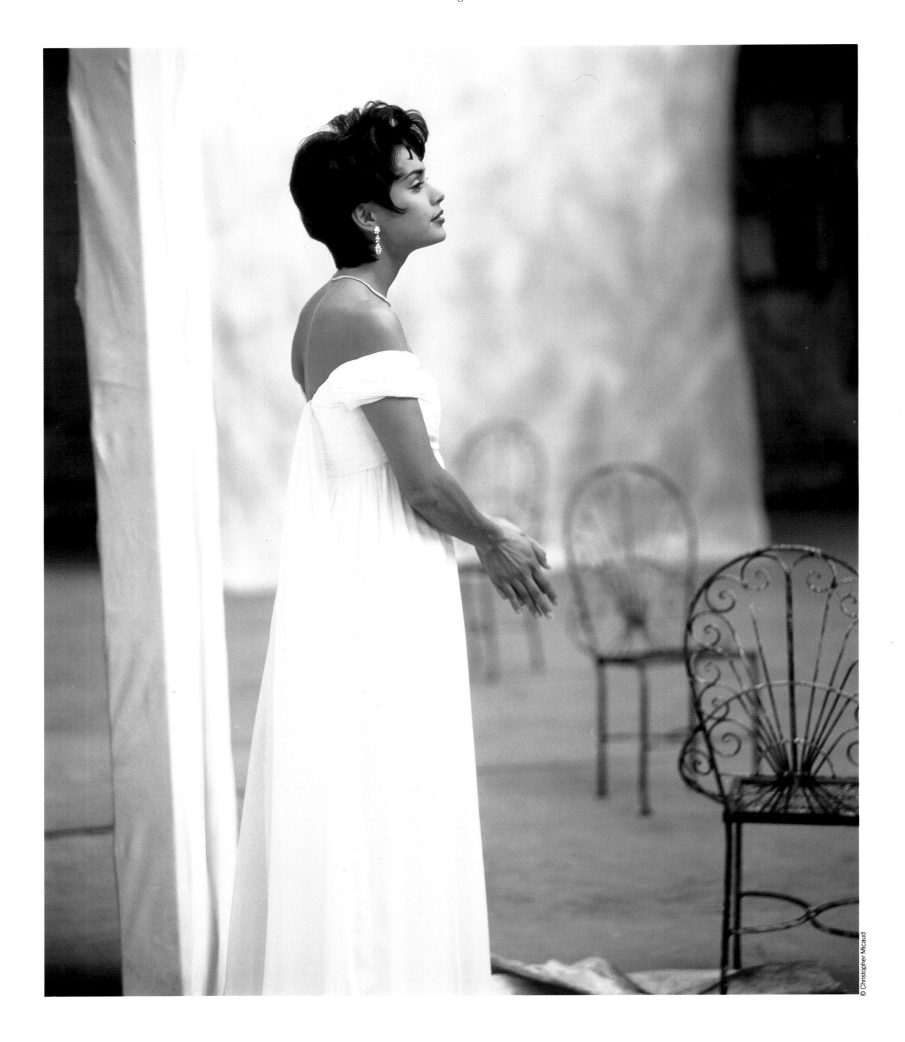

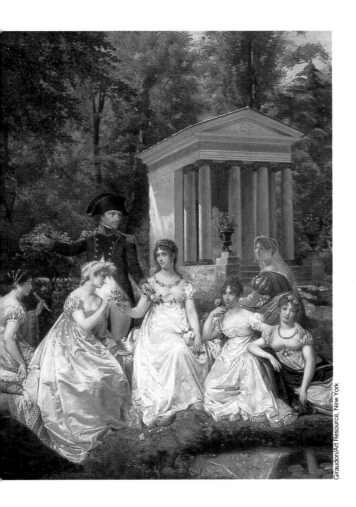

nests (sometimes real) and boats. (Women traveling to a party—or wedding—had been forced to sit on the floor of the carriage to preserve their towering coiffures.) Gone were the luxurious brocades, silks, and laces, as the bitter civil war destroyed the industries of luxury. The era that began in 1795, with France to be ruled by its citizens, called for a new political system—and a new fashion ethos to go with it. The ancient ideals of Greek democratic government were the inspiration for both new directions. Fashionable women now wore simple muslin gowns resembling narrow, ionic columns. These high-waisted dresses, known as empire (for the Napoleonic Empire), contrasted sharply with the fashions of years before. The slim silhouette was a shock after the full, wide skirts of the past, which concealed the true shape of a woman's body. Previously, women had worn undergarments known as farthingales or panniers, which were devices that extended the skirt at the sides, up to four or five feet at its most extreme width. In a dramatic departure from these styles, at the wedding of Marie Louise of Austria to Napoleon Bonaparte in 1810, the bride wore a dress of embroidered muslin over a single, lightweight petticoat. A guest noted that "all the clothes worn by the bride might have been put in my pocket."

Even more shocking, many women chose to wear no petticoat at all, and definitely no corset, while the truly risqué were known to dampen the dress, making it all the more revealing. Following the ancient pattern, brides once again wore veils, usually referred to as scarves. The diaphanous veils of lace and tulle were worn at the back of the bride's head, fastened to a wreath of roses and myrtle, an homage to Venus, which perfectly matched the neoclassic gowns. As with the Greeks, white, in all its classical purity, was the universally favored color for wedding dresses.

outrageous fashions of the court of Marie Antoinette were at once opulent and absurd. For the French aristocracy, fashion was a luxurious leisure sport: they often orchestrated fashion fads, directing court dressmakers to follow their fancy. Fashion magazines would spread the news and the public would try to keep pace. Eventually the growing demand for fashionable clothing led to major changes in the dressmaking trade. Originally, dressmakers were basically seamstresses, copying fashionable court designs for clients; later, they became designers creating original fashions and eventually setting trends and commanding a formidable following.

The French Revolution, beginning in 1789, had an immediate impact on fashion at every level. Gone were the privileged aristocrats and their extravagances. Gone were the massive hairdos, up to three and even four feet high, often topped with outrageous hats that featured items like birds and

LEFT AND BELOW: *High-waisted gowns, now defined as empire style, were worn after the French Revolution by Josephine, first wife of the Emperor Napoleon, and all fashionable mademoiselles of the time.* **OPPOSITE PAGE:** *Cut from chiffon to resemble the classic, ancient lines favored by the Greeks, a fluid reincarnation by Amsale also features a Watteau train, immortalized by the prolific eighteenth-century court painter who vividly illustrated the fashions of the time.*

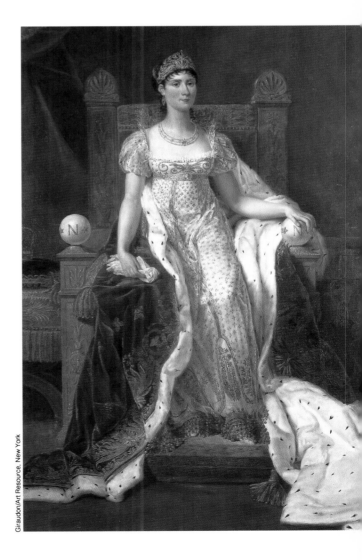

THE VICTORIAN ERA

Admired for her unwavering loyalty, sense of morality, and dedication to family, Britain's Queen Victoria (1819–1901) influenced generations. Her reign, virtually synonymous with the nineteenth century, was the longest in English history. Already a queen for three years, Victoria fell in love with her cousin Albert at first sight. Unlike most members of her royal family, Victoria married for love, and her wedding, in 1840, idealized romance and asserted a woman's right to choose her own husband. No marriage has had as significant an influence on our modern marital rites as Victoria's.

In 1840, the recent French and American revolutions with their popular disdain for royal excess remained fresh in the court's memory. Consequently, Victoria's wedding,

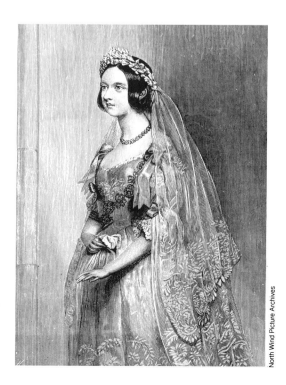

although lacking none of the requisite ceremonial pomp, was a clear departure from earlier, more extravagant, royal unions. Plighting her troth in a splendid but, for a queen, remarkably understated gown, Victoria set an example that even the most humble of her subjects might follow. Royal precedent encouraged queens and princesses to marry in gowns heavily embroidered with silver and encrusted with precious gems, and to wear jeweled crowns and velvet robes lined with rare furs. Heralding a less ornate, more simply elegant style—at least for a bride—the *Times* praised Queen Victoria's dress of "rich white satin trimmed with orange flower blossoms. On her head she wore a wreath of the same blossoms, over which, but not so to conceal her face, a beautiful veil of Honiton lace was thrown." (Since the earliest centuries royal brides, who very often had never met their affianced, could not conceal their faces, preventing a last-minute substitution.)

Seemingly austere and even bordering on the plain—by royal standards—Victoria's gown was actually exquisite and of great value. In order to promote the domestic textile industries, the heavy satin was woven in Spitalfields and the lace in a Devon village. Two hundred women were employed for eight months making the precious lace, and once finished, the designs, based on antique patterns, were destroyed to prevent reproduction. It is estimated that the lace alone cost £1,000 in 1840 (about $100,000 today).

Single-handedly, Queen Victoria set in motion the wheels of change. Even though brides continued to marry in gowns of various fashionable hues, the ideal of the white wedding was now firmly in place. Victoria's influential dedication to the ideals of romance and the perfect marriage enshrined the wedding as an extremely important institution in Victorian society. The standards were grounded in rigid rules

of etiquette, with parameters for social conduct guiding every tiny detail of daily life, not to mention major events like weddings. Executing the perfect wedding meant conforming to the numerous social rules while incorporating delicious sentimental details, such as the symbolism of the language of

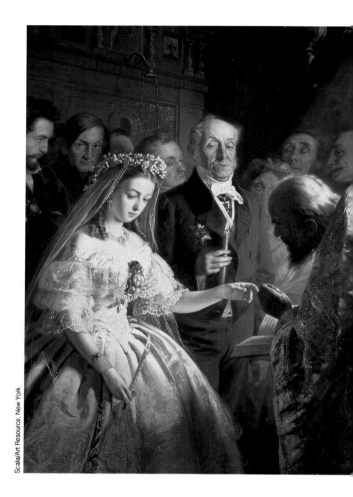

LEFT: *Queen Victoria's wedding and her gown inspired an era and an industry.* **ABOVE:** *Until the Victorian era, brides wore gowns of varying hues. The tradition of a white wedding gown began in earnest following Victoria's marriage in 1840. Most modern bridal gowns borrow some fashion details from this romantic era, like the graceful hoop-skirted ball gown,* **OPPOSITE PAGE,** *by Ada Athanassiou.*

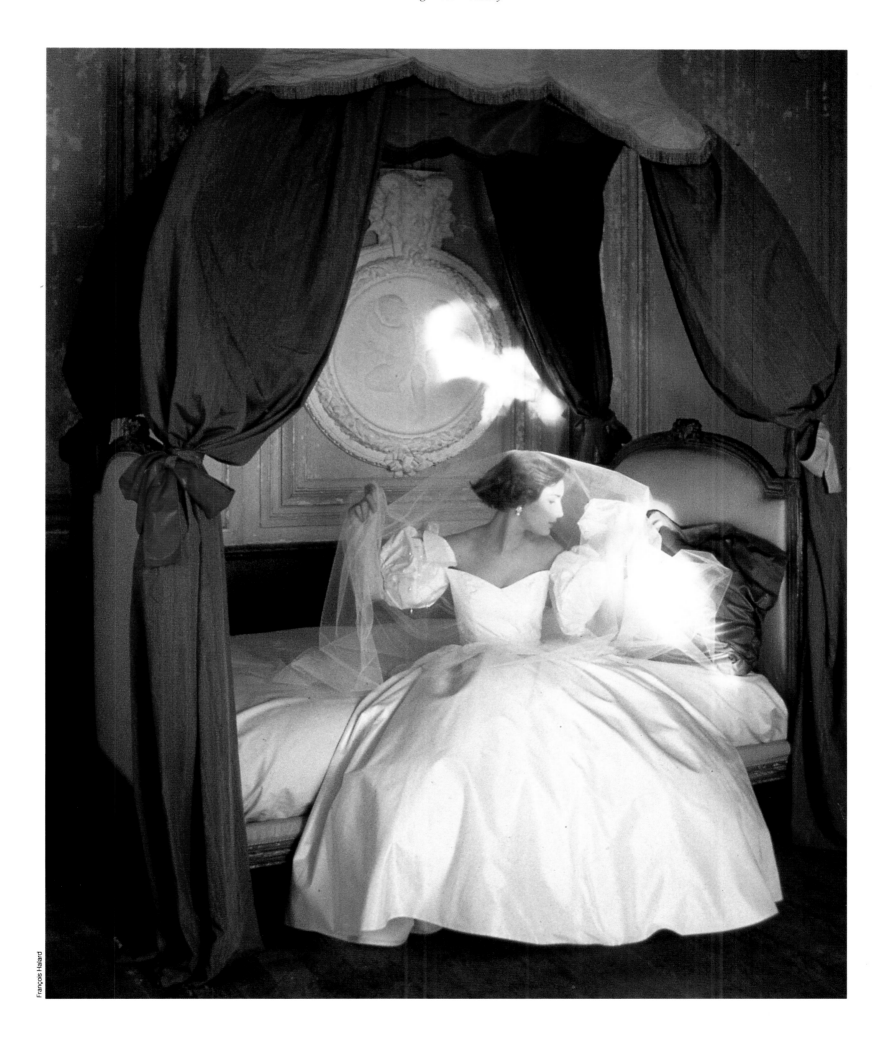

François Halard

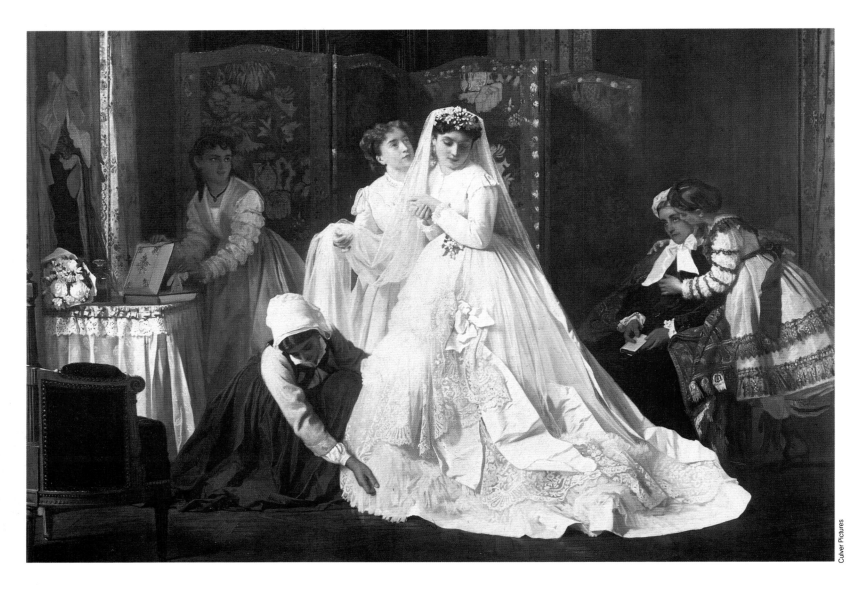

Culver Pictures

flowers, in the ceremony. Such a wedding was a grand achievement for any woman with social aspirations, and naturally, the bride's appearance was of central importance to this fanciful tableau. Victoria's nuptials initiated a popular demand for distinctive, beautiful, white wedding gowns that to this day has never abated.

The industrial revolution spawned a vast redistribution of wealth that created a sizable middle class and a nouveau riche upper class, both prepared to emulate the fashionable directions of the royal court. A booming, steam-powered textile industry provided a wide range of fabrics, even machine-made lace, at affordable prices. (No respectable bride married without at least a touch of lace in her ensemble.) The invention of the sew-

ing machine in 1846 revolutionized the dressmaking industry. Most brides, following patterns featured in fashion journals, made their own gowns or hired a dressmaker. In 1850, an Englishman named Charles Worth opened a fashion house in Paris, and thereby became the world's first couturier.

Until Worth, dressmakers were not considered designers and rarely labeled their clothing. Worth's prestigious salon was an elegant empire of high fashion. Women clamored to be dressed in his glamorous designs—a true sign of arrival in society. Many women, unable to afford a full Worth wardrobe, would insist on a Worth bridal gown, hoping to start their marriage on the right rung of the social ladder. If lack of fam-

ily connections precluded an appointment with the master, fashion magazines frequently featured designs to copy. Keeping pace with the demands of the middle class, the infant ready-made industry began to market seasonal dress styles by the 1880s, and by 1890 numerous department stores featured clothing departments, a boon to the working girl with little time to sew her own clothes. Finally, almost every bride could live out the dream of marrying in a new bridal dress.

The Victorian standards of morality dictated that the ideal woman should be modest, feminine, charming, respectable, acquiescent, and completely dependent on the male. A woman's dress clearly reflected her subscription to these values. The modest woman was always hidden under her clothes, which camouflaged her physical form, covering as much skin as possible. No respectable woman ever left home without a bonnet, her face concealed by its brim. Gloves were always worn in public, even indoors. Legs, considered terribly provocative, were buried under layers of petticoats and hoops. Any conversational reference to these limbs, even to inanimate legs, courted social disfavor; proper homes even hid their parlor piano's legs under ruffled pantaloons. Gracefulness was measured by the delicate balance a woman maintained when encircled by massive, cumbersome hoops. For over twenty years these fashionable bands of steel or whalebone tested feminine finesse.

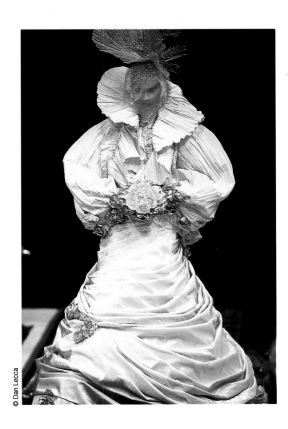

Precise draping creates sensational sweeps of fabric, an enduring signature of a beautifully finished gown. **OPPOSITE PAGE:** *A sensual swirl of skirts and floral embellishment was popular with Victorian brides.* **ABOVE:** *A flourish of gilt blossoms nestles in luxurious folds by Ungaro.* **ABOVE RIGHT:** *Orange blossom, a hallmark of maidenhood, was also de rigueur for Victorian brides.*

At their most absurd width these cages had to be lowered onto a woman's waist from a ceiling-mounted pulley—the hoops were too broad to step into or for anyone to get close enough to assist. When she was finally dressed in this frilly trap, a woman was truly a decorative object; the slightest wrong movement could wreak havoc. Crinolines, equally voluminous, were the softer alternative to hoops; a lavish bride's dress would layer at least four full skirts trimmed with flounces and ruches, incorporating at least 1,100 yards of fabric for a single gown.

The advent of railroad travel demanded a more practical silhouette. By 1875, narrower skirts with a rear bustle were the rage. These gowns, while easier to maneuver in, were not much easier to carry, as a lavishly trimmed dress often weighed ten pounds. Women's loads grew lighter by the end of the century, however, with the arrival of a new popular style, immortalized in drawings of contemporary working girls by Charles Dana Gibson: the unadorned fluid skirt with a train and topped by an elaborate bodice with wide sleeves. Propriety required that the turn-of-the-century woman—and especially the bride—still be tightly corseted and hidden under a frilly bodice with a high neck (known as a wedding band collar). "It should always be remembered that no matter how beautiful the neck and arms of a bride are, she is sinning against good form who does not have a high neck and long-sleeved bodice, for it must be remembered that she is not going to a dance or a reception, but to a religious ceremony," advised the *Ladies Home Journal* in 1890.

Today it is the mid-century Victorian fashion ideal—a narrow waist, tight bodice, and graceful, full skirt with a train—that is most reworked and widely recognized as the classic bridal silhouette. Designers today blend details from different decades—the bustle

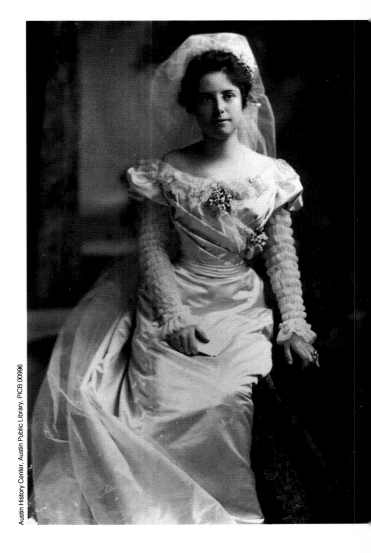

Austin History Center, Austin Public Library, PICB 00996

and the Gibson gigot sleeve—to invoke nineteenth-century fantasy for a twentieth-century woman.

Ladies' journals proliferated during the nineteenth century. *New Monthly Belle Assemble, Ladies Cabinet, World of Fashion,* and *Godey's Lady's Book,* to name a few, documented the feminine sports: society events, fashion, and etiquette. The new bourgeois valued the news and advice, those with social pretensions doing their best to strictly follow the magazine's dictates. Weddings, often described in detail in the journals, were an important occasion to parade the latest feminine fashions. After Queen Victoria's wedding, fashion plates illustrating white wedding gowns became a regular feature of the journals. According to *Godey's Lady's Book* in 1849, "Custom has decided, from the

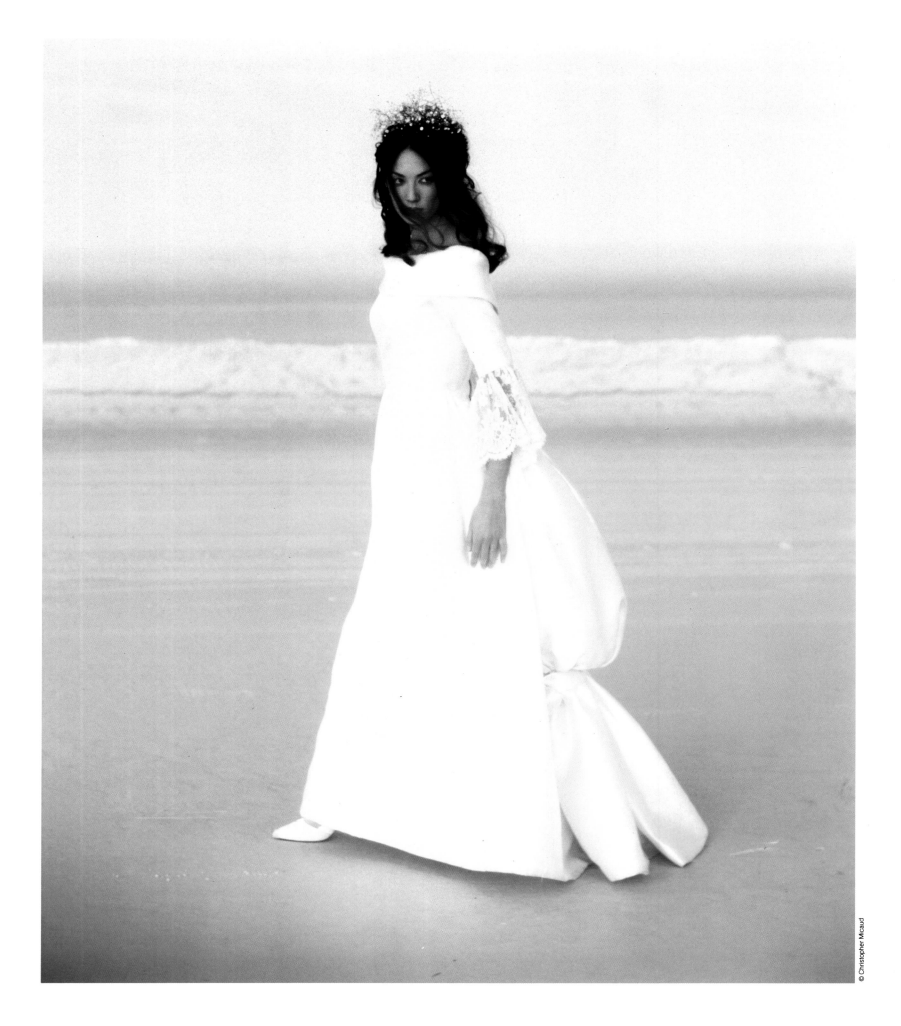

earliest ages, that white is the most fitting hue, whatever may be the material. It is an emblem of innocence and purity of girlhood, and the unsullied heart she now yields to the keeping of the chosen one. This should also be the hue of the flowers which compose the wreath and bouquet, for both are now considered indispensable." However, despite the editorial support for the all-white bridal gown, many women still chose to wear one of the fashionable hues—for example, in 1886 brown and blue were popular—which made for a more practical best dress for after the nuptials. Nevertheless, with consistent promotion white bridals steadily gained favor through the century. A bride would be reminded in an 1889 issue of the *Delineator* that since her "wedding is the most important event in a young girl's life, it seems, therefore, right not only that all appropriate pomp and ceremony should be displayed, but that the insignia of bridehood should be adhered to. The illusion veil, the orange blossoms and the pure white gown are the bride's, not only because of her position, but also from time-honored custom." Finally white became so accepted as the bride's banner that the *Ladies Home Journal* noted in 1890: "from time immemorial the bride's gown has been white." While not quite accurate, this reference highlights how deeply instilled the image of the bride in white had become.

Although there are early records noting the presence of orange blossoms—a guest at U.S. president John Adams' son's wedding reported that the bride wore white satin, orange blossoms, and pearls—it earned a royal association when, as a bride, Queen Victoria prominently displayed this Mediterranean symbol of fertility. Its sentimental symbolism appealed to most Victorian brides who, for extra measure, festooned their gowns with garlands of sweet-smelling orange blossoms. The royal approval trans-

formed these tiny blooms into a vital element of bridal regalia. In fact, noted *Harper's Bazar,* the wedding was "the only time in a woman's life [when] she [could] wear these fragrant blossoms." (Unfortunately for brides living in northern climes, the delicate, short-lived flowers rarely survived being transported—wax copies were necessary for these weddings.) It is a measure of the power wielded by these ladies' journals that every bride, despite her circumstances or the look or newness of her gown, tried her best to wear orange blossoms and a veil. Indeed, many photographs survive of Wild West brides severely posed in their best dress and sporting a veil and orange bloom.

Recognizing their leadership role for readers, the journals abounded in practical advice for the average bride. "It is to the careful young woman with but a few hundred dollars to spend that we hope to give some assistance," noted *Harper's Bazar* in 1868. "The price of satin varies from seven to fifteen dollars a yard, the popular quality, 27 inches wide, is sold at eight dollars. Faille and soft poult de soie [sic] are the next choice after satin, and cost about the same. Very handsome corded silk at four to six dollars a yard and plain taffetas as low as three dollars, but these require an over skirt of illusion that add considerably to the outlay." The wise bride was also reminded by the *Ladies Home Journal* in 1894 that with "a white gown thought must be given to the becomingness of the shade, for after all, there are as many tones in white as in other colors; the one that most suits the pale blonde is absolutely unbecoming to the rosy brunette."

In addition, no magazine could afford to ignore the accessories of the bridal dress. After highlighting the favorite bridal dresses of the season—silver-flecked tulle over white satin, white crepe lisse over a slip of white silk—*Godey's Lady's Book,* in 1850, went on

to inform the bride that "tulle veils, very full, are still worn more than any other. They are inexpensive and always give a peculiar grace and delicacy to the face and figure." Whether tulle or lace, "the wedding veil is certainly the most necessary part of a bride's costume, and it is much more a matter for great care in arranging it on the head than people seem to think necessary," cautioned *Harper's Bazar* in 1895. The magazine wisely suggested that a bride make several attempts, before her wedding, to attach her veil to her head. Otherwise, the editors warned, "the prettiest woman can be made to look like a fright with her veil put on unbecomingly, and the handsome lace veil badly adjusted would look worse than even a coarse tulle one." The veil

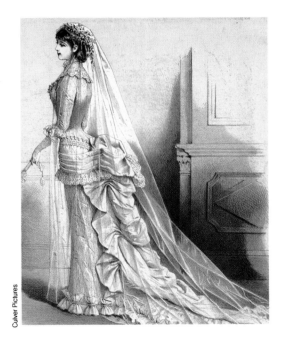

ABOVE: *By the end of the 1870s, hooped skirts were no longer stylish; fashionable women opted instead for gowns with elaborate bustles.*
OPPOSITE PAGE: *A modern variation by Josephus Melchoir for Balenciaga pairs the same sleek bodice with a lavish bustle.*

was sacrosanct, and even if a bride opted to be wed in a fetching bonnet, it would have a veil. Lace veils were the preferred, but more expensive, choice. Even Queen Victoria wore a veil of net—although lavishly adorned with floral lace appliqués. As successive generations of nineteenth-century brides married, it became popular to wear an heirloom veil—something borrowed. And to complete the picture, *Godey's Lady's Book,* in 1849, reminded brides that "white silk stockings and satin slippers should always be the accompaniment of a bridal dress. Kid or prunella have a vulgar look."

Although nineteenth-century etiquette demanded that the bridal veil and orange blossom garland be removed immediately after the wedding, it was widely recommended that a bride rewear her wedding dress as often as possible in the early days of her married life, for both sentimental and practical considerations. The *Delineator* insisted, in 1889, that "the orange blossoms and the veil are never worn again after the wedding; even if the gown be assumed the next day, white roses or some other flower must be substituted for the orange blossom, [for] they are sacred to the bride and not to the wife." In fact, most brides ordered or made their bridal gown with the intention of having it redesigned for later use. Since the bride's garb closely resembled the fashions of the day, with slight changes the wedding dress was perfectly appropriate for wear on other occasions. The ever-practical *Ladies Home Journal* advised brides to always use plenty of fabric rather than extra trimmings when making the gown, as "you will always be able to make it over into another style, whereas with less material and a few odds

and ends of trimming, this is doubtful." It was also quite common to have a second bodice made at the same time as the bridal bodice and skirt to allow for an immediate option for rewear.

By the end of the century, the Victorian wedding was big business, supported by a booming fashion trade. Traditional, laden with sentimental trappings, and endorsed by nostalgic brides, Victorian style has been well documented, captured forever in photographs and numerous illustrations, to serve as inspiration for many of today's brides.

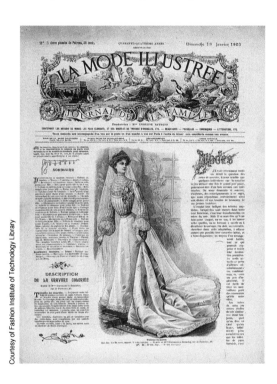

Courtesy of Fashion Institute of Technology Library

Brides at the turn of the century were dedicated to the white wedding gown and ethereal veil, yet the style of their gowns closely echoed the fashions of the times. **ABOVE:** *The shirt-waist blouse with leg-o'-mutton sleeves and S-shape style typical of the Gibson girls.* **OPPOSITE PAGE:** *The typically pleated Edwardian bodice and plain skirt.*

THE TWENTIETH CENTURY

During the first few years of the new century, the Edwardian bride enthusiastically embraced the traditions promoted by her Victorian predecessors and made them larger than life. As for the Victorians, a busy social life was a significant goal of members of the Belle Epoque society, and fashion was a preeminent indicator of social success. It was typical for Edwardian ladies to change at least five times daily, as a different costume was required for each social event and time of day, including motoring, luncheons, sporting events, European court functions, and the grandest events of all, weddings. And changing was no easy feat, as Jean Cocteau noted: "To undress one of these ladies was obviously a complicated enterprise that had to be planned well in advance, like moving a house." The ideal of the big wedding with its own costume took on theatrical proportions: the bride and her (usually large) wedding party dressed thematically. A popular motif required the bridesmaids to be outfitted in wide-brimmed, flower-bedecked hats and to carry garlanded crooks, creating the image of a bevy of shepherdesses escorting the bride. This idyllic picture was completed with monstrous bouquets of hothouse blooms and ferns dripping with ribbons and love knots. As the *Delineator* noted in 1900, "Simplicity…is not a feature of wedding

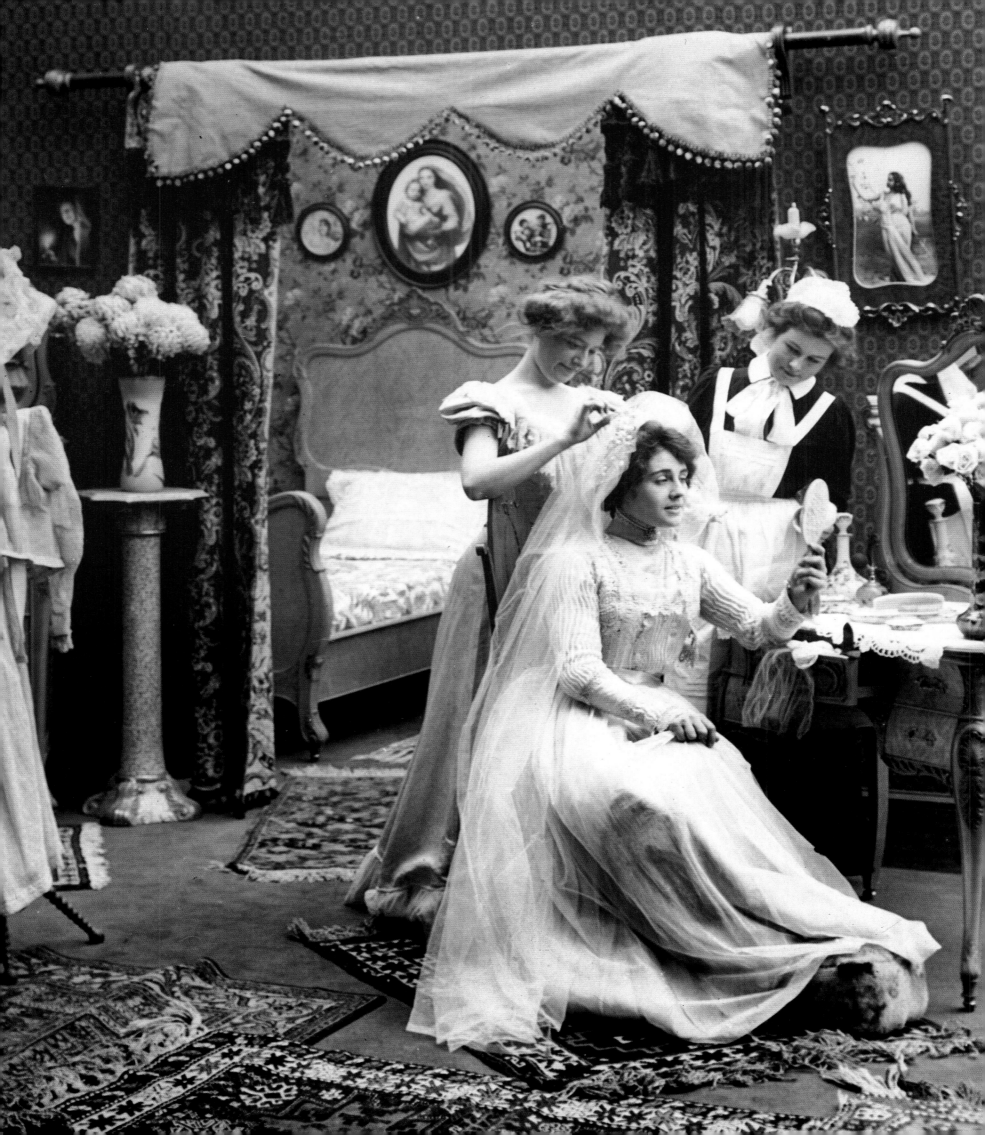

dresses this year. No fabric is considered too rich…whether it be cloth of silver or white velvet worked with seed pearls." Confronting a new century, a new world, and a new life on her wedding day, the bride attempted to rekindle a measure of Old World charm. No one knew how soon the world would change forever.

As fashion evolved, bridal details provided a comforting link with tradition. **BELOW:** *A bride married in 1912 followed prim Victorian standards by wearing a high neckline and long gloves.* **RIGHT:** *The bridal bouquet, a small posy in the 1800s, had grown to a lush bouquet by 1913.* **OPPOSITE PAGE:** *By the 1920s, massive shower bouquets laden with beribboned loveknots were all the rage.*

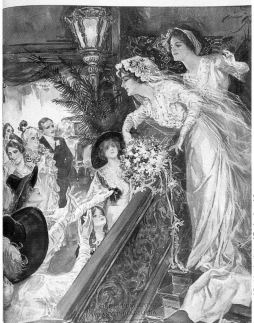

THE LADIES' HOME JOURNAL

OCTOBER 1913 · FIFTEEN CENTS

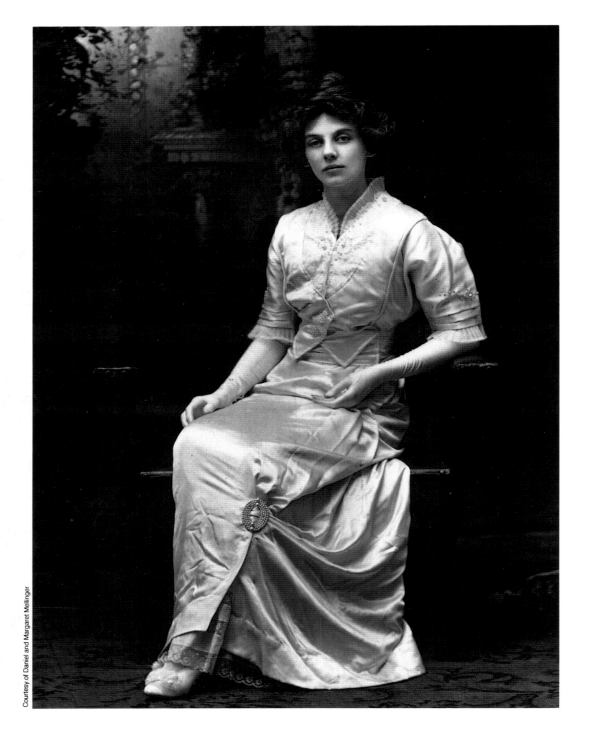

The "war to end all wars" began in 1914, a cataclysm that is well documented in the changing fashions of the times. As the world situation became more serious, it was considered appropriate and necessary for women to wear functional, not purely ornamental clothes. The body was finally freed from the restrictive corset, revealing a natural waistline and bust. Skirts became shorter, showing ankles for the first time. After the war, the freedom of fashion reflected women's fight against their traditional roles; in 1920, the Nineteenth Amendment was passed in the United States, finally granting women personhood and the right to vote.

As women awoke to their new freedom, a designer named Coco Chanel captured the energy of the new era with her distinctive style: tubular, easy-to-wear knee-length tunic dresses, bobbed hair requiring less daily maintenance, and manly but fluid blazers worn with, of all things, trousers. A major fashion force, Chanel officially introduced the short wedding dress, worn just below the knee with a court train. The gown was white. From this point on, even though other colors were occasionally favored by some brides, white was the universal color of choice. Veils survived in the '20s as a link to traditional wedding garb, with a general rule of the shorter the dress, the longer the veil.

Reality came crashing down on the fun and frivolity of the flapper era in 1929 as the stock market crashed and the Great Depression brought economic disaster. As many Depression brides made do with their best dresses, Hollywood flourished, providing an antidote to the painful times with glamour, wealth, and romance combating the dismal poverty and low spirits of the public. The power of film reached a peak as beautiful women and handsome men became instant celebrities when captured on celluloid. For most women, the excitement of the silver screen could be captured only by emulating the exquisite fashions and orchestrating their own glamorous event—like a wedding. By the end of the 1930s, as the economy rebounded, creative designers in Europe and America took their cues from this new assertive glamour: cut undeniably sexy and sleek, their new fashions evoked a refined modernism that swept the world in every art from architecture to literature.

When Princess Marina of Greece married the Duke of Kent in 1934, she wore a gown designed by Molyneux: a slim sheath of white and silver lamé with slender, fitted sleeves and a court train that cascaded from her shoulders to pool on the floor. A beautiful, elegantly dressed woman, she captured the spirit of the 1930s. Her headpiece was not of orange blossoms—too old-fashioned for the modern woman—but was a fringed tiara of diamonds, patterned like the sun's rays, with a sweeping tulle veil that was ten feet wide at its base. The

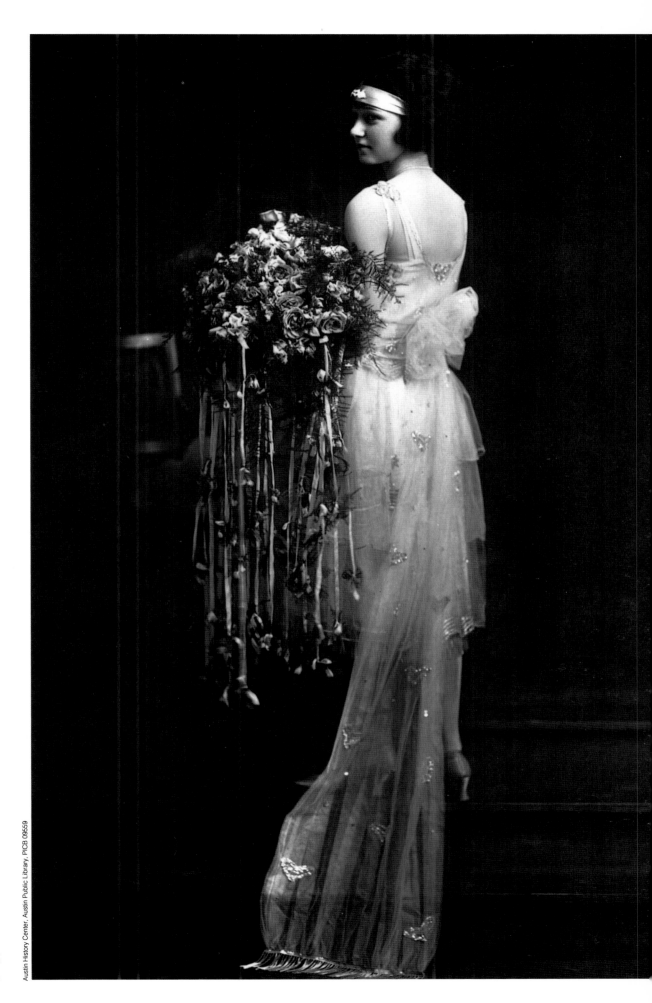

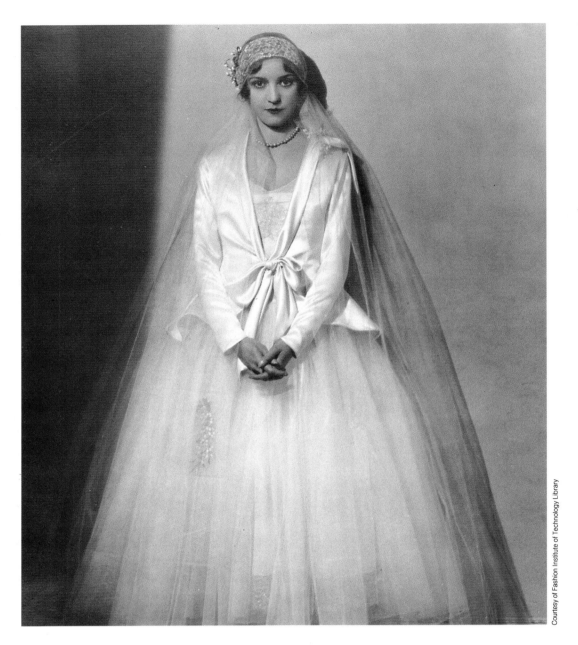

Fashionable brides of the 1920s often wore cloche caps with very long veils, and typically the shorter the dress, the longer the veil. The thoroughly modern alternative was a short, tiered skirt of charmeuse **(OPPOSITE PAGE)** *or an ankle-skimming skirt of tulle, designed by J. Whitehead in 1927* **(ABOVE)***; but always, the veils swept the floor in lieu of a train.*

Courtesy of Fashion Institute of Technology Library

lisher who introduced, in 1934, a quarterly magazine dedicated to the bride: *So You're Going To Be Married.* The first issue breathlessly announced "...you have set the date for the great day. Your day. It is the one day you have dreamed about since first romance was born in your heart...it must be perfect in every particular. Everything about it should be just as you desire.... It's the culmination of exciting weeks of preparation—hectic shopping, sending out invitations, opening presents; it's the symbol of great adventures to some—your honeymoon, your home, your role as hostess." Renamed in 1936, *The Bride's Magazine* eventually shortened its name to just *Bride's* but added hundreds of pages of valuable, effervescent advice each issue to guide the bride through every moment of her exciting engagement to its thrilling conclusion. The bridal bible featured the latest bridal fashions, so that brides would never again question what to wear.

power of communications transmitted her glorious image round the world, creating an instant demand for this new look, especially the regal headpiece. The efforts of marketers and of manufacturers to respond rapidly to the new trend made it possible for brides to have costume copies of Marina's tiara almost immediately: now every bride could be queen for a day. Retailing empires grew with stores crisscrossing the country, providing mass access to fashion. Bridal departments were a staple of the best stores: Lord & Taylor, John Wanamaker and Company, Bonwit Teller, and others advertised just to the bride. All this bridal brouhaha caught the attention of a pub-

World War II (1939–1945) had a profound effect on every aspect of American life. Men and women went to war, women staffed the work force of domestic industries, "frivolous" manufacturing was aborted, and rationing became a fact of life. The War Production Board legislated domestic restrictions in order to channel every resource toward the fight. The fashion industry was not exempt: turned-up cuffs, double yokes, sashes, patch pockets, and attached hoods were all banned. Not only did the war restrictions affect everyday fashion—for example, hosiery was out of production—but luxury industries, including bridal manufacturing, were also hard hit. The Association of Bridal Manufacturers vigorously lobbied Congress and the War Production

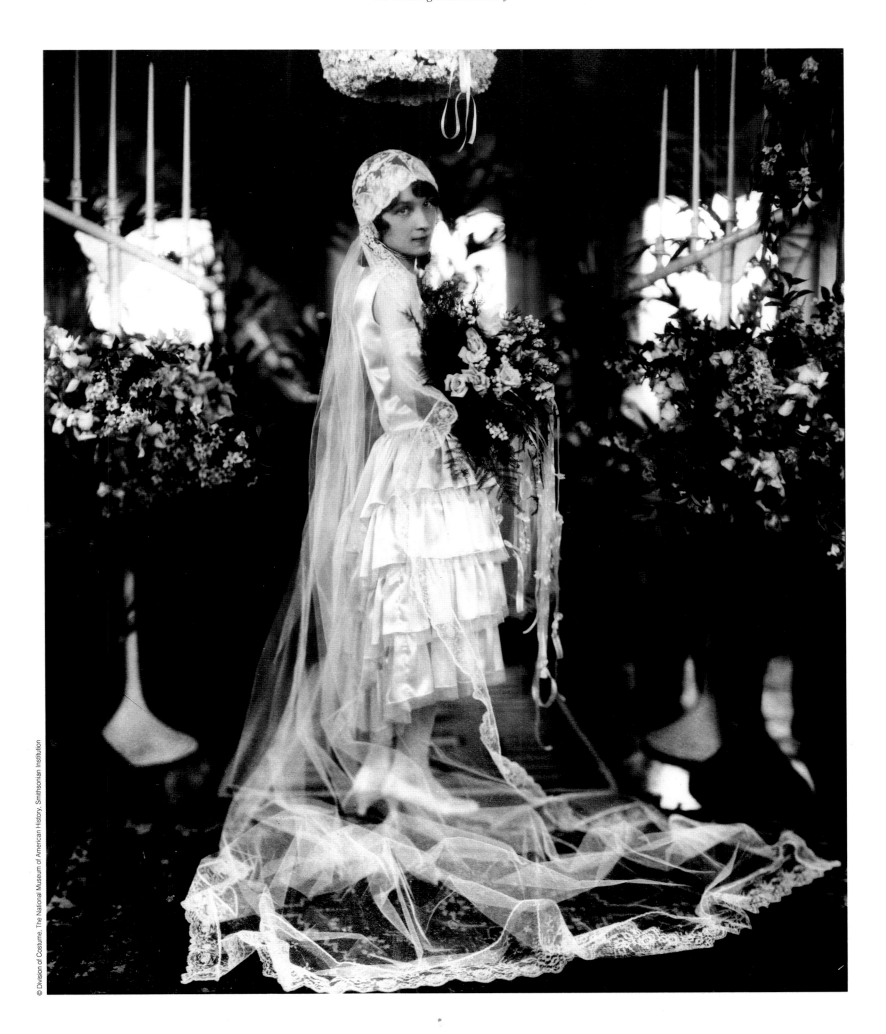

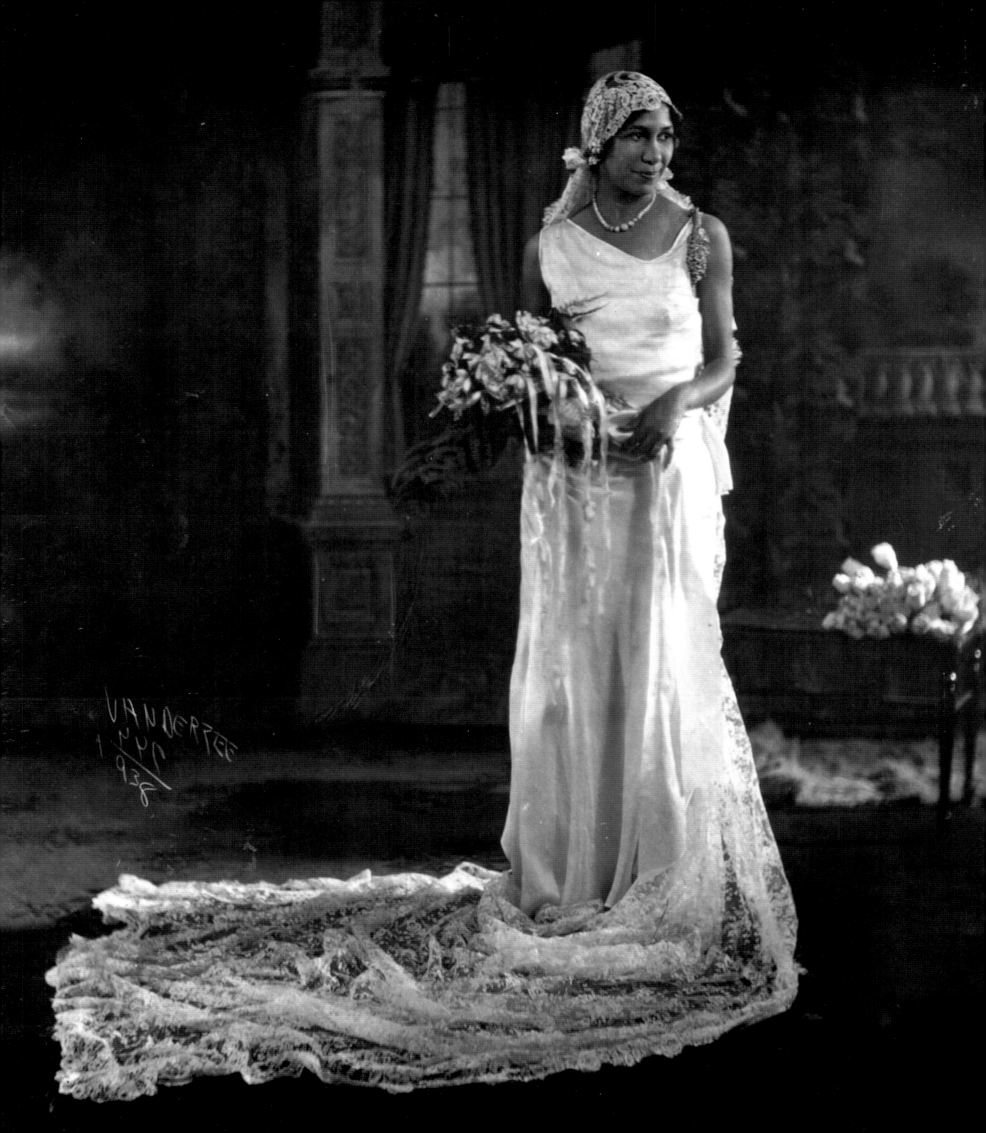

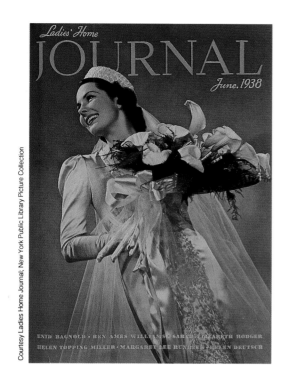

Board to change their decision to cut back on fabric availability (silk, used in parachutes, was particularly hard to get) for bridal designers. After all, the association argued, what is America fighting for, if it isn't to maintain the traditional values represented by the ceremony of marriage? The American government proved it had a soft spot for romance by easing some restrictions on the bridal industry.

During wartime, most brides felt it was their patriotic duty to forsake a traditional wedding. With engagements lasting only days or weeks, there really was no time to plan to wear anything but their best suit. Women who wanted to wear a white wedding gown would borrow or rent one, an acceptable wartime option. There is one woman who remembers passing her gown on to so many different friends—and friends of friends—that it was eventually lost. Brides who could afford a custom-made gown at this time had to search hard for prewar satin and silk—or use the fabric from an old gown. Military couples who fell in love were wed in their respective dress uniforms. Although the world was gripped by a violent battle for freedom, romance and marriage

not only persevered but thrived. A regular wartime column in *Vogue* titled "Marrying in Haste, Accelerated Wedding Plans" blithely acknowledged that "weddings nowadays hang not on the bride's whim, but on the decision of the groom's commanding officer. He names the day—when he grants that unexpected furlough….The 1942 schedule may run something like this: engagement announced, if it hasn't already been announced, on Monday, invitations sent out by telegram on Wednesday….the last handful of rice and rose petals flung on Saturday." The columnist happily reminded the nervous bride, "You can still have all the trimmings that really count. A pretty dress; flowers; the people you like (and most of them will manage to get there, somehow, at the last minute); music; toasts; gaiety. These aren't trimmings, anyway. They are essentials."

In the postwar 1950s, men and women reverted to their traditional roles: men in the work force and women at home. Once again, fashion reflected the change in values. A fabulously feminine form, credited to Christian Dior in 1947, was the new look: a high, round bosom; a tiny waist; knee-length, full skirts worn over crisp crinolines; and tight bodices with scoop necklines. This modern reinterpretation of nineteenth-century style was enthusiastically embraced by the bridal industry. Nylon, invented in 1938, was a postwar bridal fashion phenomenon. Crinolines, bridal veils, and dress fabrics were crafted from this stiff net. Once again, following but also transcending the fashion of the times, the 1950s bride often married in an ankle-length, trainless bridal gown of nylon lace, point d'esprit, or organdy over stiff crinolines and a short bouffant veil. The classic

image of the traditional bridal gown, created in the nineteenth century, was reborn in the fashions and values of the 1950s. And not unlike their Victorian counterparts, brides of this time wanted weddings with all the trimmings. Postwar prosperity made this an option for almost every bride.

The tremendous publicity generated from grand weddings, like that of Grace Kelly in 1956, fueled society's fantasies of big weddings and beautifully gowned brides. When royalty married quintessential Hollywood glamour, a magical bridal gown was in order: 25 yards of peau de soie, 25 yards of silk taffeta, 100 yards of silk net, and 300 yards of Valencienne lace combined to dress the princess. Bridal salons, dedicated to fulfilling the individual needs of the everyday bride, opened up across the country

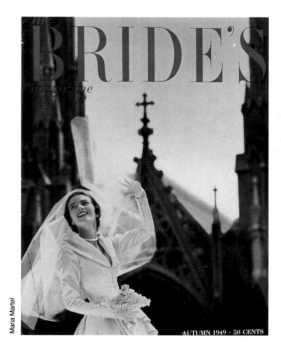

The art deco spirit was clearly evident in streamlined gowns from the 1930s. A cloche, a veil of lace, and a bouquet with loveknots **(OPPOSITE PAGE)** *was inspired by days past, while the pillbox cap and armful of calla lilies* **(ABOVE LEFT)** *pointed to the future.* **ABOVE:** *After a decade of wartime austerity, brides rallied to the altar in complete bridal regalia.*

in response to the demand for equally Cinderella-like events. Emporiums devoted to promoting the bridal industry and catering to the bride were fundamental in establishing an unwavering feminine predisposition for a custom-ordered, all-white wedding gown that would be worn only once.

Until the last few years of the 1960s formal weddings were the standard. The most popular bridal gowns were conservative by design, less frivolous, longer versions of the 1950s wedding dress. Men and women exchanged vows without questioning the stereotyped roles they were about to assume.

Recognizing the profound merits of tradition, *Bride's* magazine reminded its readers in 1961 that "there is something infinitely dignified and reassuring in knowing that the etiquette of the formal wedding is not a hodgepodge of arbitrary rules but a beautifully integrated procedure that is full of meaning." However, faced with the painful reality that traditional values were question-

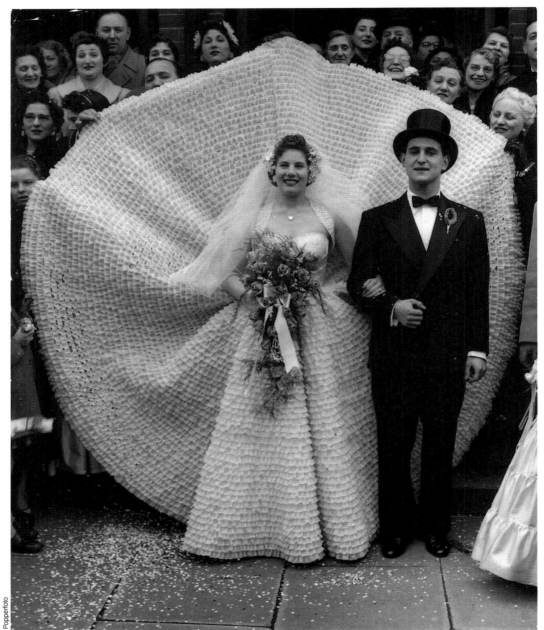

able and no longer met the needs of many modern young people, a whole generation rebelled. Anti-war, anti-fashion, anti-conservative, but pro-love, pro-peace, pro-people young people in the 1960s uprooted long-standing bridal traditions in favor of earthier ceremonies that celebrated their modern values. Young couples still fell in love and vowed to share their lives—but in their own words, on beaches at twilight instead of cathedrals at noon. Reaching out for natural, simple options that did not smack of their parents' generation, many young women chose cotton caftans and

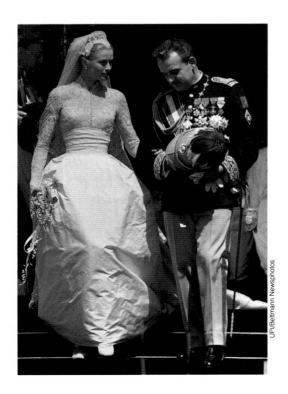

Quintessential 1950s fashion—a tight, molded bodice, a defined waist, and a full skirt—is still the prototypical bridal silhouette. **OPPOSITE PAGE:** *Fine lace, by Valentino for his sister's wedding, is always classic.* **LEFT:** *Hundreds of yards of precious peau de soie and lace by Helen Rose, a Hollywood studio designer, were worn by former movie star Princess Grace.* **ABOVE:** *Crinolines supported the fullest skirt and protected the modesty of the '50s bride when necessary.*

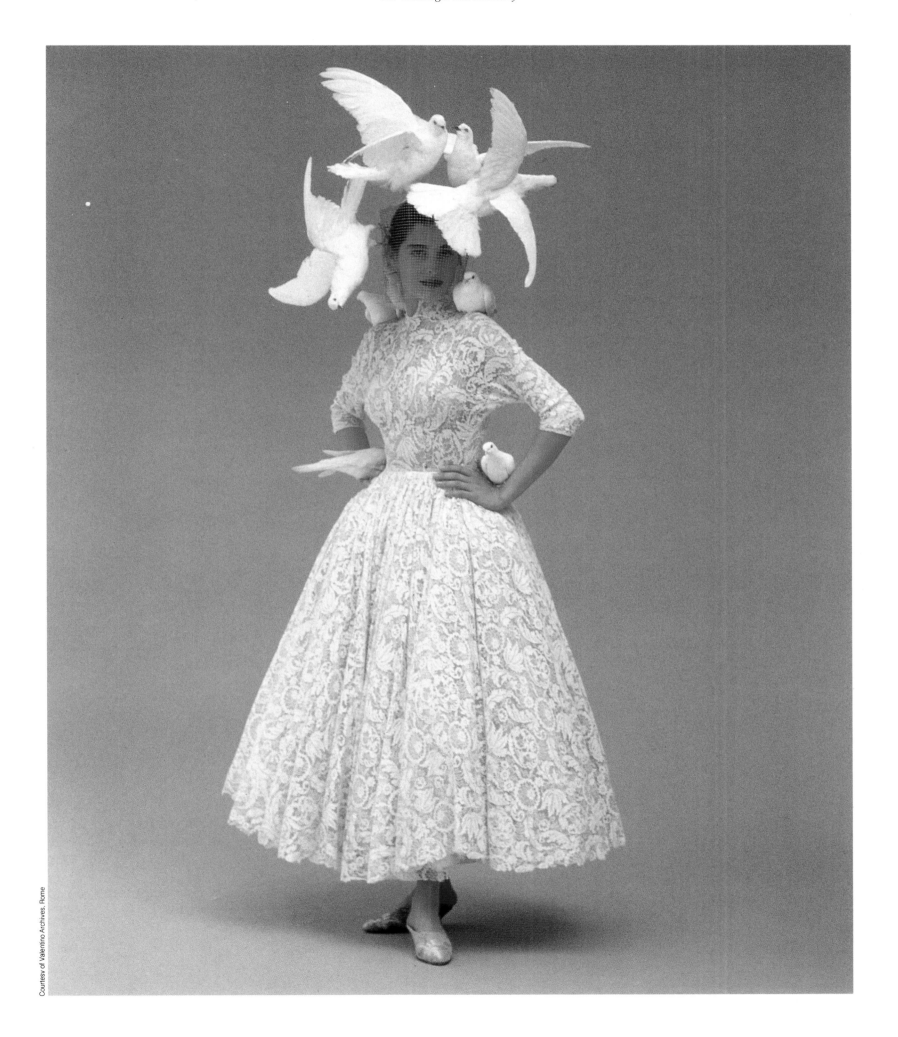

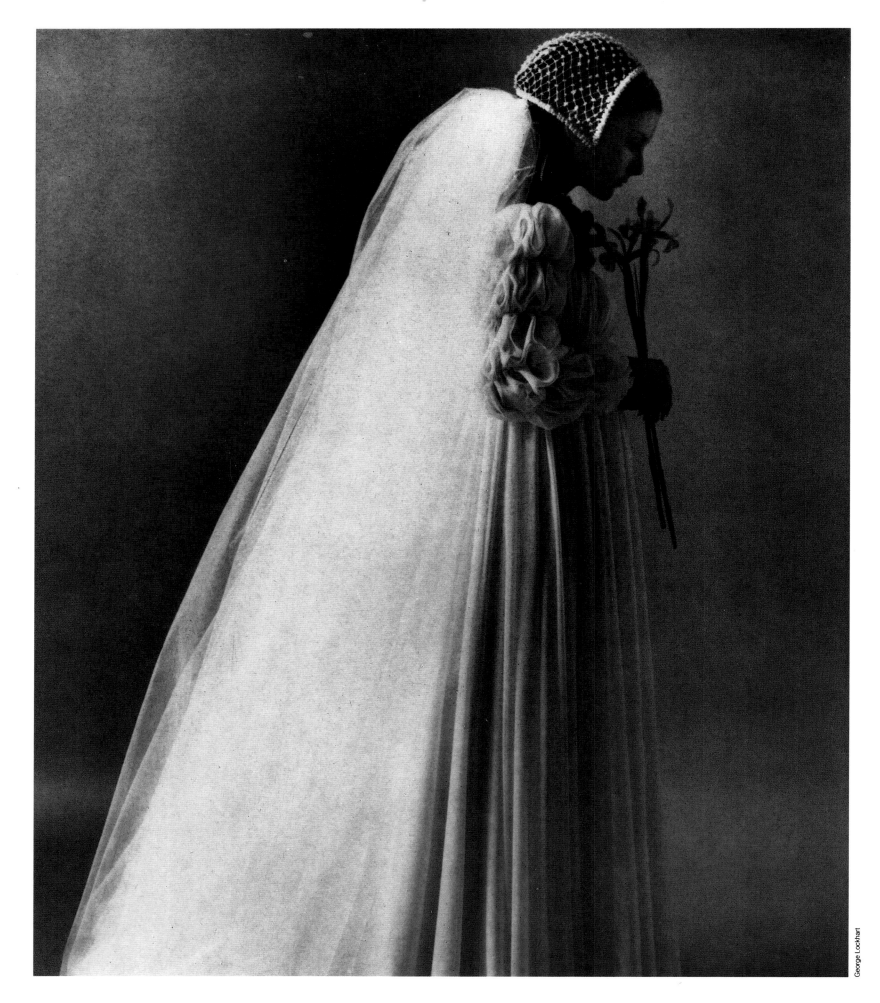

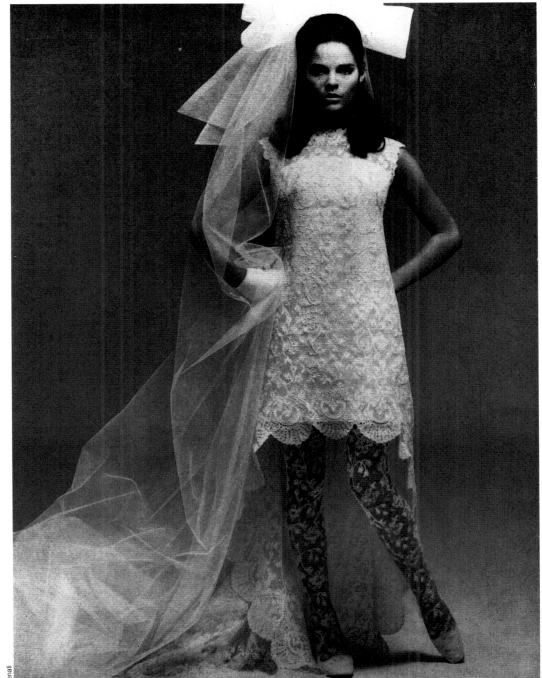

Penati

peasant smocks to replace tulle and silk ballgowns as the bride's garb. Specifically for this bride, a store called the Barefoot Bride opened in New York City in 1972 stocking muslin, cotton lace, and eyelet dresses; hats rather than veils; Mexican wedding gowns of embroidered white cotton; and medieval-style caftans and hoods.

Despite the popularity of these new directions, most brides could not help but be emotionally linked to the past—these brides still coveted a measure of tradition. In 1971, 94 percent of the wedding gowns sold were white and, although minis were the rage, 87 percent of the bridal dresses were floor-length; although women fought for equality, went to work, opposed the war, and burned their bras, the universal dream of an all-white wedding never really faded. At a time of tremendous reevaluation of personal and social values, this gown offered a measure of security in tradition.

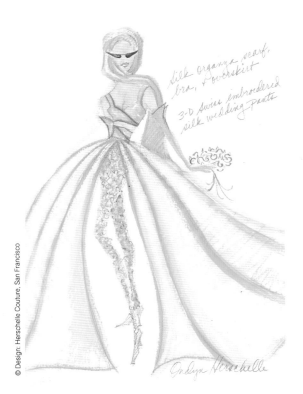

silk organza scarf,
bra, Overskirt
3-D Swiss embroidered
silk wedding Pants

© Design: Herschelle Couture, San Francisco

Ondyn Herschelle

In 1981 Lady Diana Spencer married Prince Charles of England, reminding everyone how truly romantic traditional pomp and circumstance can be. The world watched as Diana emerged from her horse-drawn carriage in a taffeta gown trimmed with thousands of pearls and sequins, bows, and antique lace, and a seemingly endless twenty-five-foot train. Diana was young, lovely, and apparently in love, just the right romantic incarnation to rejuvenate the bridal industry. After a decade of swinging singles and disco infernos, suddenly everyone

Widely heralded as the decade of revolt, the 1960s featured brides who exemplified the contrasting tempos of youth. **FAR LEFT:** *The romantic bride, inspired by Shakespeare's heroine, wore a beaded juliet cap and chiffon wedding gown by Miller.* **ABOVE:** *The groovy, albeit tradition-edged, alternative was an Alençon lace minidress that cascaded into a train, by Frank Massandrea.* **CENTER:** *Ondyn Herschelle updates the mod spirit with a midriff-baring bra paired with pencil-slim silk pants and a full, sheer overskirt of organza.*

Centuries of refinement have shaped today's bridal gown. The legacy balances tradition with feminine elegance. **BELOW:** *Sumptuous fabrics and inspired lines make this tiered A-line lace gown by Gianfranco Ferre for Christian Dior Boutique an ethereal option for today's bride.* **OPPOSITE PAGE:** *Exquisite details inspired by the past include a close-fitting bodice bedecked with three-dimensional beaded flowers on a dress by Ronald Mann for Victoria Royal.*

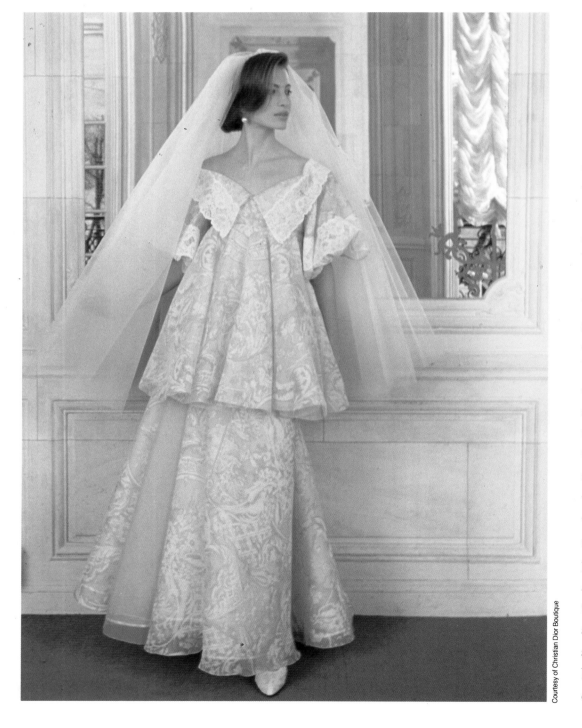

wanted to be married and every bride wanted a gown fit for a queen: regal and ornate, with a lengthy train, and a jeweled veil. The big white wedding was back in style and no expense seemed too great. When the scions of the Tisch and Steinberg families were married in 1987, at least $2 million was spent on the wedding celebrations. Five hundred guests enjoyed an elaborate full-course dinner, the best champagne, and a wedding cake estimated to have cost $18,000. The 12,000 white French tulips and 50,000 white French roses, lilies, and dogwood may have cost another million dollars. The bride's gown was by Scaasi. Lavish, opulent, glittering, luxurious, and bejeweled were descriptions that fit the bridal gowns of even the most ordinary bride during this decade of enormous prosperity and conspicuous consumption.

Settling into the 1990s and looking ahead to the next century, weddings are more popular than ever. Millions of couples seek the fundamental security and pleasure that marriage offers. As people rebound from the excesses of the previous decade, ostentatious displays of wealth are no longer considered in good taste; similarly, in the face of another major recession, the excessively ornate gown of the 1980s has become unfashionable. Today's bridal gown is most often classically but simply styled, borrowing details from the past but remaining true to the present, appealing to the tradition-loving but modern bride. Her dress is elegant without being fussy, and almost always long and white, but the generalities end here. Unlike the bridal gown typical of the nineteenth century and earlier, today's bridal gown echoes fashion, but doesn't follow it—it has a look all its own. Recognizing the diverse personalities, ages, life-styles, ethnic heritages, and fortunes that comprise the bridal population today, the fashion industry offers a dress for everyone. No longer is one limited style of wedding gown considered appropriate; what's more important is the way the wedding gown is styled—to express the bride's personality and the romance of the occasion. Although it is the nature of fashion to change, the wedding gown has always retained its aura of romance; over centuries of cultural and stylistic evolution, the wedding dress has endured as a magical, powerful symbol of love and romance.

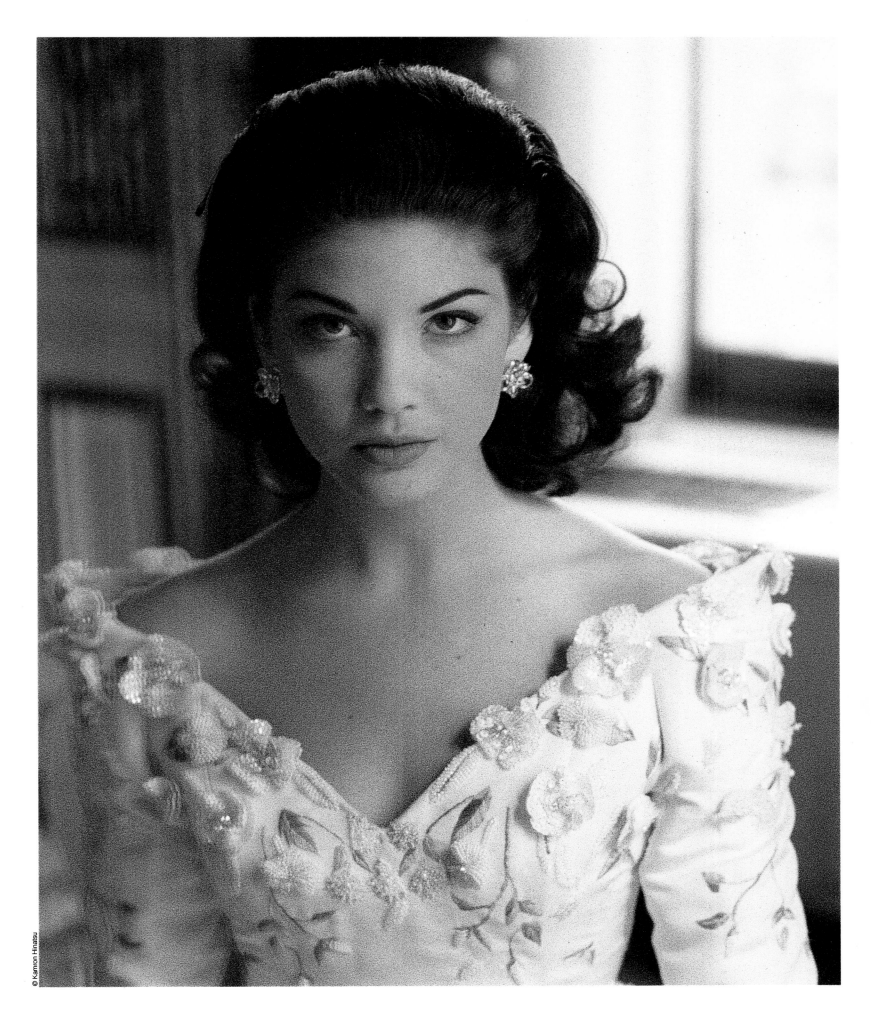

PART TWO

THE

MODERN

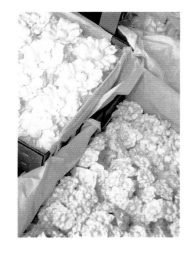 WEDDING

DRESS

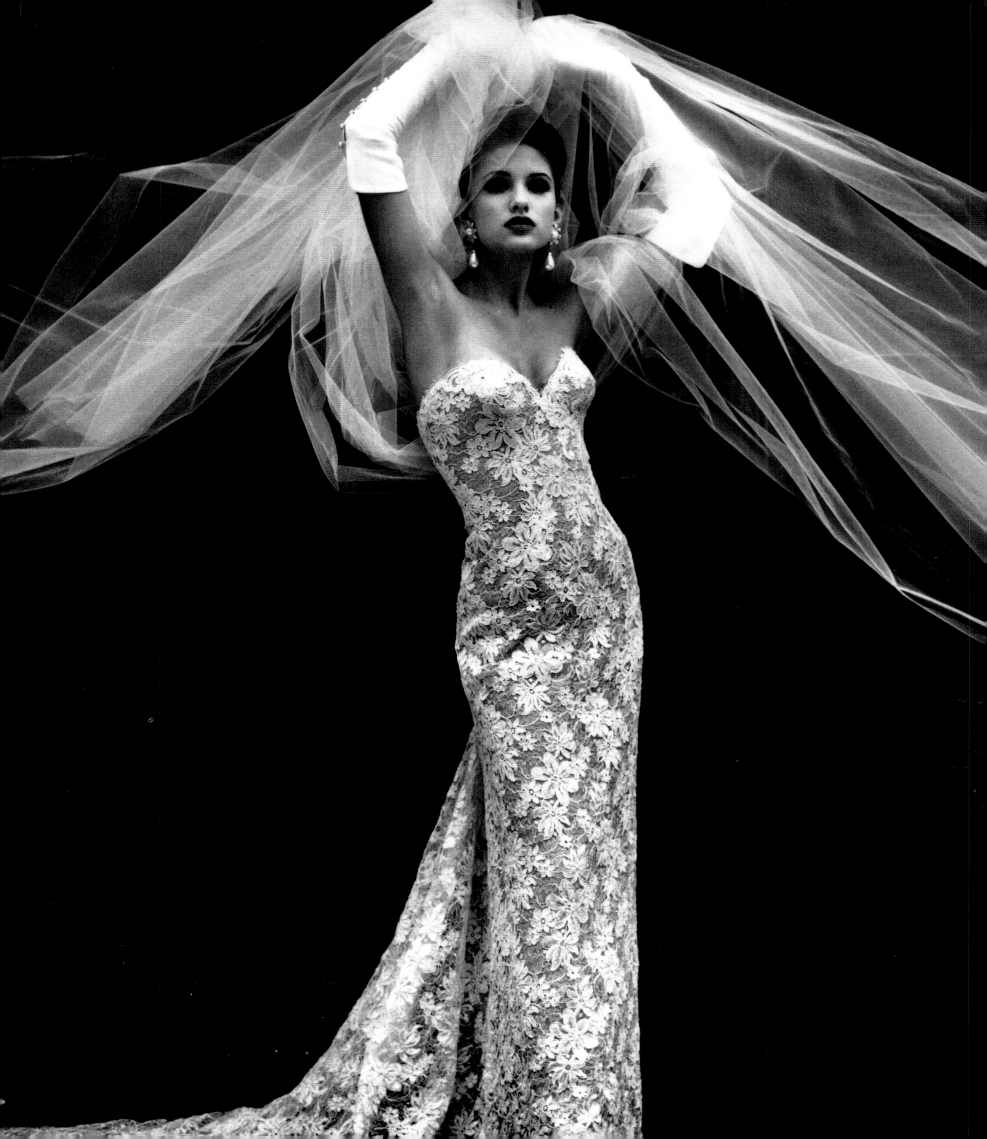

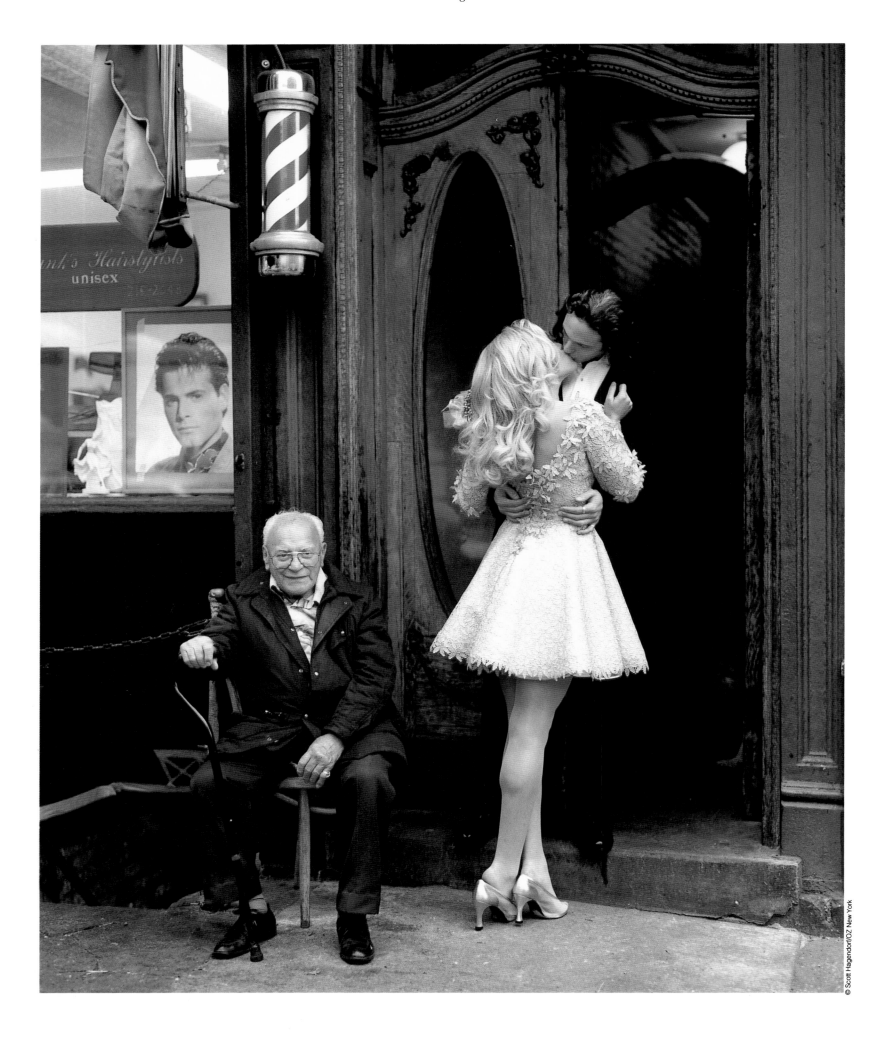

FACT AND FANTASY

Everyone is getting married—young and old, counterculture and conservative, never-married and often-married! All over the world, even as the times, styles, and values have changed, the wedding has remained an enduring institution, its popularity undiminished over time. As technology has made the world a smaller place, the grand old tradition of a bride attired in a big, beautiful white wedding gown has become an almost universally accepted image. We see her everywhere—exchanging vows in an ancient shrine near Tokyo; at a royal Zulu ceremony in Africa; trailed by a thirty-foot embroidered silk train at Westminster Abbey; in front of a roaring fire in a cozy Quebec inn; at the base of Ayers Rock in Australia; and even pulling up to an all-night drive-through wedding chapel in Las Vegas. History, the media, and loyal traditionalists have together molded an image of the bride that is a modern icon: the romantic, radiant, blushing bride, incandescent in layers of billowing, snowy white tulle and lace—yet, in truth, although this bride is an often-emulated fantasy, she is not always the reality.

Today's typical bride differs from the traditional image in two significant aspects: her age, a worldly twenty-eight today, compared to only nineteen in 1975, and the proliferation of second and third marriages, with 34 percent of all brides marrying again. Unlike the ingenue bride of earlier decades, this confident woman with seasoned taste is comfortable with her own personal style.

And not only will she want to wear a dress that embodies her own bridal fantasies, she'll be able to find it. On average, months, and frequently up to two years are spent piecing together all the important details of a modern wedding and carefully choosing the right dress. While still popular, the church wedding and club reception have just as often been traded for an exchange of vows at weekend-long gatherings of family and friends; holiday weddings at tropical resorts with guests flying or sailing to the celebration; private civil ceremonies followed by swank twilight receptions; stroke-of-midnight "I dos" and late-night revelry ending with an early-morning breakfast; plighting troths in medieval castles; promises to love and cherish have even been exchanged on a bus, traveling to a glitzy theme park. Certainly no one gown is right for every wedding, or for every bride. The modern woman has worked hard to establish her own identity, to craft a loving relationship with an equally unique man—she doesn't plan to ignore her own stylish instincts on her wedding day, nor should she.

Savvy fashion experts offer bridal ensembles ranging from leather to antique lace for today's bride, and they all agree that there is no single look appropriate for all weddings. Couture designers, ready-to-wear manufacturers, and vintage specialists unanimously concede that whatever the bride chooses to wear, she should feel—and therefore look—beautiful. Most brides try to achieve a look of timeless elegance that is at once modern but also classically rooted and personally significant. Even brides who opt for an untraditional, uniquely styled gown may yearn for some aspect of the traditional aesthetic. Thus, the essence of charming, captivating bridal beauty is a comfortable, compatible mix of personal style with a nod to tradition and a blush of fantasy.

Although the bride is dressing for one perfect day, she is ultimately dressing for a lifetime of memories. "It's important to accommodate the bride, to tailor a dress to her whims—it's the most important day, and she must feel beautiful in her dress, but she should be reminded not to be trendy," affirms Carolina Herrera, noted for her dedication to minimal, elegant gowns that underscore the personal beauty of the bride. "You must be aware of fashion but not be its slave," agrees Ann Stephens, the bridal designer for Laura Ashley. "If a gown is to become an heirloom to be passed down from one generation to another, it must keep its integrity without becoming overpowered by trends and looks that will quickly date it." An underlying sense of style, of what's right in line and fabric, is as important as ever for a truly striking gown. Norma Kamali's urbane brides "increasingly demand untraditional gowns"; however, these thoroughly modern dresses must "have a timeless beauty and be finished with beautiful details on the finest of fabrics." Without question, creating a palpable spirit of beauty is itself a goal in bridal design—to imbue the dress with a quality that is inspirational for the bride. A bride so attired is resonant with a beauty and happiness that is always apparent to her guests.

The best bridal gowns demand an intimate inspection of their beauty: "Elegant dresses don't shout at you from across the room, they force you to come closer to appreciate the details; you should always notice the woman first," reminds Jean Hoffman, the co-proprietor of a vintage bridal boutique. Of course, pure beauty is not the only consideration in dressing a bride. Mary McFadden believes in celebrating the sense of history behind the traditional wedding dress, no matter how modern the bride: "I think every bride should wear some shade of white. It represents the joy of the moment; it

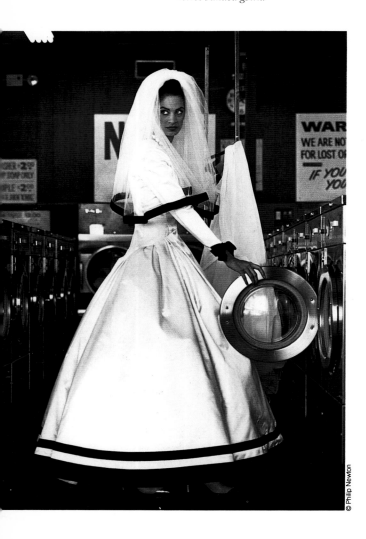

© Philip Newton

is symbolic of the wedding." For the couture bridal designer, the power of white is understood. As anyone who has seen a bride enter a room unannounced knows, this luminous hue focuses all attention on the bride. The demand for tradition notwithstanding, the color's tonal symbolism aside, a bride garbed in white is the center of all attention, and that, after all, is the point.

White remains the overwhelming favorite of brides and designers—it is traditional, dramatic, and beautiful. Yves Saint-Laurent shocked a few fashion followers during the 1980s, when his bride was layered head to toe in ultra-traditional silk and tulle—all of it apparently black—although a closer look revealed it to be a deep aubergine. Monsieur Saint-Laurent's leap across the color spectrum did not ignore bridal tradition but actually returned to its roots, recalling the time when it was typical for brides to wear their best dress, not infrequently black, to marry. In the 1930s, there was a vogue for black wedding gowns with contrasting bouquets of white calla lilies. Saint-Laurent's modern version inspired a fashion renaissance, a recognition that it was time for a newly glamorous, invigorating, sophisticated approach to design. The enduring sophistication of black was apparent to Vera Wang, who in 1990 banded an otherwise classically cut all-white bridal gown with black, using it to trim the hem, the neckline, and the edge of the veil. The elegant, daring, but simple contrast of color and line made it very clear that this would be the decade during which bridal fashion would transcend traditional design —the key would be to do it well.

Designer Frank Massandrea, credited by many on New York's Seventh Avenue for revitalizing the tradition-choked American bridal market, understood what the older, smart, stylish bride wanted: luscious, feminine, extravagant, frankly sexy wedding dresses as fabulous as anything walking down Parisian runways. Bridal designers from the 1960s and 1970s remember the conservatism—the demure, covered-up, unwavering bridal styles in two basic shapes: the narrow empire or princess-line and the full-skirted ball gown with fitted bodices. Noteworthy was the strict "two-and-a-half-inch rule": measuring from the hollow at the

base of the bride's throat, no neckline could be cut any lower than two and a half inches. Massandrea's imaginative use of previously underutilized fabrics—pastel silk, dotted net, allover beaded lace with nude-tone lining—and his new approach to color, cut, and workmanship propelled the bridal industry forward. At last a bride could realize her fantasy of waltzing down an aisle wearing an ethereal, fashionable, sensual, wonderful modern but classically inspired gown. Change was in the air: necklines lowered until they fell right off the shoulder—where they still popularly linger; gowns even changed color, as subtle hues proliferated. Dresses began to feature pastel linings of delicate pink, peach, and lime worn under white silk, organza, or tulle to give the bridal gown a delicate flush of color.

Striking splashes of colorful silk flowers, bows, embroidery, beading, and fabric adorning cleverly cut gowns are favored by bridal designers all over the world. The freshest techniques give the dresses a painterly quality. Both Norma le Nain, a California-based bridal designer, and well-known couturier Arnold Scaasi embroidered gowns with brilliant crystal beads in the shapes of flowers and stems. The colorful blooms, made of minute hand-stitched pieces of glass, seem almost alive as they gracefully climb up skirts and encircle shoulders. Flower blossoms, the most ancient adornment of brides, continue to be a favorite design element of David Fielden, a London-based bridal designer, who uses three-dimensional, hand-rolled silk flowers in true rose hues to line hems, finish necklines, and bustle backs. Colorful floral embroideries and brocades are popular among other British designers as well; Victorian-inspired gowns of old English rose prints by Marilyn Martin and Ritva Westinius are beautiful examples. No gown by Ron LoVece, a

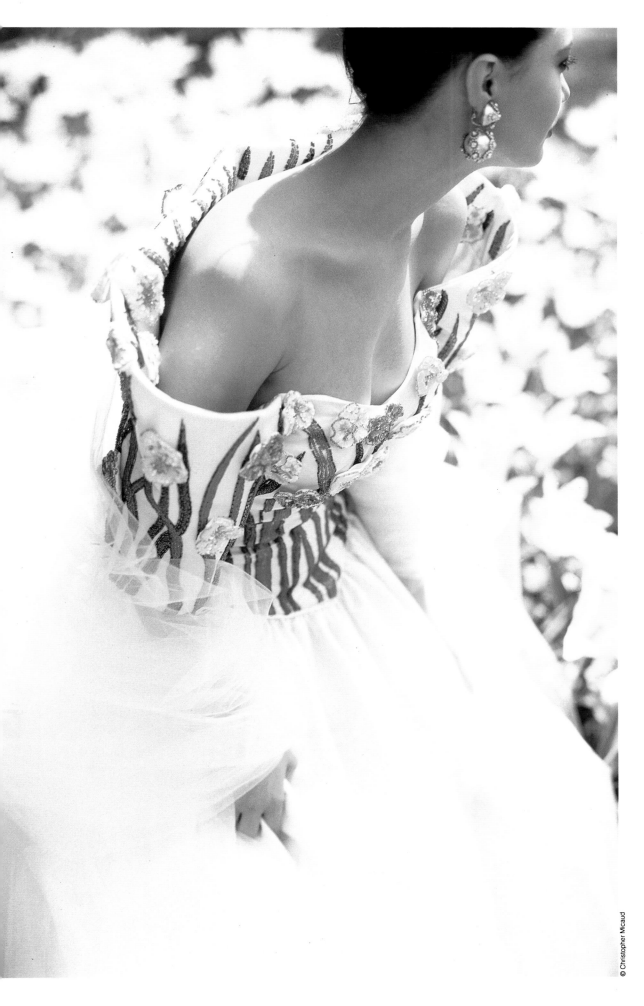

renowned New York designer, is complete without a profusion of his signature rosebuds tucked in lace. Even Christian Lacroix can't resist the allure of the colorful blossom: one memorable Lacroix gown featured a floating tulle skirt under a jacket thoroughly embroidered with vivid flowers.

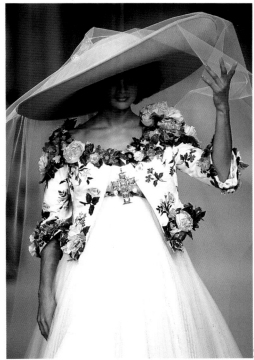

Continually reinvented, the traditional white wedding gown is actually alive with color. **ABOVE:** *A jacket by Christian Lacroix is festooned with blossoms.* **LEFT:** *A hand-beaded peau de soie bodice by Norma LeNain.* **FOLLOWING PAGES:** *The confident implications of Yves Saint Laurent's dark tulle and silk wedding gown ushered in an era of creativity in bridal gowns. Today, the appropriate vestments for a bride are the ones she loves.*

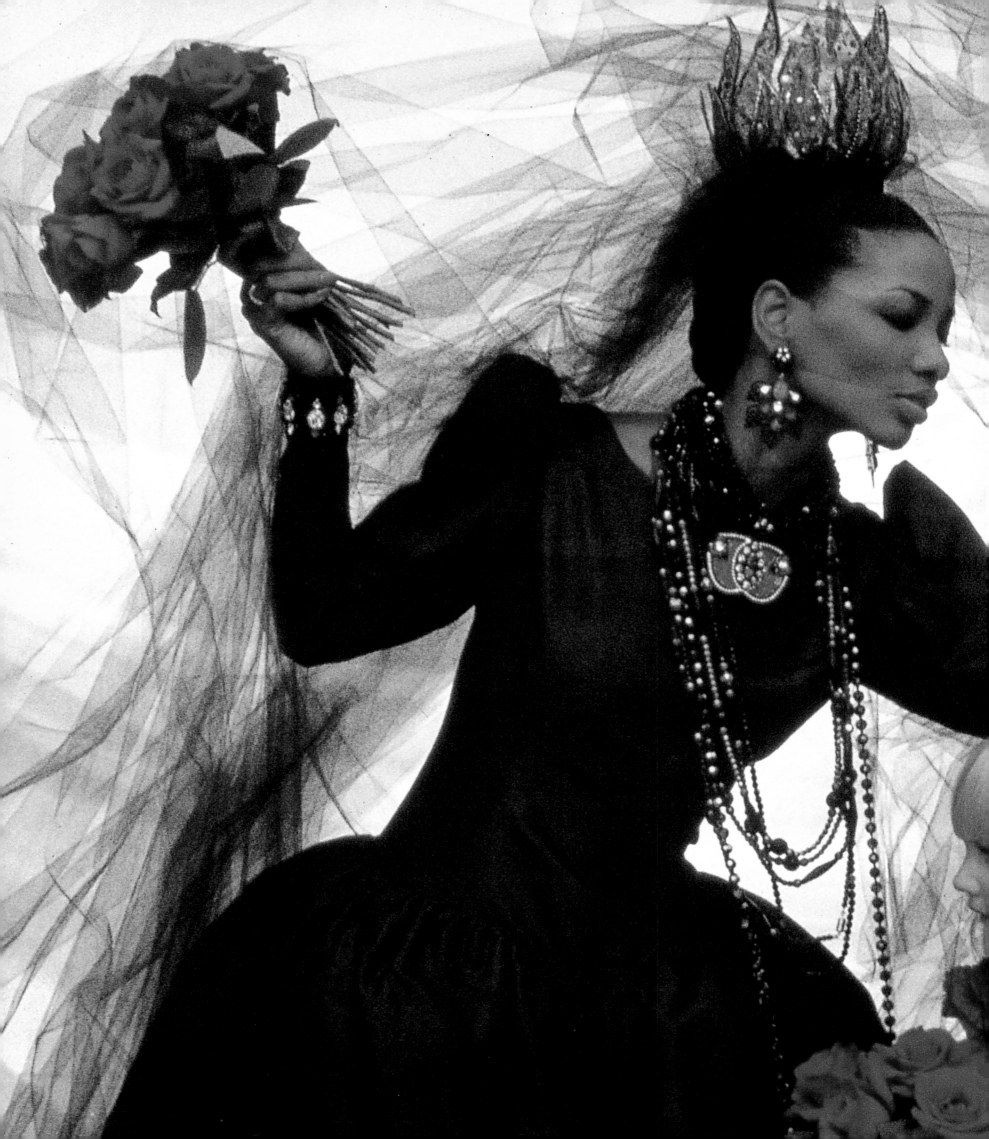

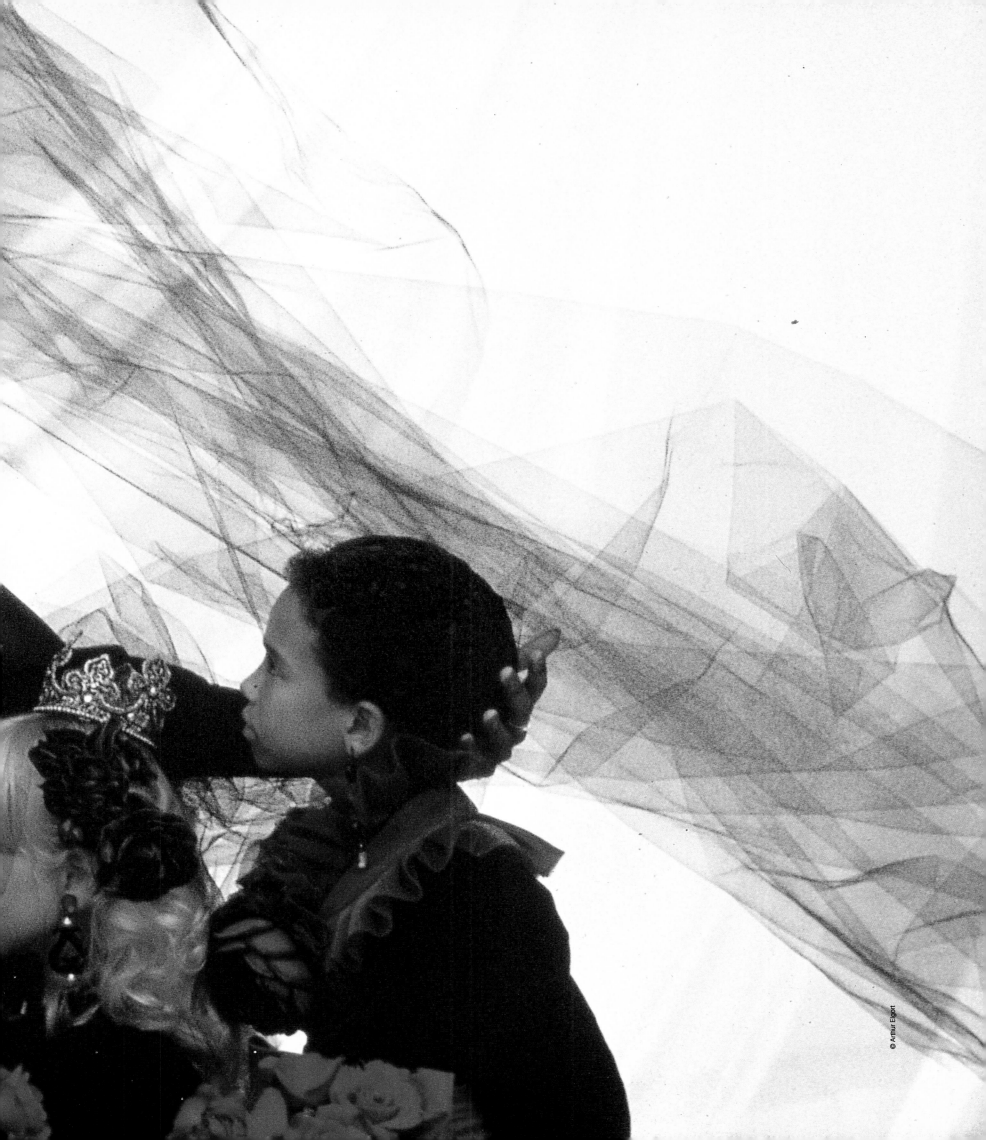

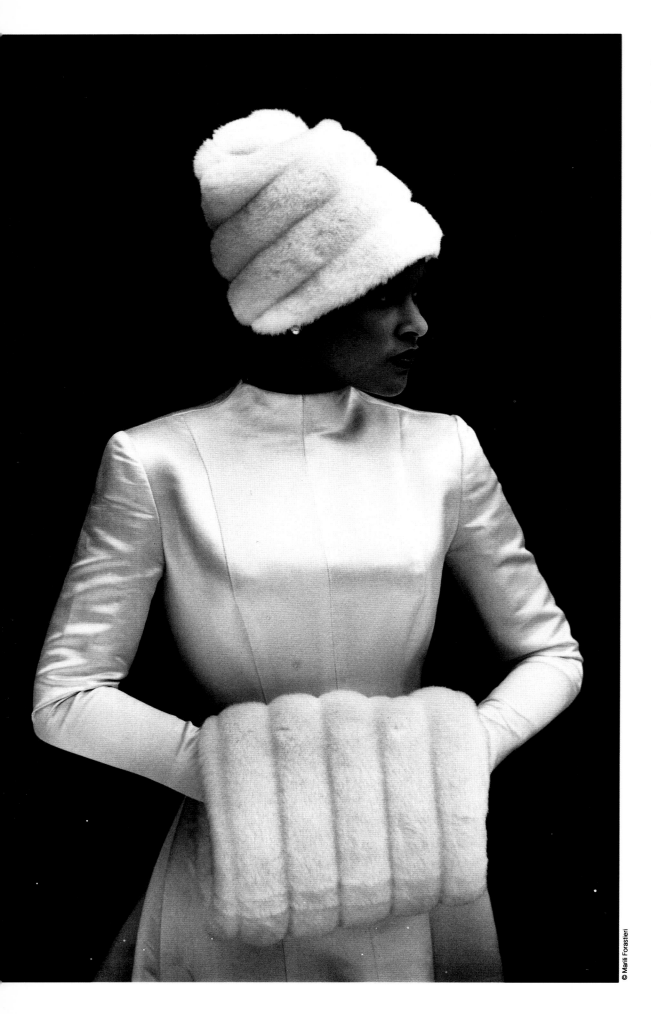

Today's bridal gown comes in dozens of other romantic incarnations. Color and ornamentation are two of the elements the modern bridal designer manipulates to change the look of the wedding dress; shape is another. The most significant evolution of the classic bridal gown is its recent return to simple, elegant lines. In many gowns of the 1990s ornamentation is minimal or used with judicious, deliberate restraint—the lavish, conspicuously consumptive overbeading typical of the 1980s is considered passé. In an attempt to mimic the excessive opulence of the past, bridal manufacturers in the 1980s layered beads and pearls and ruffles and ribbons and passementerie and sequins and palliettes on gowns. The "more is better" principle seemed to satisfy some brides who thought the decorative superfluousness was the fashionable mode. Yet couturiers have always executed their best designs when they relied on nothing but the most exquisite fabrics, beautifully cut and meticulously constructed into a simple, elegant gown. Cut, construction, and fabrication form the basis of the perfect dress; indeed, the more minimal the gown, the more apparent its perfection. Givenchy noted decades ago that: "It isn't necessary to put a button where it doesn't belong, or to add a flower to make a dress beautiful. It is beautiful of itself."

As the 1980s drew to a close, a spiraling boom of weddings and sophisticated brides demanding more choices drew increasing numbers of American couture designers into bridal design. The clarity of their design perspective was timely and refreshing, neither rooted in nor confined by traditional bridal demands. Indeed, they could design bridal gowns as they did evening wear—inspired by pure fantasy and simplicity of form. This point of view invigorated the bridal market as the streamlined elegance of designs by Carolina Herrera, the clever juxtaposition of fabrics by Carolyne Roehm, and the luxurious femininity of Oscar de la Renta hit a nerve. Stunning simplicity, manifest quality, refined ease, and classic beauty characterize the best bridal gowns—whether they are dramatic ball gowns of pleated tulle with molded satin bodices, body-skimming lace sheaths, or perfectly fitted, smart suits of faille and gazar.

The soignée but decidedly untraditional bride doesn't have to look far to find her perfect gown. Dedicated costumers of the elegant and irreverent, including ready-to-wear sportswear designers, outrageous couturiers, imaginative private designers, vintage enthusiasts, and even some traditional but spirited bridal designers, offer fashion for the bride who wants to marry in a gown more suited to her avant-garde temperament. For example, white leather motorcycle jackets worn over

tulle skirts hit the bridal runway recently, designed by Robert Legere for the Diamond Collection—a look that ensures the couple a smooth getaway after requisite "I dos." Ondyn Herschelle, a San Francisco–based private designer, updates 1960s cool into 1990s sleek-chic with a white lace catsuit under a sheer organza caftan. Fluid, ruffled palazzo pants and an allover pearl-studded jacket, by Norma Kamali, are boldly modern but perfectly feminine. A double-breasted crepe coat dress is a spring favorite of Ralph Lauren—not originally intended for a bride, it becomes the perfect bridal suit when finished with a tulle-veiled straw boater and a posy of flowers. Pearls, lace, and tulle, all classic bridal elements, are reworked by numerous modern designers to give an edge of romance and formality to many different styles.

Today, fashion is all about variety, about catering to the most individual stylistic instincts. Thigh baring, knee skimming, or ankle concealing; sophisticated, romantic, or casual; made to order, off the rack, or inherited; lace, leather, or lamé—there is a style for everyone. What is fashion but an opportunity to express your identity? What is a wedding but an occasion to affirm your identity? And what is your bridal gown but a chance to revel in the fantasy of all you ever wanted to be? Fantasy should never be overlooked, especially on your wedding day. Fantasy is a creative process, one that uses the imagination to build an idea, or create an event. Your bridal gown is a delicious, rare opportunity to indulge yourself, to enjoy an exercise of extravagance, to step away, for a moment, from the carelessness of an increasingly informal world. "Every woman wants to feel that she's the most beautiful bride, like a star on an MGM set—her dress is the ultimate costume," says Ron LoVece, who has dressed enough brides over the years to know.

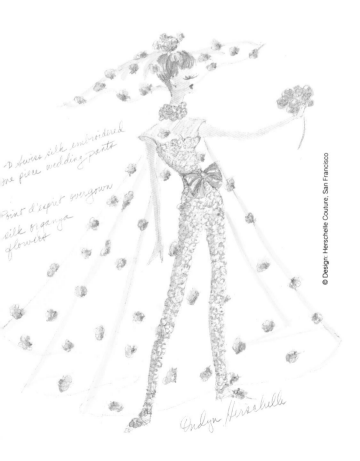

Swiss silk embroidered one piece wedding pants

Point d'esprit overgown

silk organza flowers

Ondyn Herschelle

© Design: Herschelle Couture, San Francisco

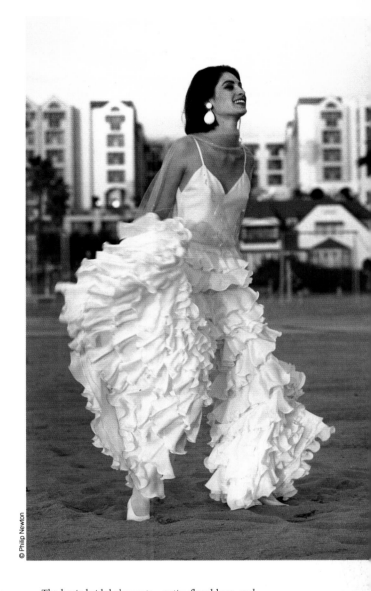

© Philip Newton

The basic bridal elements—satin, floral lace, and tiers of ruffles—are reworked by clever designers to entice every bride. **OPPOSITE PAGE:** *Sculpted fur balances the sleek silhouette of Eva Chun's luminous satin gown.* **CENTER:** *Ondyn Herschelle's embroidered catsuit under crisp, sheer point d'esprit.* **ABOVE:** *Norma Kamali's palazzo pants.*

FINE FABRICS

Brilliant brocade, sensuous satin, feathery lace, cool silk, crisp cotton, and sheer linen: these delicate threads, sculpted by talented hands, have traditionally adorned the bride. The finest fabrics of the world have always been used for the bride's vestments. A close look at history and art attest to the significance of fabric in our lives: primitive cultures used skins and rough weaves for warmth, adornment, and protection; the advancements of entire civilizations were measured by the quality of their cloth; tapestries recorded heroic tales in finely loomed threads; nations and their leaders have dedicated themselves to cultivating, owning, and wearing the finest of fabrics; the economies of empires depended on the commerce of fibers and fabric, with the secrets of production—the key to wealth and power—fiercely guarded; sumptuary laws were frequently enacted to limit access to the finest cloths; and all significant social and cultural events—coronations, tournaments, balls, and especially weddings—have been distinguished by guests wearing the finest fabrics affordable. It's no exaggeration to state that fabric is the foundation of society; centuries ago, Queen Elizabeth I of England decreed that nobles should pledge their oath to the crown while kneeling on a wool sack to remind them that the power of England was built on cloth. Today, access to fabric and finished goods is so universal that the significance of the simple thread is lost on most. Yet every bride who approaches the altar in a gown of gleaming silk, a sheath of

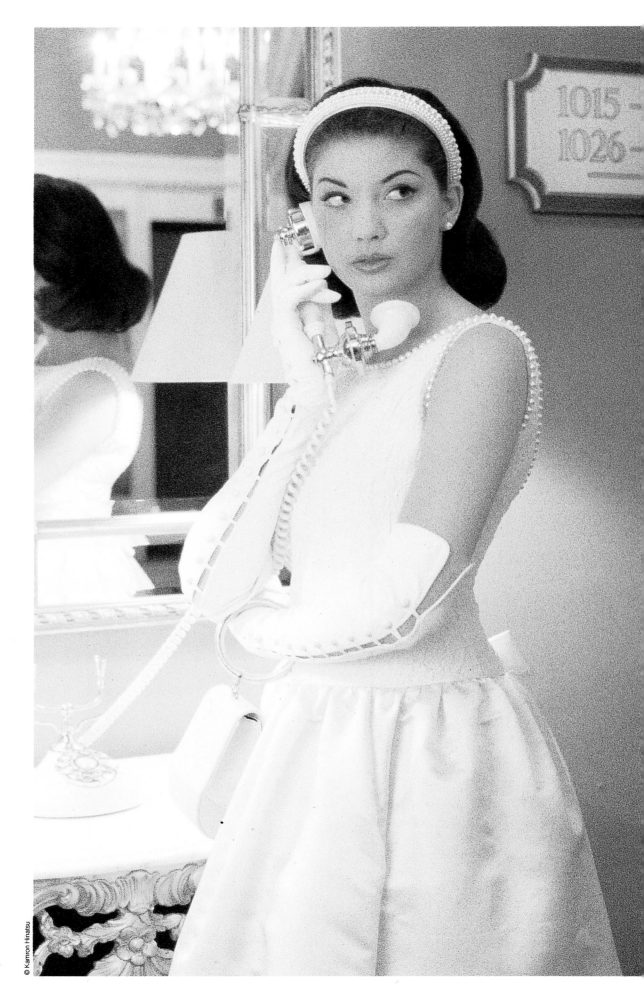

© Kamon Hinatsu

lace, a swirling skirt of mohair, or a crisp cotton suit is cloaking herself in the history of the world.

SILK

About 2640 B.C., a young empress in China was seated under a mulberry tree, enjoying a cup of tea, when a moth's cocoon fell into her drink. The tea's warmth unraveled the delicate filaments of the cocoon, revealing the first threads of silk, a fiber that would transform the world. The Chinese exported raw silk thread and lustrous cloth to the West as soon as the first merchants traversed the "Silk Road"—six thousand tortuous miles over desert land and across a vast sea—between the Far East and Greece. Early nobles, from Cleopatra to Nero, favored the precious threads, creating a tremendous demand for this rarified cloth. The silk threads traveled so far, through so many countries—each of which imposed a tariff—that by the second century A.D., silk, the only fabric sold by the pound, was worth its weight in gold. The cultivation of silk was a zealously guarded Chinese imperial secret. Any attempt to export the eggs of the silkworm or the seeds of the mulberry tree it nested in and ate was punishable by death. A Chinese royal daughter who married a Byzantine emperor is credited with successfully smuggling the first eggs and seeds out of China in her hair. As the art of producing raw silk, or sericulture, moved West, traveling only to the most powerful capitals—from Byzantium to Venice by way of Spain and the Moors—it brought its practitioners vast wealth. By the twelfth century, Italian weavers were producing the finest cloth in the world, a distinction they continue to hold. By that time, the availability of glorious, exquisite, brilliant silks had transformed the way people dressed. The sensual drape of the sleek cloth inspired fashions that con-

toured the body for the first time since the Roman Empire. Proud of their silks, people typically wore as many different layers and colors as possible: it became the rage to wear clothes slashed so all the underlayers were visible. Silk merchants, the first arbiters of style, dressed miniature dolls in the newest silks cut to the latest fashion and sent the little models to prospective customers everywhere.

When a daughter of the powerful Florentine de' Medici family married the king of France in 1533, she wore a glorious white silk gown made in her hometown of Florence. The nuptial festivities lasted thirty days, but the French fascination for silk never ended. Silk masters were bribed to relocate in France, and by the reign of Louis XIV there were over one million silk workers in Lyons and every type of silk fabric was produced there. Although the fashionable

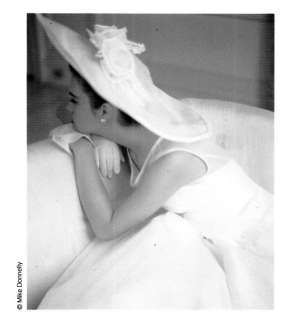

Style, cut, drapability, and, of course, the season are all important factors in determining the best fabric for a wedding gown. **OPPOSITE PAGE:** *Puckered silk cloqué edged with pearls contrasts with a silk satin skirt for a tailored gown with a feminine edge by Amsale.* **ABOVE:** *Sheer but crisp silk organza cleverly underscores the gamine style of Dior's simply-cut button-front gown.*

excess of royalty and nobility kept the silk looms busy, most members of the nobility neglected to pay the vast sums of money owed their costumers and threatened blacklisting if attempts were made to collect. It is a little-known fact of the French Revolution that the upheaval was supported by a legion of dressmakers and silk weavers who had depended on the silk paraders for business. When the French Revolution erupted, the luxury fabric industries died, not only because all the looms were destroyed but because all the best customers were killed or fled the country. No one wore silk for fear of being mistaken for a member of the hated nobility. About sixty years passed before the French silk industry was fully resuscitated, due, to a large extent, to the concerted efforts of Empress Eugenie, wife of Napoleon III. During the Second Empire (1851–1870) Eugenie typically traveled with at least 500 silk dresses, dubbing her cargo "political wardrobe." The empress's fondness for extravagant fashions prompted a renaissance in Parisian dressmaking and was a potent influence on women everywhere. As the demand for silk grew to unprecedented levels, it became clear that the popularity of other fabrics would come and go, but the value and beauty of silk would make it an enduring favorite.

Across the Atlantic, Americans craved the lustrous yardage, too. As the domestic garment industry developed in America, so did the need for vast quantities of the silkworm's labor. Dressmakers imported tremendous amounts of silk goods directly from the Orient: cargo landed in Seattle or San Francisco and headed to New York City. Demand was so high that in 1919, the trains known as "silk specials," each bearing an average of $2 million worth of silk goods, were given an unprecedented direct right-of-way, coast to coast.

When the United States government appropriated and rationed all the silk stocks during World War II, the bridal industry lobbied to make sure that a bit of this precious fabric remained available to American brides. Just before the war, rayon, man-made from woody plants, was perfected as an alternative to silk. With the wartime restrictions on silk, textile manufacturers widely promoted the use of rayon for all clothing. Its cool, fluid silkiness made it a fabulous fabric for bridal gowns. Rayon was marketed as an affordable artificial silk thread—indeed, it is still widely used in better blends of fabrics and laces. During the late 1960s and 1970s, polyester fabrics were new and popular. These man-made fibers were viewed as modern wash-and-wear alternatives to silk and rayon—even brides wore polyester, in the form of wrinkle-free Qiana fabric. The 1990s bride has come full circle, marrying in a gown cut from the same cloth favored by brides a hundred years ago. At a time when the earth seems overpopulated and overwhelmed, the silk-clad bride shows a nostalgic respect for nature's resources, for the precious materials that have inspired people since their first discovery. This decade's renewed appreciation of quality and enduring value means that there is no place for disposability and inferior workmanship. Today, as a result of consumer demand, most traditionally styled bridal gowns are made of silk. There is a new importance attached to having and recognizing the best, not for showmanship but for quality's sake. The finest gowns today are made from the purest fabrics. Natural fibers exude an innate quality of unadulterated refinement, and give an impression of easy elegance and superior quality that is exactly what brides want.

When drawn from a cocoon, silk is a single continuous length of durable thread; anywhere from 500 to 1,300 yards long, silk is the only natural fiber that doesn't need to be spun before weaving. Its natural color is a creamy white, the most popular color of bridal gowns today. Silk is the only fabric that initially (in the production process) is sold by weight; the heavier and denser the final weave of silk, the more expensive it is. Extra weight was commonly added to silk goods in the late nineteenth century to inflate the price of the fabric. This shady commercial practice, known as silk weighting, would involve washing or finishing the threads with a metallic salt, such as iron, tin, or magnesium. Even sugar, paraffin, and tannin were used for this purpose. These products could easily add three to four pounds of extra weight to each pound of raw silk before any of the outwardly apparent, natural qualities of the silk were lost. Many fabulous dresses from this era did not survive intact because of this destructive practice, as the abrasive salts crumbled the naturally durable silk fibers. The most abused silks, with up to nine pounds of added weight, were corroded within months of the salt baths. Heirloom gowns from the seventeenth and eighteenth centuries that did not suffer salt baths have survived in better condition than those from the late nineteenth century. Tragically, some of these brilliant gowns look intact, but they are brittle and crumble in the hand, and there is no technique that can rescue the fibers.

Silk threads are woven to create various fabrics, including satin. Satin is silk that is densely woven into a bolt of cloth in a manner that finishes one face of the fabric with a superior, lustrous sheen, while the "wrong" side is a shineless matte. Satin's gloss has always been impressive; indeed, there are descriptions of "mirror" satin dating to the Elizabethan era. The tightness and brilliance of the weave make satin a favorite for bridal gowns. The weight of the fabric makes it especially popular for skirts, where it provides an elegant sweep and dramatic body with regal character. Weighty satin skirts must be supported by petticoats; the fabric's heaviness also makes it a good choice over hoops, keeping them properly in place. Wrinkles are rarely a problem with satin because the weight of the cloth draws them out. The name is derived from Zaytoun, China, the ancient port from which fabric was exported during the Middle Ages.

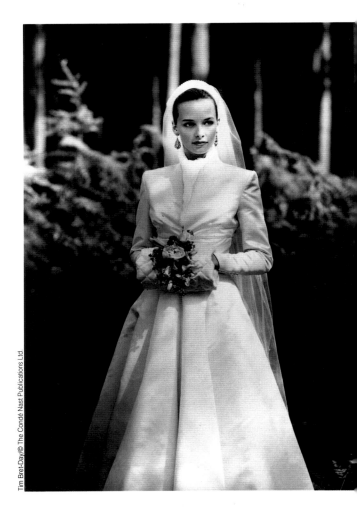

Tim Bret-Day/© The Condé Nast Publications Ltd.

Favorite bridal fabrics have luxurious texture, beautiful drapability, and magnificent presence. **ABOVE:** *A Ritva Westenius gown cut from sensual duchesse satin resembles a collarless jacket with a soft silk chiffon scarf at the neckline.* **OPPOSITE PAGE:** *A skirt of crisp taffeta by Cynthia Rowley paired with a cashmere sweater set is fabulous the day of the wedding and after.*

Less expensive but widely favored for its similarity to silk satin is silk-faced satin, sometimes called duchesse satin, which is a blend of silk and rayon. Woven like traditional satin, this blend is less heavy than pure silk satin and is therefore a good choice for warm-weather weddings. Often priced at least twenty dollars a yard less than silk satin, duchesse satin makes a more affordable dress.

Peau de soie, or "skin of silk," is a heavyweight smooth satin woven with an extremely fine ribbing that gives the finished satin its distinctive dull luster. Luxurious peau de soie is a perennial favorite with brides.

Charmeuse (from the French word meaning "enchantress") is a lightweight, rich, very soft satin woven from silk or rayon. Charmeuse is distinguished by a more subdued luster and is sometimes woven with crepe, a pebbly-textured yarn, for an even flatter texture and more clinginess. Crepe charmeuse is a sophisticated option for a wedding dress. Its softness gives it wonderful drapability that is perfect for less architectural gowns.

Another extremely popular bridal fabric is taffeta, also originally woven from silk. One of the most ancient and simple weaves, with a fine, smooth-finished surface, taffeta is often classified as a plain weave. Mentioned in the *Thousand and One Nights*, its name comes from the Persian word *taftan*, which means "to spin or twist." Taffeta is characterized by a crisp body, and is known for its gentle rustling sound. A popular choice for ball-gown skirts, the crispest versions are labeled paper taffeta. This silk fabric, which is relatively lightweight compared to satin, has excellent body, making it a favorite with brides who, by the time they are completely dressed, are supporting plenty of weight with all the layers of fabric, lining, and petticoats. There are many varieties and blends of this versatile weave, which is now often

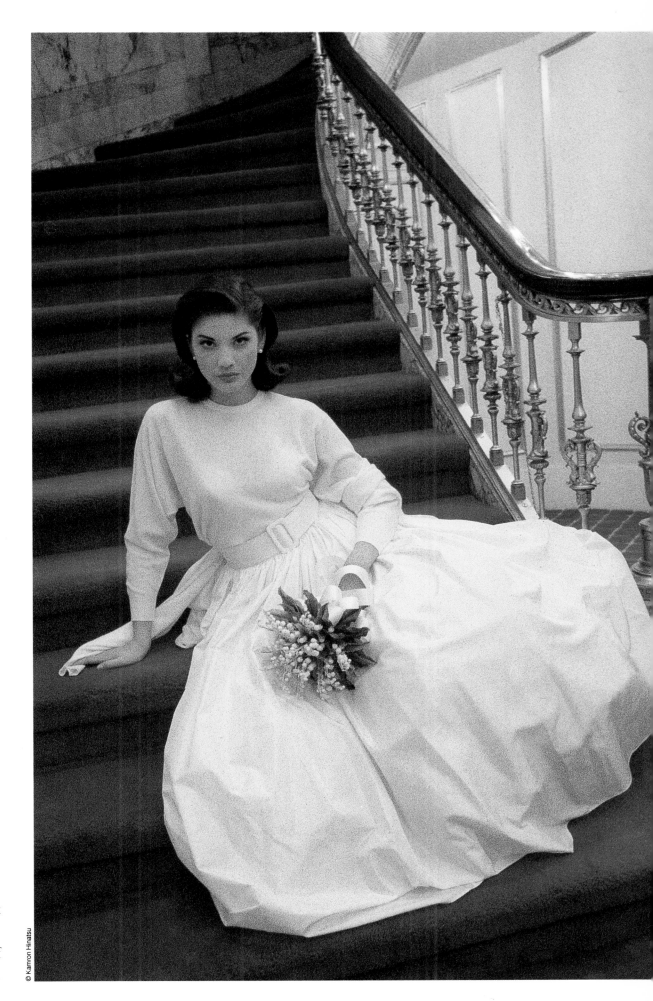

© Karron Hinatsu

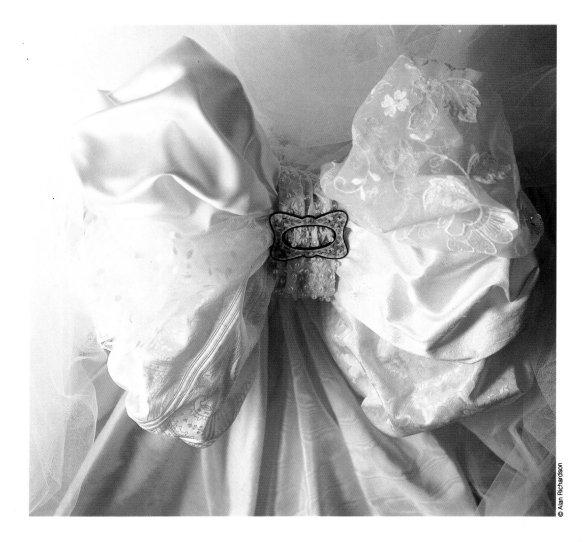

© Alan Richardson

Textured fabrics add interest to bridal gowns without the risk of overembellishment. **ABOVE:** *A bow of bridal fabrics is knotted from swatches of double-faced satin, dotted net, paisley striped jacquard, shantung silk, moiré, floral jacquard, shantung silk, embroidered net, and a center of beaded shantung. The right fabric selection is critical for successfully bringing a design to life.* **OPPOSITE PAGE, LEFT:** *Robert Legere's gown sculpted from golden brocade for the Diamond Collection.* **OPPOSITE PAGE, RIGHT:** *A shantung silk creation by Ondyn Herschelle.*

made from rayon and acetate. Tissue taffeta is an almost transparent fabric. Moiré taffeta has a distinctive watermarked pattern that resembles melting jagged stripes. Moiré is commonly embossed on silks, rayons, and cottons with a riblike texture, like failles.

Silks woven into a pattern, typically floral or geometric designs, are broadly classified as damask. Marco Polo returned from the Orient with this decorative silk fabric in the thirteenth century. It was originally distributed from Damascus, which was at that time a major distribution center between East and West. Today any fiber can be woven in a damask pattern. The weaving is produced on a Jacquard loom, invented in the early 1800s by Joseph-Marie Jacquard. The term *jacquard* now refers not only to the loom but also generically to a wide variety of patterned dress-weight cloth. The rising popularity of

unadorned bridal gowns has sparked a renewed fascination for textured fabrics, especially silk, rayon, and even polyester Jacquard. This fabric has the sheen and weight popular for bridals with the added interest of pattern—a white-on-white Jacquard makes a subtle but striking bridal gown. Brocade, heavier and more three-dimensional than damask, is also woven on the Jacquard loom, and it often has silver or gold threads running through the pattern.

Lamé is woven from metallic threads often blended with silk or rayon into burnished fabrics that appear to be molten silver or gold. Lamé was a debonair choice for 1930s brides. Cloth of real gold and silver, woven from hammered threads of the metal, was a precursor to lamé and was de rigueur for every royal bride until the nineteenth century.

Textured silks are immensely popular for modern bridal gowns. Textured fabric may be used for the entire dress or to make a contrasting bodice matched with a satin or taffeta skirt. Shantung silk, named for its Chinese province of origin, was originally woven from wild silk. Shantung silk's characteristic natural imperfection—the rough, randomly nubby texture—was caused by the moth breaking through the cocoon and damaging the fiber. Commercial production typically kills the moth before it can damage the cocoon. The knotty quality is now deliberately produced by weaving uneven fibers together, creating irregular slubs throughout the fabric. This low-luster, textured silk is sometimes mistakenly referred to as raw silk, which is really unprocessed silk fiber. Dupioni silk is also a slubby silk. Its name derives from the double- or multiple-nested cocoons from which it is spun. Dupioni fibers are thick, coarse, double filaments often woven together in a taffeta weave that is also known as antique taffeta, in an imitation of eighteenth-century fabrics.

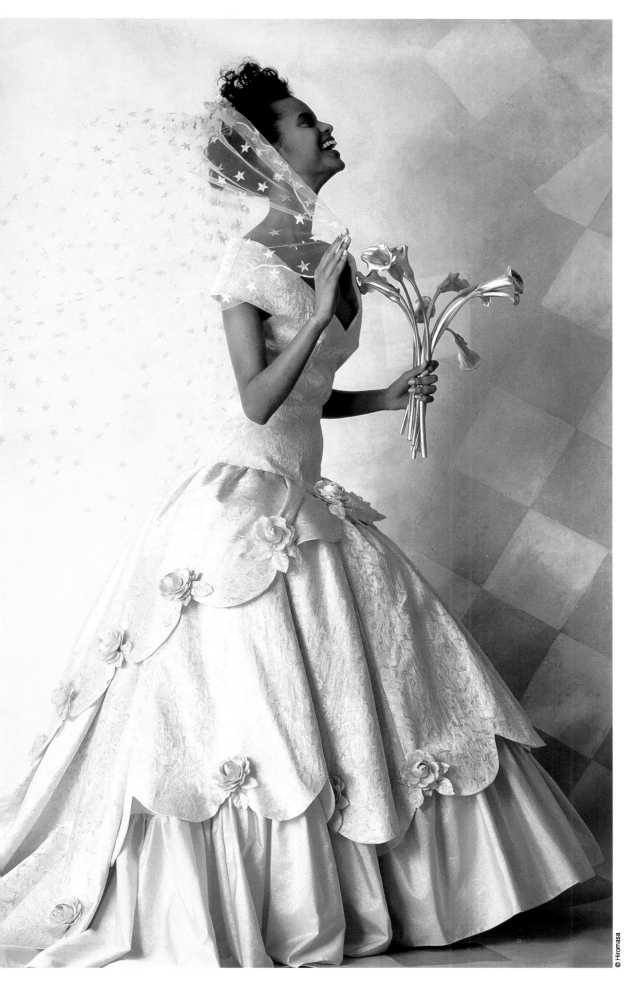

Gros de Londres, faille, bengaline, and ottoman are all ribbed weaves listed in order of thickness of the cord or rib. Gros de Londres is the finest and the flattest. Originally made in silk but now woven from cotton, rayon, polyester, and even wool, these refined fabrics are perfect for tailored gowns, suits, or jackets matched with skirts of another fabric, such as tulle.

Matelassé is a silk that has undergone a quilting technique to create a lustrous puckered fabric. Today rayon, cotton, and synthetics are similarly processed. Matelassé has a unique texture that works very well when contrasted with another fabric, such as satin; Lycra blends make wonderful, fitted jacket-like bodices.

Sheer, transparent silk fabrics with gossamer texture are classic warm-weather bridal cloths. Often used for skirts of gowns, these fabrics must be used in multiple layers because of their transparency—but since the fabrics are so lightweight, the layered approach seems to emphasize their inherent

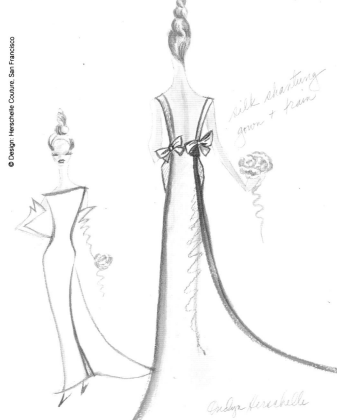

© Design: Herschelle Couture, San Francisco

© Hiromasa

beauty rather than hide it. Silk chiffon, which Coco Chanel described as a "fluttering breeze," has a diaphanous but lusterless texture that makes it an excellent choice for spring or summer day gowns. Soft silk chiffon skirts are so light that they billow with the slightest bit of wind; indeed, they seem to move even when still. Modern chiffon is also woven from rayon, cotton, or synthetics.

Organza is heavier and stiffer than chiffon and today is more commonly woven from rayon than silk. It has a soft luster, giving it a more formal effect than chiffon. Organdy is a similarly crisp, sheer cloth that is woven from cotton. Organza and organdy gowns are naturally more sculptural than chiffon, which depends upon construction and movement to bring it to life. Georgette, also a sheer silk, is woven with twisted threads for a crepey, pebble-like surface. It is named for the nineteenth-century modiste, Madame Georgette de la Plante, who first used the fabric.

Tulle, illusion, maline, and net all refer to the same type of sheer meshlike weave widely used for bridal veils. Tulle is also frequently used in layers to create skirts that float with the grace of ballet tutus, making a delicate contrast to bodices of satin, brocade, or even cashmere. As *Harper's Bazar* wisely noted in 1895, "Tulle makes any other material look well, and the more of it used, the better." Tulle originated in Tulle, France. Pure silk tulle is very fragile and expensive; because of its delicacy, synthetic tulle is commonly substituted in the best gowns. A very new processed tulle that is accordion pleated is beginning to make an appearance in the skirts of updated but romantic bridal gowns.

Another novelty net is dotted or flocked tulle, marked by white-on-white, metallic-on-white, or pastel-on-white polka dots scattered all over the tulle. Maline, named for its Belgian town of origin, is finer than silk

tulle. Illusion is a generic term for tulle, frequently used when describing the nature of the veiling. Net is the heaviest, coarsest weight, typically synthetic, and is generally used for petticoats or underskirts to give a skirt lift and body.

The last of the great bridal silks is velvet. There are records of velvet weavers' guilds in Florence as far back as 1247. The word *velvet* comes from the Italian word *velluto,* which implies a wooly feel to the touch. Originally

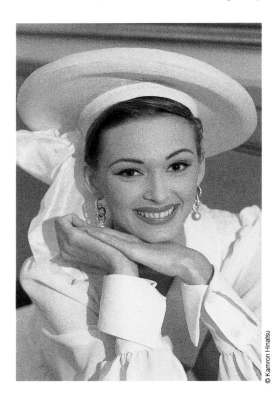

The essential nature of any fabric defines its best use. **ABOVE:** *Billowy, fluid chiffon is ideal for a poetic blouse by Cross & Spellan.* **OPPOSITE PAGE:** *Languid silk tulle is perfect for a Raffaella gown cut with an old-fashioned drape reminiscent of turn-of-the-century lawn dresses.*

woven of pure silk, today's velvets are often silk blends, with rayon or cotton as the back. Velvet is often woven double on the loom and cut apart by a shuttle knife. Piles deeper than one-eighth of an inch are classified as plush. Chiffon velvet is a soft, lightweight velvet most commonly used for gowns; crushed velvet is processed to exhibit a shimmering, irregular, barklike surface. Velveteen is cotton or rayon velvet, woven singly with loops that are finally cut, or sheared, into a very soft surface. The weight and texture of velvet lends any gown a warmth and sensuality, making it particularly popular with brides in the cooler, winter months.

COTTON AND LINEN

Many exquisite linen and cotton fabrics are also popular with brides. The best linens and cottons are not less expensive than silks, but their unique crisp qualities and light weights make them versatile options for the warmer months. Along with wool, flax, from which linen yarn is made, is one of the most ancient fibers known to civilization. The ancient Egyptians first attained perfection in linen fabrication. Ancient Phoenician mariners traded linen between Egypt and Athens, where the Romans eventually found and adopted it as a replacement for wool, particularly in hot climes. The Romans took their knowledge of flax and linen north on their conquering quests to Flanders, where the cultivation and weaving later flourished.

Flax plants are still harvested in much the same way as in ancient days. The long silky fiber comes from inside the bark of the flax plant. Most linen is woven using variations on a universal technique, although the weights and the qualities of the threads—and therefore the fabrics—differ. As a result, compared to silk, there are far fewer choices of finished goods in linen for the bride. Today, the best linens come from Belgium

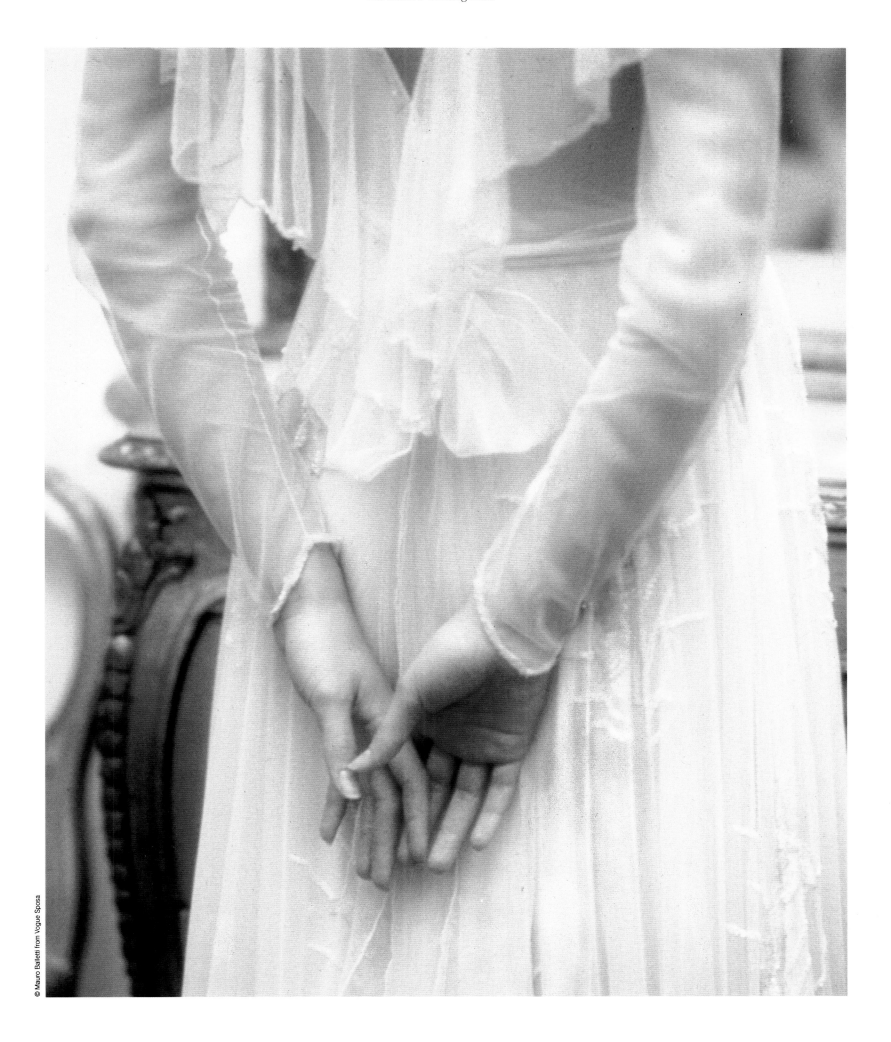

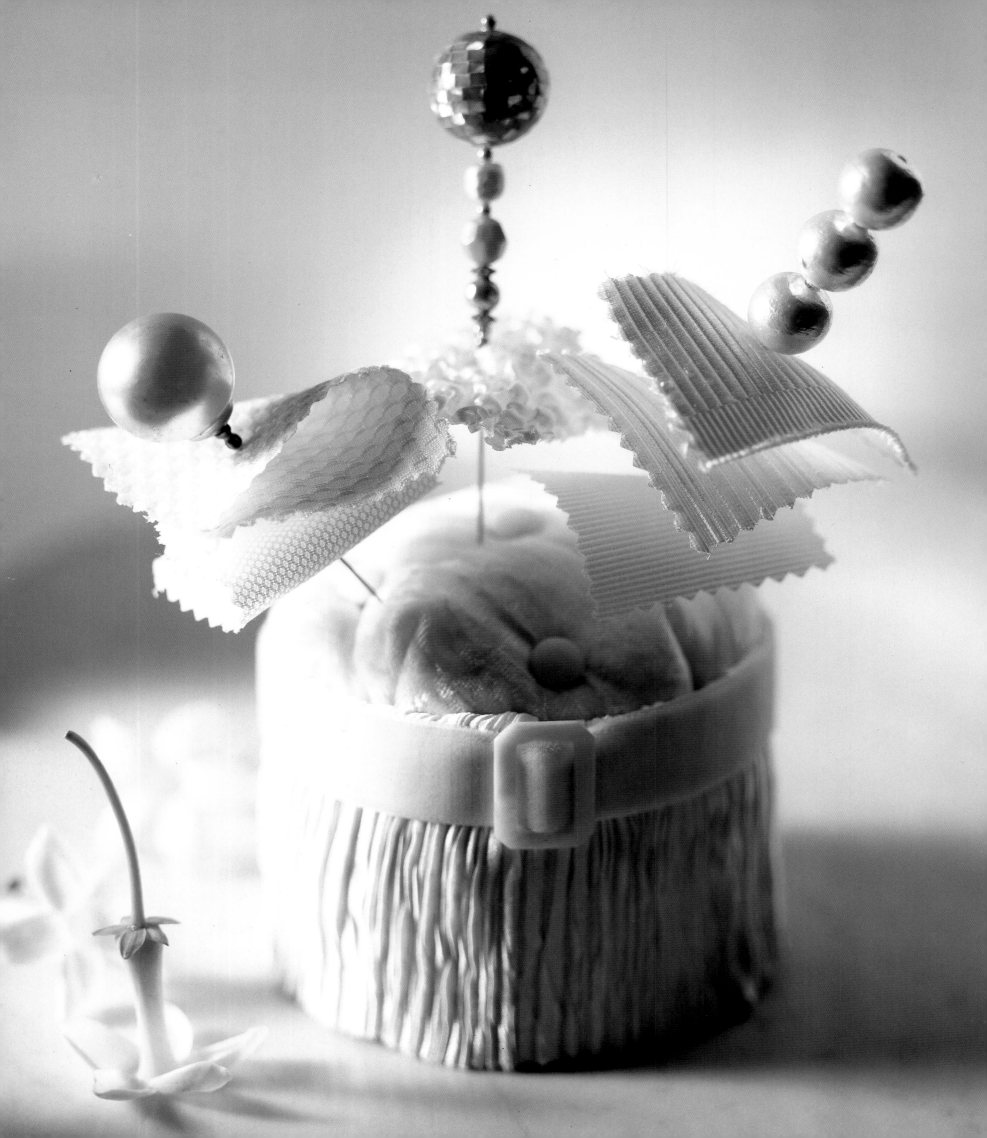

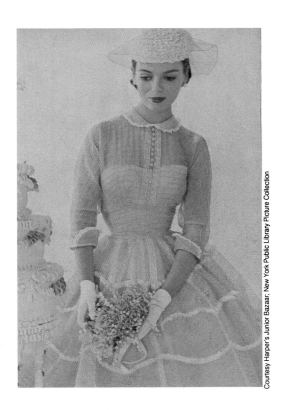

and Ireland. Cooler and stronger than fine cotton, linen is noted for its tendency to wrinkle, but it can be sized with a crease-resistant finish. The firm but fine linen threads make this fabric excellent for embroidery, particularly pulled or cutwork. The first technique requires threads to be pulled or removed from an area, while the second technique actually cuts holes in the fabric. In both processes, the remaining edges are reinforced with embroidery, creating open blocks of pattern, usually striped across the width of the fabric. A beautiful bodice might feature a stripe of pulled work across the decolletage, while an exquisite skirt could have a dozen concentric rings of pulled work (or just one) near the hem. Mary Tudor, Queen of England from 1553 to 1558, so valued cutwork that she passed sumptuary laws forbidding anyone under the rank of baron to wear it.

We know that cotton was grown, spun, and woven in India about 600 B.C., but it was known and revered by Indians as far back as 3000 B.C. The ancient Greek scholar, Pliny the Elder (A.D. 23–79) noted that the Chinese

"are famous for the wool that is found in their forest, and after steeping it in water, they comb off a white down that adheres to the leaves." In the ancient world, cotton became known as tree wool or vegetable lamb. It wasn't until the seventeenth century that cotton was widely worn, and even then, the expense of importing the fabric ensured its place as a favorite of royalty and the rich. After the French Revolution, cotton became a more commonly worn fabric. Not only was its durable quality well suited to the neo-classical fashions of the time, but its less rarified status differentiated it from aristocratic silk, making cotton the patriotic option. In England, Edwardian ladies favored crisp white cotton lawn and tea dresses. Many of these gowns survive today. Almost always embroidered, and featuring extremely feminine, simple, gentle curving silhouettes with sweeping trains, these dresses are favored by brides who want to wear an heirloom gown.

Favorite bridal fabrics woven from cotton can be broken down into three broad groups, sheers, embroidered cottons, and textured fine cottons. Sheers, finely woven, virtually weightless fabrics, have a transparent but (because of their whiteness) veiled quality. Batiste and marquisette are soft sheers, while organdy is a crisp sheer. Eyelet is any embroidered cotton in which an allover, openwork pattern is punched out of the fabric with the embroidery worked around each hole to finish the edges. This wonderful, classically romantic fabric would be perfect for a country-garden gown, topped with a wreath of fresh flowers or a broad-brimmed straw hat. Finally, there are the textured fine cottons. Piqué and ottoman are ribbed designs, with the finer ribbed pique often used for cuffs and collars to add schoolgirl charm to the right gown. Waffle piqué is a honeycomb weave; dotted Swiss and point d'esprit are sheer cottons flecked with tiny

white dots, perfect for the bride who wants a dress that is the essence of eternal spring and eternal youth; damask designs, fabulous in silk, are just as popular in cotton.

LACE

Richly symbolic and steeped in tradition, lace is a popular, even de rigueur, bridal fabric. Few brides would consider exchanging vows without at least a touch of this ethereal webbing somewhere in their bridal regalia. As a craft, lace making is even more ancient than cloth weaving, as the knotting techniques were first used to make fishnets and baskets. A Belgian folktale recounts the origin of lace. A romantically inclined knight,

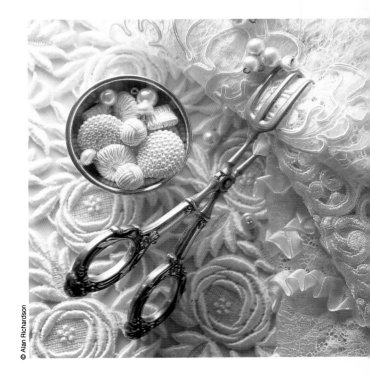

Textured fabrics add subtle allure to wedding gowns. **OPPOSITE PAGE:** *A pincushion of velvet with a skirt of pleated charmeuse highlights some of the best* **(FROM LEFT TO RIGHT, TOP TO BOTTOM)** *waffle cotton, cotton piqué, matelassé, bengaline, ottoman, and faille.* **ABOVE LEFT:** *Tailored details like pleating are wonderfully feminine when executed in organdy or graphic patterned laces.* **ABOVE, LEFT TO RIGHT:** *Guipure, ribbon, guipure and reembroidered Alençon laces.*

off to the Crusades, left his lady a perfect rose as a token of his love. Time passed, and the rose bloomed. To preserve her precious gift, as each petal fell, the lady tenderly sewed it back into the rose. Eventually, the original rose was gone, but a delicate, even more precious lace one remained.

Heirloom, or antique lace, was made from either silk or linen threads, some so fine they were impossible to see, and were manipulated by the lace maker by touch. Although numerous patterns existed, there were only two major techniques of making lace, either bobbin or needle.

For bobbin lace, a series of threads, often dozens, were anchored with pins to a pillow (this technique was also referred to as pillow lace) with bobbins—like spools—holding the length of each thread. Following a pattern marked by pins, lace makers would cross and twist the threads into lace. Bobbin lace was also known as bone lace, because in the days before brass pins were widely available, lace makers used splintered chicken bones and fine fish bones as pins, with slightly larger bones used as bobbins. The earliest bobbin lace was knotted in thin lengths, resembling a lace ribbon, often called bride lace. This lace was used to trim the traditional wedding cup or was tied around sixteenth-century bridal nosegays. The name of the lace may have originated in the groom's custom of wearing lace in his hat as a symbol of love.

Needlepoint lace, or *punto in aria,* meaning "stitches in air," was developed in the fifteenth century. Stitches were basted into a pattern over parchment paper. A simple, tiny, repetitious buttonhole stitch was used to cover and connect the pattern threads, creating lace. Often ten or more different workers would craft a single length of lace, with each lace maker creating a single motif and yet another stitching them all together. Not only

was this a more efficient method of production, it also protected the secrets of the pattern. Interestingly, the connecting stitches or bridges of threads between designs were called brides, presumably because these stitches securely "married" the motifs together forever. Many lace makers lived and died in the same home, knotting the same

In the Victorian era few brides would marry without a touch of lace. **BELOW, TOP TO BOTTOM:** *Bolts of bold lace designs— Alençon, ribbon lace, beaded Alençon, and guipure.* **OPPOSITE PAGE:** *This gown of traditional tulle and Alençon lace by Victor Edelstein has a decidedly contemporary twist.*

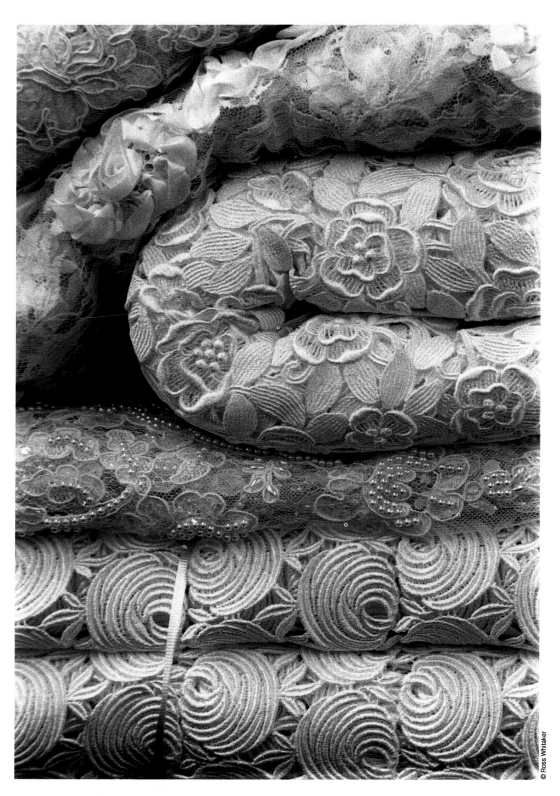

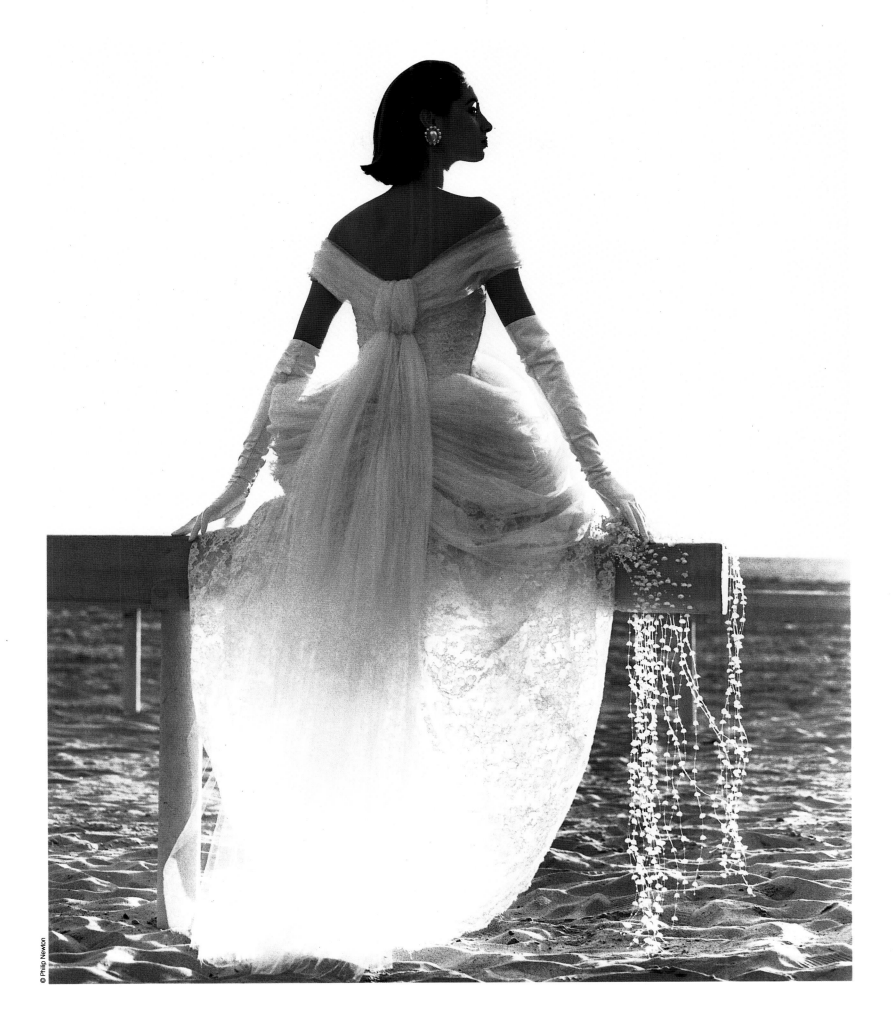

exact pattern of stitches taught to them by their mothers and grandmothers. Each town of lace makers was known for its own pattern; indeed, lace was usually named for the town, such as Chantilly, Lyons, or Alençon.

The series of knots that we recognize as lace was the delicate thread that supported the economy of entire nations. The medieval nation of Flanders perfected lace making in the sixteenth century, when by royal command all girls, upon reaching the age of five, were taught the art of lace making in schools and convents. Children living in convents were expected to make enough lace to pay for their expenses. During the Renaissance, lace was so valuable and profitable that Venetians were forbidden by law to wear their own art, as all Venetian lace was being sent abroad in exchange for gold. The high price of lace was a reflection not only of its beauty and the aristocratic demand for these showy threads but also of the time required to make it. Lace makers, although adequately compensated at the time, nevertheless suffered for their craft. The best and finest flax threads for lace had to be kept moist, cool, and protected from bright light; thread and lace making often were carried out in damp, dark underground cellars. Since soot, a by-product of flame heat, could also damage white lace, lace makers often worked in barns during winter, warmed only by the body heat produced by the stabled animals. Blonde lace, a popular French lace made from the late eighteenth century to the mid-nineteenth century, was made in two colors, white during the summer and black in the winter—a smart solution to the problem of white lace dirtied by smoky winter fires.

Once lace was introduced, the demand for it never waned, and like other fine fabrics, lace influenced the fashion of the times. Indeed, as soon as lace became available, styles were developed purely to show off this

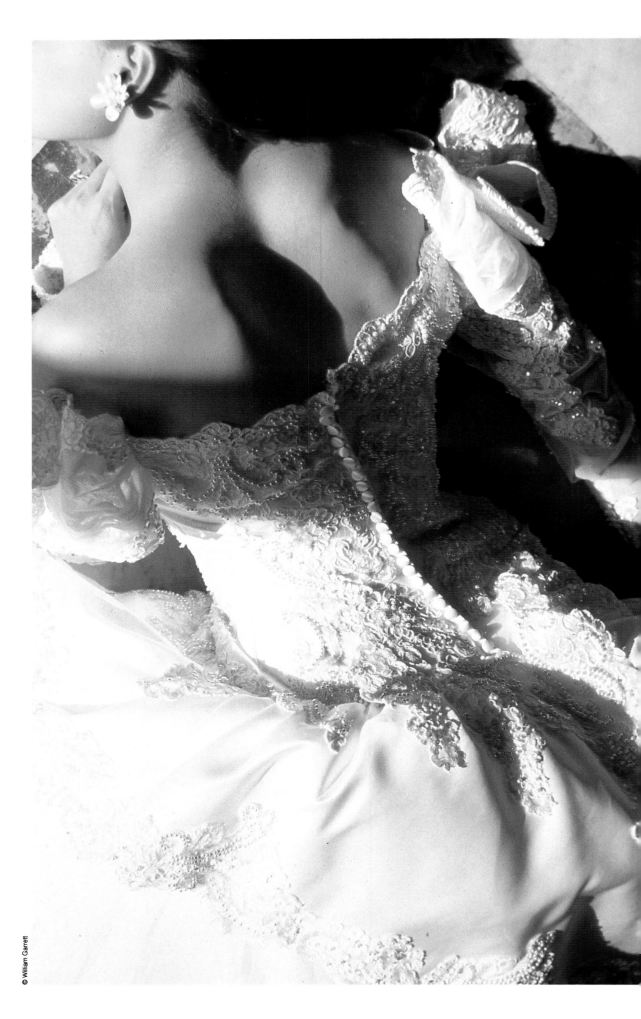

© William Garrett

incredible finery, including lace ruffs and collars. Pleated and fluted lace collars that encircled the neck were a favorite of Queen Elizabeth I, whose ruffs were often three-quarters of a yard deep. Utilizing as much as twenty-five yards of lace, Queen Elizabeth's ruffs were so broad that they had to be supported by hoops of iron or wire. It became the mode among the aristocracy to attempt to outdo one another with wider and more elaborate ruffs. There is a story about the resourcefulness of Lady Renée Margot, who, in order to dine while wearing her enormous ruff, ate with a special spoon that had a handle two feet long.

France is the undisputed center of lace making today. Upon her marriage to the French monarch Henry II, Catherine de' Medici introduced this Venetian craft to the French court. Her son, Henry III, was so enamored of the ethereal, delicate fibers that he refused to allow his servants to handle his ruffs, preferring to wash and iron them himself. It wasn't until the reign of Louis XIV that lace making flourished in France, when the finance minister, Jean-Baptiste Colbert, became alarmed at the enormous sums being spent for Italian lace and established lace schools near Alençon that eventually produced some of the best lace in the world. Fearful of losing lace makers—and their potential earnings—to the French, the rulers of Venice issued a decree:

If any artist or handcraftsman practices his art in any foreign land for the detriment of the Republic, orders for his return will be sent to him; if he disobeys them, his nearest kin will be put into prison in order that through his interest in their welfare, his obedience may be compelled. If he comes back, his past offense will be condoned and employment for him will be found in

Venice, but if notwithstanding the imprisonment of his nearest kin he obstinately decides to continue living abroad, an emissary will be commissioned to kill him, and his next of kin will be liberated only on his death.

Not to be outdone, Louis XIV proclaimed a sentence of death for anyone who carried lace secrets beyond the borders of France.

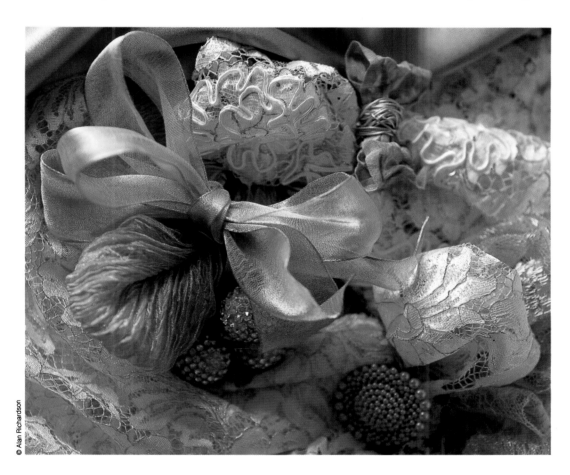

© Alan Richardson

Two revolutions virtually ended the art of lace making by hand. The French Revolution temporarily destroyed the demand for lace, but the revolution that struck the coup de grace was the industrial revolution, which transformed not only the lace business but fabric industries throughout the Western world. After the French Revolution, Napoleon Bonaparte tried to revive the lace industry by making the wearing of lace compulsory at court and even personally designing a lace pattern, but it was too late.

Machine-made net was the first invention, woven at a pace hand lace makers could never match. At first, machine net was used by the lace makers as a background to their still hand-stitched art. Queen Victoria's wedding veil of Honiton lace was a combination of machine-made net and handmade motifs. Her veil was one of the last celebrated efforts at handmade lace. The new machines were producing not

OPPOSITE PAGE: *Regal beaded Alençon lace has the body and the stature to measure up to grand bridal designs and its graceful edge makes it ideal for a bodice with looped lace sleeves by Eve Muscio.* **ABOVE, CLOCKWISE FROM BOW:** *Organza ribbon, gilt soutache lace, gilt Chantilly, charmeuse, and pleated gauze lamé.*

merely net, but entire lace patterns quickly and thus affordably, and suddenly lace was no longer the privilege of nobility.

Although lace had always been popular with wealthy aristocrats, the advent of machine lace spawned a passionate demand among average Victorians. Technology made it possible for every woman to copy the fashions of queens. Following the style set by Victoria at her own wedding in 1840, lace became an important hallmark of the bride, frequently used for veils and also as a trimming for gowns. In 1853, *Godey's Lady's Book* announced to prospective American brides the latest wedding fashion: "We copy the following from the *London Lady's Newspaper,* 'She was magnificently attired in a white moiré antique dress, with two deep flounces

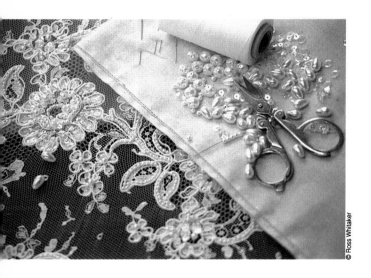

© Ross Whitaker

Virtually all lace—whether it is a copy of classic rose point and duchesse **(OPPOSITE PAGE)** *or Alençon* **(ABOVE)** *—is made by machine today. Yet whenever lace is beaded or cut into a bridal gown, it is done by hand. Even mass-produced wedding gowns feature the same old-fashioned workmanship that is elemental in the best designer gowns.*

of the finest Brussels lace…a superb Brussels lace veil, reaching to the ground, was thrown over her head." Even though well-made machine lace was replacing handmade lace among the burgeoning middle class, the handsewn variety was still available to wealthy brides.

Many Victorian women were schooled in the fine, feminine art of lace making, and they slowly wove family heirlooms. "Lace veils, of course, must be used just as they are …no one buys a [handmade] lace veil, but merely uses one that has been worn in the family," reminded *Harper's Bazar* in 1895. Perhaps it was the rarity of heirloom lace and the proliferation of the nouveau riche by the end of the eighteenth century that prompted *Harper's Bazar* to comment on Consuelo Vanderbilt's 1895 wedding, "as a bride still in her teens is too young for a lace veil, Miss Vanderbilt wore a tulle veil." Machine-made lace has sustained an art that would be otherwise lost today. As ancient patterns are copied and preserved, the legacy of lace offers each bride "something borrowed" from history.

Although brides today will almost always wear machine-made lace, there are hand-made heirloom lace gowns and veils that survive to be reworn or reworked. Pat Kerr, a Memphis-based designer and collector of antique textiles, creates one-of-a-kind gowns from old lace. Antique, hand-made lace is as expensive as it is rare—fine Belgium lace has sold recently for $1,500 an inch. Most machine lace is made in France and it is usually a blend of cotton and rayon, all rayon, or synthetics, in order of quality.

Many antique styles of lace are made by machine today although no longer in the original town and with variations on design that are broadly classified by the basic weaving technique. There are a handful of laces that continue to be favored by bridal designers and brides. Alençon, a regal lace for any

bride, was originally known as Point de France when the town of Alençon was established as the lace-making center of France in the 1650s. Alençon has a delicate background of neatly arranged flowers and swags, and its distinctive character is the outlining or reembroidering along the edge of each design with cord. Originally this cording was made of true horsehair that was stitched over with the traditional buttonhole stitch. Battenberg lace, a coarser version of Renaissance lace, is made by using a tape, braid, or ribbon of Battenberg linen and stitching it into a pattern, which is then connected with decorative stitches. Ribbon lace is the modern derivation. Chantilly lace, a favorite of Marie Antoinette, was originally a black bobbin lace of delicate floral sprays and intertwining ribbons on a plain mesh background edged with a finer, less defined cord than Alençon. Guipure lace, originally a design cut from fine cotton and embroidered with needlepoint stitches, is similar to Irish lace. Today, guipure is applied to heavy, defined work. *Guipe* actually refers to a cord around which silk is rolled. This tape lace is characterized by large motifs with few connecting bars. In the final stages of manufacturing, the background supporting net is removed by heat, leaving the distinctive lace. Irish lace broadly refers to net embroideries and Irish crochet, some of which is still made by hand. The most popular is Carrickmacross, a guipure-type lace made from cotton or linen. Due to its popularity at the turn of the nineteenth century, excellent samples and dresses survive. Schiffli lace is a very lightweight, modern lace made on the Schiffli machine. Its design is really an allover embroidery—with running stitches instead of knots—on a mesh background. Venise lace is the machine-made version of old Venetian Point, a needlepoint lace of floral motifs connected with irregularly spaced brides.

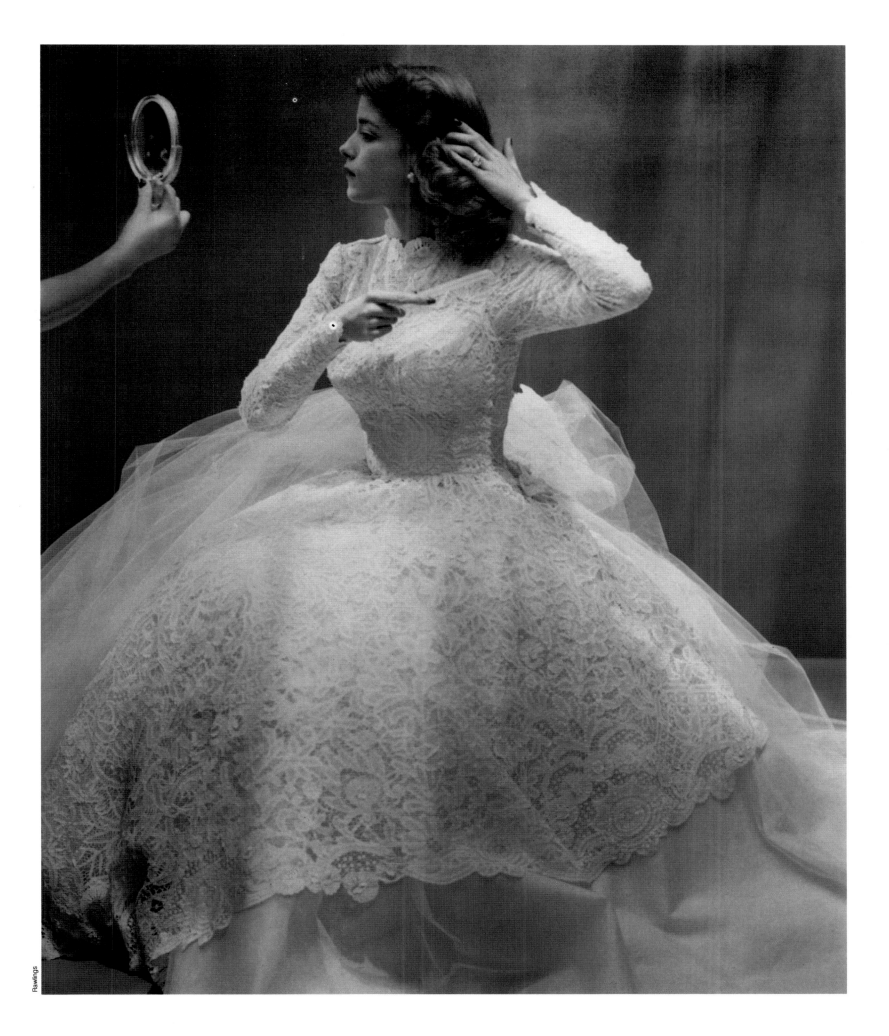

Rawlings

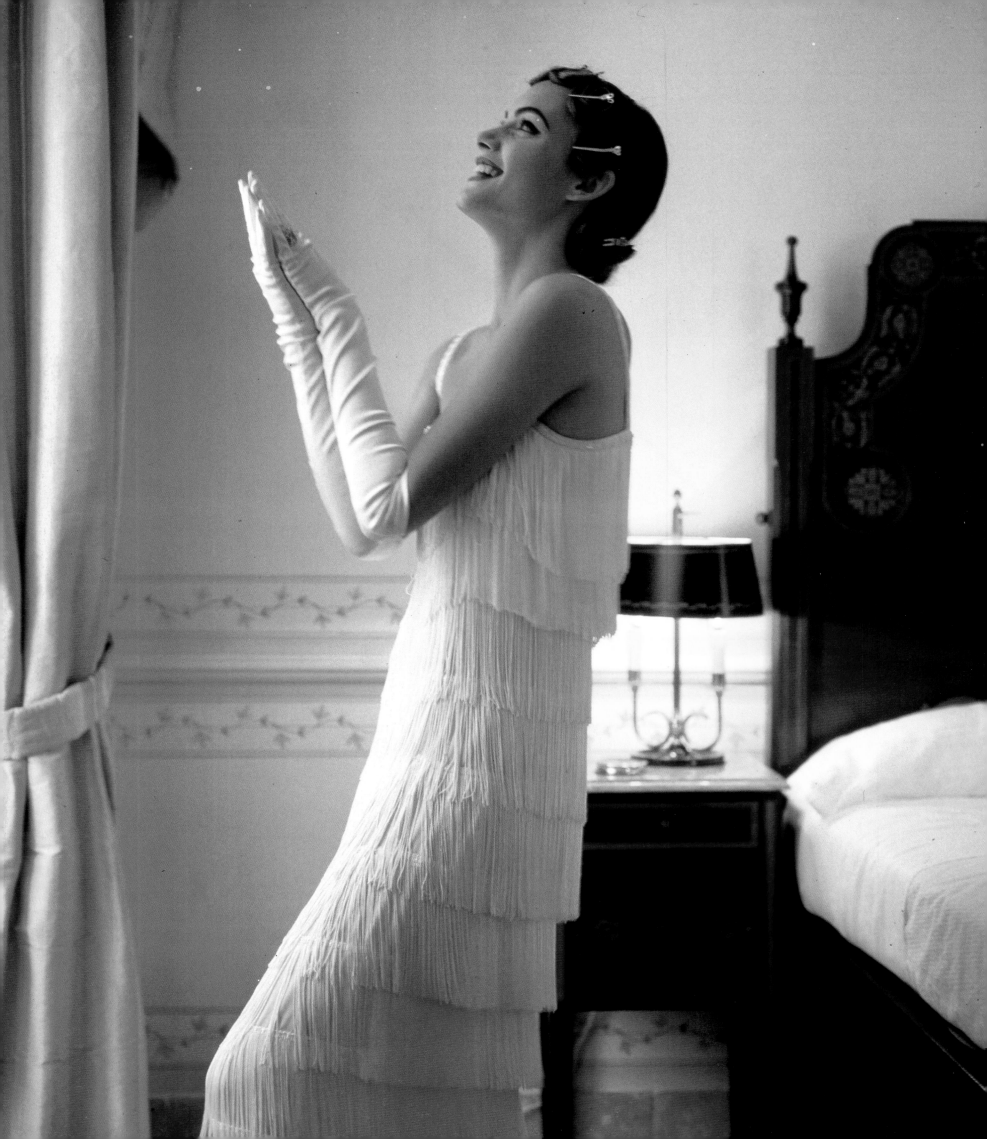

EMBELLISHMENTS

Brides have always adorned their bridal gowns with some element that suitably embellished the fabric to give the bride an even more glamorous appearance. Precious jewels were royal favorites, but today's bride has many more options. Lace has always been a popular flourish: flounces, ruffles, ribbons, bows, and three-dimensional flowers were all made of lace. Beading is often used to finish lace. If applied properly, says Richard Glasgow, a couture bridal designer, "beads can make the lace flower bloom, but too many beads can make it impossible to recognize the lace." Beads are always applied by hand, sewn on the costliest gowns and glued onto less expensive dresses. Crystal

beads, real or synthetic, are subtle and are best used to highlight a lace; opaque white or metallic beads can create a pattern on a plain fabric—a chain of hearts around a neckline, a gilded bow on the bodice, an allover mesh-patterned train; and even colorful beads are found on wedding gowns, as a bouquet of beaded flowers that spills over a skirt.

Seed pearls, real or synthetic, are tiny irregular jewels often embroidered in

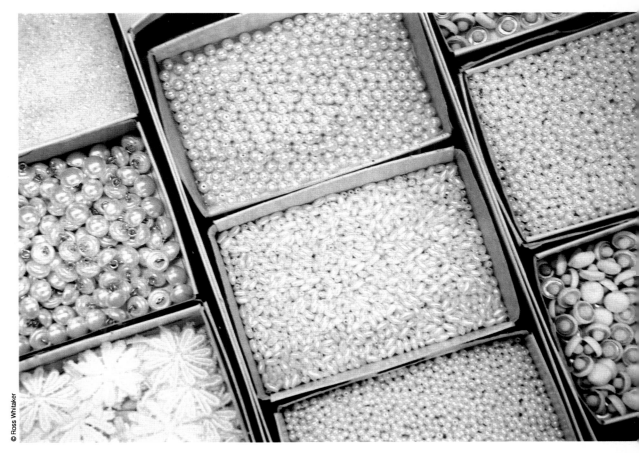

to create a shimmering, metallic fabric. Norma Kamali has used allover matte gold sequins on extra-long scarves that can wrap around the bride and trail to the floor and on jackets worn with flowing skirts of jersey for the less traditional bride.

During the nineteenth century, gowns were always finished with decorative passementerie, a heavily embroidered braid used as an edging. A beautiful bridal gown today

patterns onto a dress. Carolina Herrera designed her daughter's wedding gown with a delicate seed-pearl pattern of lilies-of-the valley blooming across the bodice; Andrew Koval, a couture bridal designer, creates handmade ribbon lace for a bodice with each curve of the lace beaded with a single pearl.

Sequins, tiny metal or synthetic disks with a center pinhole, and larger versions called paillettes, are used to add a decorative sparkle to part of a dress or in an allover pattern

ABOVE: *Imaginative manipulation of embellishments—from buttons to crystal beads to tiny lace florets to miniature seed pearls—can transform an ordinary gown into one marked by personality.* **OPPOSITE PAGE:** *Layers of fringe by Atelier Rosalba.* **LEFT:** *Ondyn Herschelle's spaghetti fringe ensemble is scattered with pearls.*

silk ottoman wedding pants

—spaghetti fringe scattered with pearls

Ondyn Herschelle

© Reto Gunter from Vogue Sposa

© Design: Herschelle Couture, San Francisco

© Ross Whitaker

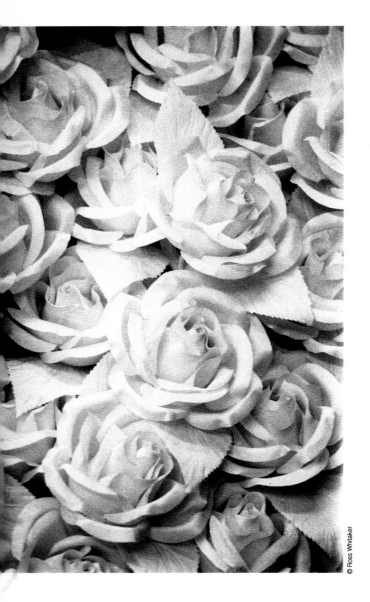

might use passementerie to outline the cuff of a sleeve or to create a trompe-l'oeil jacket on an elongated bodice of shantung silk.

The Victorians were also well versed in the language of flowers, trimming their gowns with sentimental favorites. Today, blooming brides often opt for silk flowers. The best silk flowers are handmade, either cut from multiple layers of silk or rolled from a single swatch of silk. The House of Chanel has its trademark camellias. Richard Glasgow is known for trimming his dresses with full-blown roses, highlighting the curve of a neckline or the back of the waist.

Silk ribbons and bows are also favorite bridal adornments. A massive bow is a perennially popular highlight for the back waist of a gown, marking the start of the train. Skirts that are to be bustled do well with some back waist adornment to set off the folds of fabric. Medium-sized bows may graduate in size all the way down a train or be used singly for a headpiece. And the tiniest bows are delightful when scattered across a skirt of net. Satin and grosgrain ribbons, sewn into three-dimensional, undulating ribbon lace, could form an entire bodice. Sewn flat on bridal gowns, ribbons may outline necklines and sleeves for a tailored finish or, to create subtle stripes, off-white ribbons may be sewn to a white skirt.

In the eighteenth and nineteenth centuries, bridal gowns were distinguished by an overabundance of decoration. The wealthier a woman was, the finer the fabric of her gown—and the more lavishly trimmed and bejeweled her gown. Today, however, it is the mark of quality rather than wealth that is the aim of the perfect wedding gown. The best gowns wisely use the finest of fabrics in a deliberate, well-executed manner. The incredible range of ornamentation is not a license to riot—the most exquisite dresses are designed with judicious restraint.

Silk is not only the foundation of most bridal gowns, it's also a favorite flourish. **ABOVE:** *Dozens of handmade silk roses await placement across an undulating neckline or a swirling hemline.* **RIGHT:** *Slender silk ribbons are knotted into bows, a tempting closure for the sheer organza sleeves of this Yumi Katsura gown.*

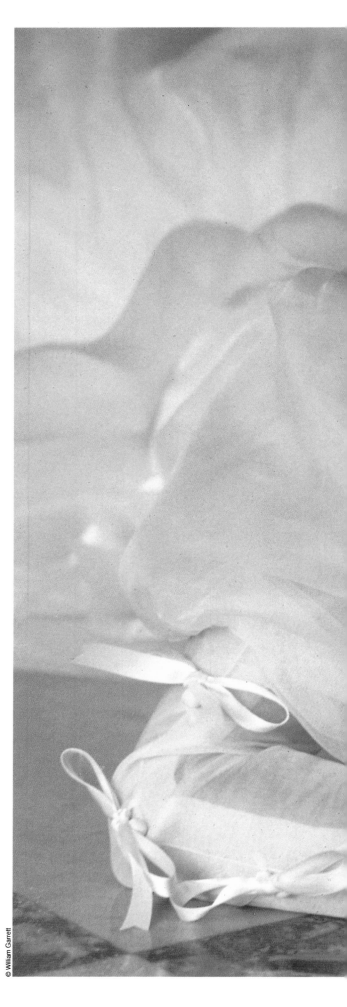

© Ross Whitaker

© William Garrett

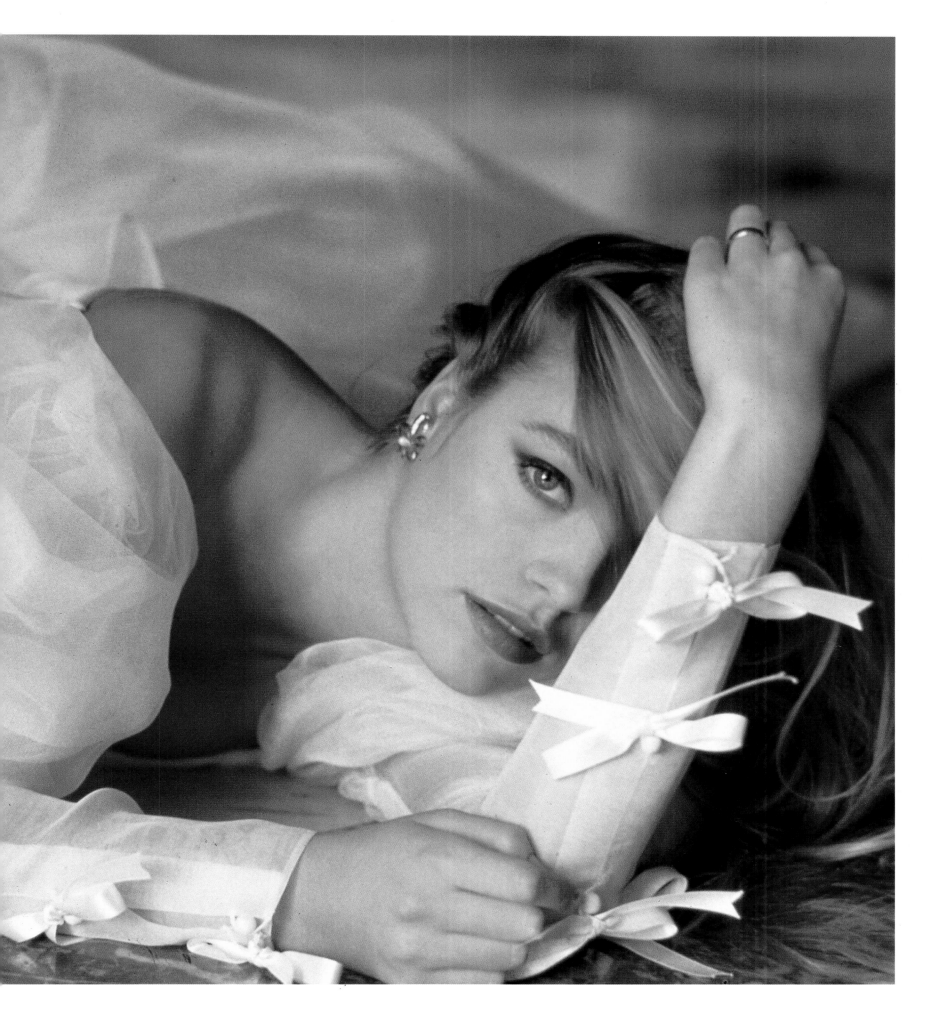

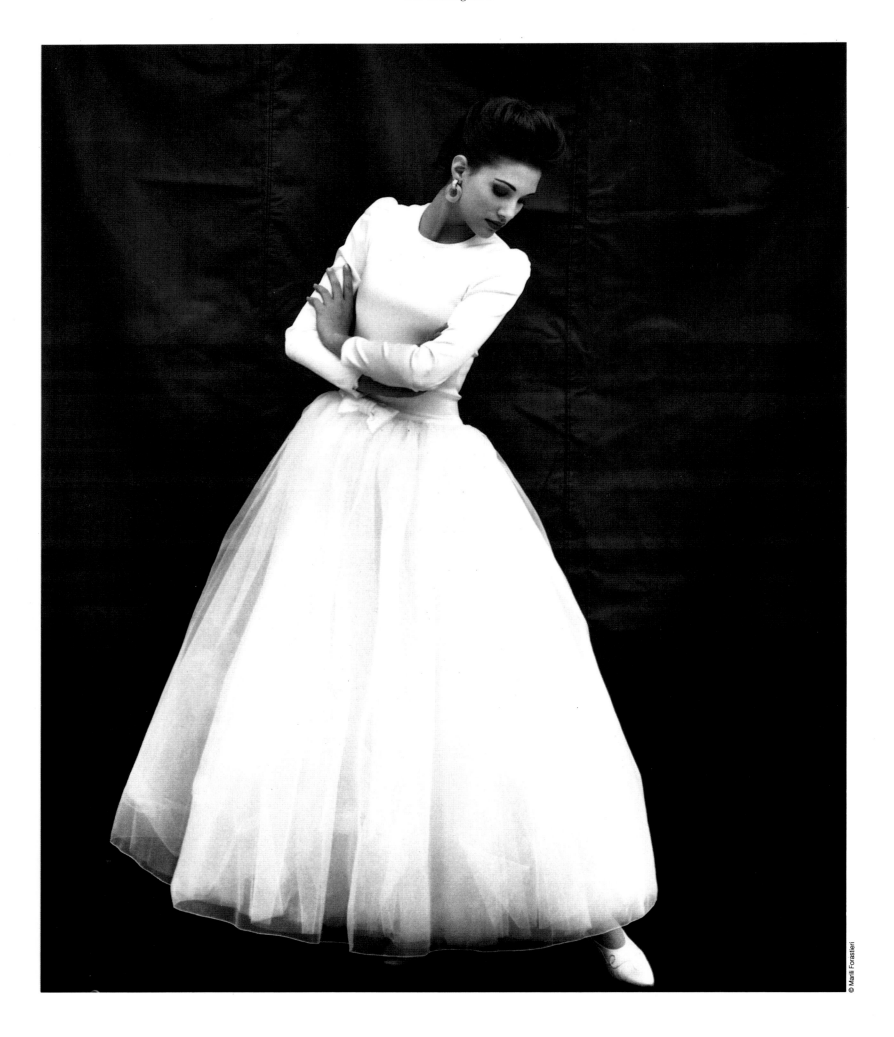

STYLE AND SHAPE

The cut of a bridal gown is the preeminently important detail in a field of important details. The task of the designer is not merely to cut, but to sculpt and manipulate fabric to fit, mold, and drape a bride's body—with the goal not to conceal but to glorify her. The cut of a gown is its foundation, with the choice of sleeve, neckline, and train combining to give each dress its own style and a look that is the signature of the designer. The perfect gown is one with elegance and a seemingly natural, aesthetic balance. No bridal gown is naturally elegant, however; each one is painstakingly designed to achieve that state. The right fiber must be cut into the right shapes, which must be sewn together in the right manner and finished with the right detail—and each element must not only be right by itself, but must combine to be perfect together.

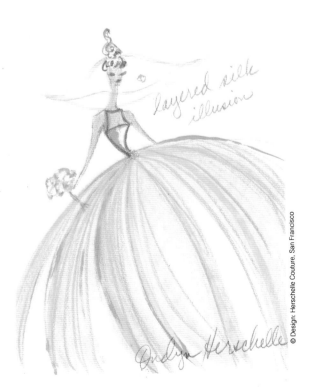

The basic line of a bridal gown directs the choice of details, the resulting silhouette shapes the final style, which will, in turn, determine the overall look of the wedding. The ball gown is the most traditional bridal shape, evoking romantic images that range from Cinderella to Scarlett O'Hara in her dress made from curtains to Princess Grace as a royal bride. The basic ball gown has a big, full, bell-shaped skirt, supported by petticoats or hoops, a bell shape, and a fitted bodice. The ball gown is the most universal style, and its basic silhouette can be reworked to flatter every figure. Its narrow waistline can flatter or camouflage. A ball gown with a basque waist makes a Rembrandt woman look slender—the full skirts emphasize the smaller waist—match this with an off-the-shoulder neckline edged with flowers and the bride instantly has an hourglass figure. Indeed, this shape has hundreds of incarnations when paired with a different sleeve, neckline, waistline, or train. The ball gown is always proper, from the most formal weddings to tradition-minded garden ceremonies.

The sheath is a svelte alternative, a less traditional choice that is excellent for physically fit brides. This body-contouring silhouette seems revealing even when the bride's body is completely covered. The most daring sheath is one of allover lace with a nude lining. Because of their tight fit, sheaths are worn without a petticoat and may be less comfortable for a long ceremony and a reception with a lively band made for dancing. Stepping in and out of a limousine can be tricky, too, unless the sheath is also a mini. A sheath is often finished with a detachable train or overskirt, which can conceal the sheath until removed.

The A-line and similar princess-line gowns are less restricting than sheath styles. Equally fitted through the shoulders and

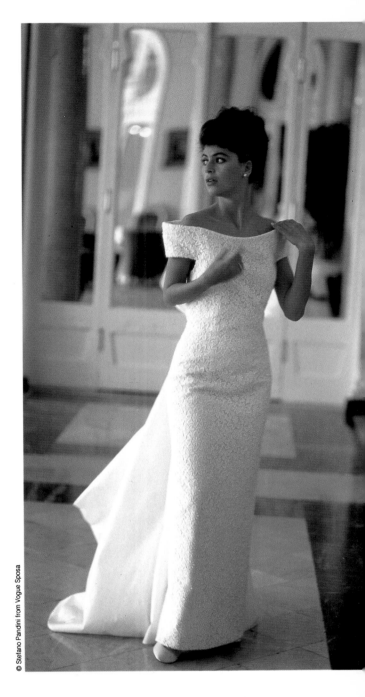

Two silhouettes—the ball gown and the sheath—dominate the cut of bridal gowns. A full-skirted ball gown with a natural waistline is the sentimental favorite, shaped from layers of organza by Guy Laroche **(OPPOSITE PAGE)** or ethereal tulle by Ondyn Herschelle **(LEFT)**.
ABOVE: The ball gown's alter ego is the narrow sheath. With its off-the-shoulder neckline, this streamlined version by Laura Dionisi is frankly sexy.

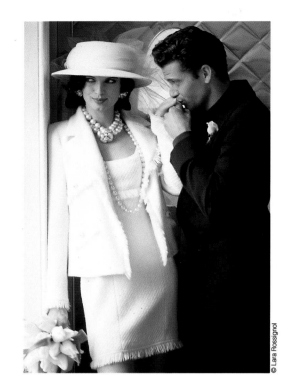

Contrasting textures, color, and embellishments underscore the cut of modern classics. **BELOW:** *Frank Massandrea's bold juxtaposition of soutache, pearls, and rhinestones vividly demarcates the empire waist.* **RIGHT:** *Wool bouclé edged with fringe by Karl Lagerfeld for Chanel invests a civil suit with whimsical panache.* **OPPOSITE PAGE:** *Pale ivory skirting blushing pink cleverly delineates the gentle curve of this princess-line gown by Phillipa Lepley.*

bodice, above the waistline the gown begins to flare gently away from the body down to the hem. The first princess cut is credited to Worth, who constructed a waistless gown for Alexandra, Princess of Wales, in 1873. The nearly synonymous term "A-line" was introduced by Christian Dior, whose silhouettes were often graded with a letter that embodied the shape of the style. A high-waisted petticoat with a gentle flare works best under the princess gown; its higher waist lies flat and unnoticeable, while the soft flare keeps the skirt from collapsing, protecting its distinctive line. This style is flattering on almost every bride, and is especially ben-

eficial for a petite bride, because its elongated, fluid lines give the illusion of length.

The empire silhouette is a return to the neoclassical styles of the early eighteenth century: a high-waisted design with the skirt falling from directly under the bust line. The bodice can be molded—an excellent choice for a bride with a perfect bosom—or soft, more typical of the style Empress Josephine favored during the First Empire. Contrasting the bodice fabric with the skirt fabric—either in color, such as an ivory satin bodice with a white skirt, or texture, such as a beaded or lace bodice over a plain skirt—can further emphasize the simple, understated line of this style.

The suit is a modern silhouette that is always finished with a jacket or a coat. It can take on many combinations: a lace minidress with a coat of the same length in lace or otto-man; a long crepe Edwardian riding jacket over a chiffon blouse with wide ruffled cuffs and a pencil-thin skirt; a three-quarter-length quilted satin jacket with a short lace skirt and a pile of pearl necklaces. The wedding suit is de rigueur for civil ceremonies, logical for second or third or more weddings, and perfect for a woman with a tailored personal style.

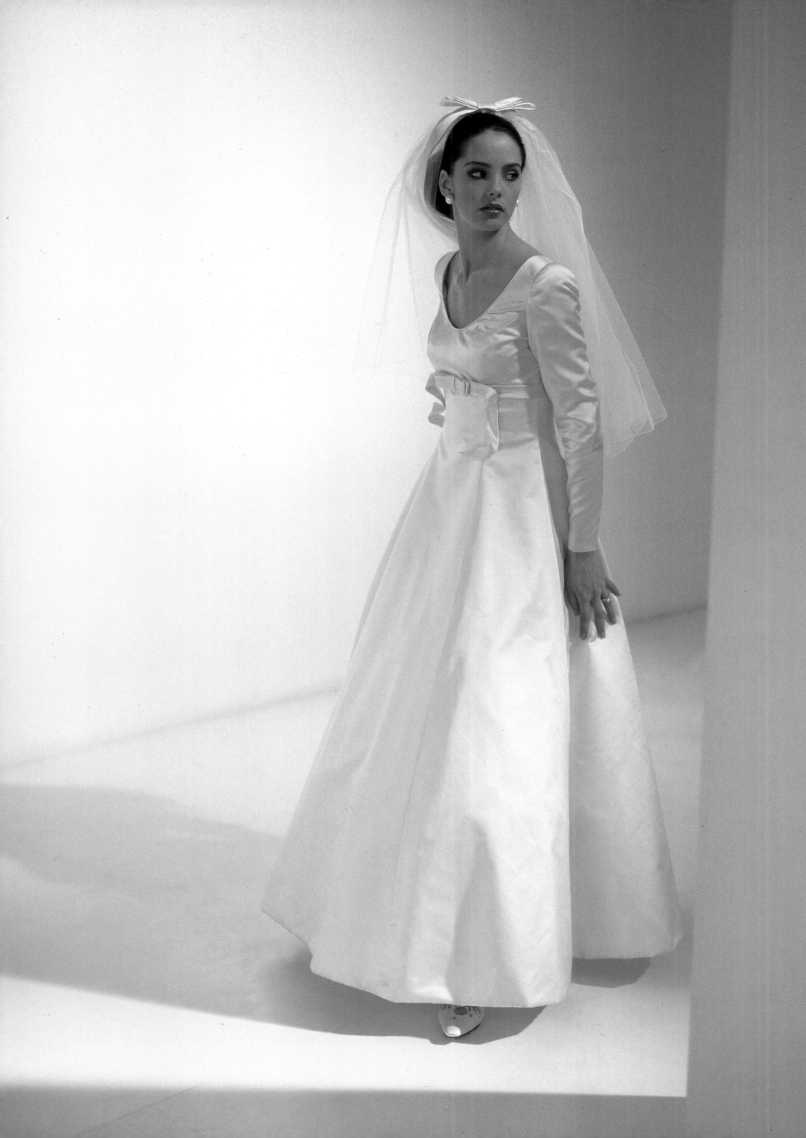

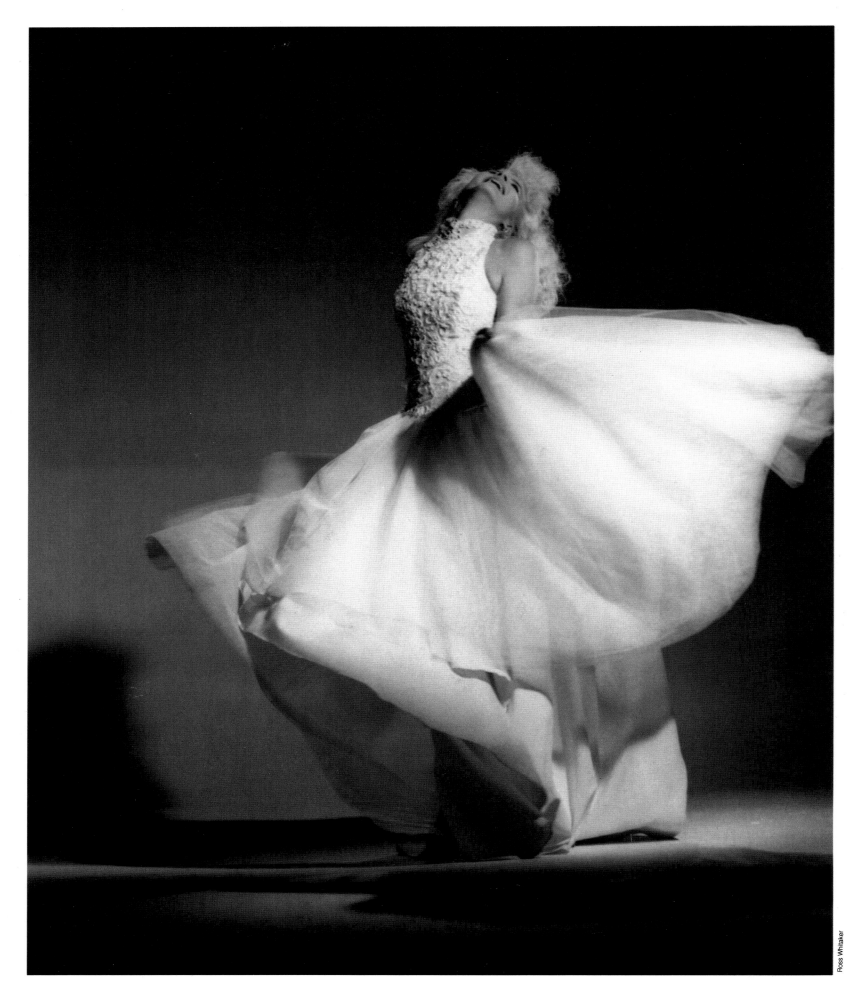

DESIGN DETAILS

The overall line of the bridal gown is refined by distinctive traditional details—the shape of the neckline, the sweep of a train, the style of the sleeves—that give each dress its particular style. These design elements are usually borrowed from the past, making the bridal gown a modern link to fashions gone by. Indeed, little else in our modern dress is as visually derivative of the history of fashion as the wedding gown. Exchanging "I dos" in a gown with period details is a celebration not only of sentimental tradition, but also of the heritage of fashion.

Most of the descriptive names of the favorite bridal necklines, waistlines, sleeves, and trains are logically rooted and easy to understand. These elements are critically important to the finished look of the gown—to make a harmonious whole, each detail must work well with the line of the dress and the choice of fabric. Necklines are a critical focus of the wedding gown, because this is the section of the dress that most people notice first. The right neckline should flatter your face and draw attention to your strongest features. If the neckline is wrong, the dress is wrong.

A wedding band collar is a high, fitted collar, popular in the 1890s, when it received its name. The sweetheart neckline is a low neckline that is cut to resemble the rounded curves of a heart. This slightly revealing décolletage was first popular in the 1930s and 1940s and has been a classic bridal neckline ever since. An off-the-shoulder neckline falls below the shoulders with a col-

lar or sleeve on the arm. A bodice with this cut needs to be boned for support, and many designers also include a few inches of elastic under the sleeve to "hold" the dress. Women with beautiful shoulders should select an off-the-shoulder style. The aptly named portrait collar perfectly frames and highlights the bride's face and neckline. An open neckline that often extends off the shoulders, it is always finished with extra fabric to frame the bride's neckline. Also known as a *fichu*, the collar wraps around the shoulders and is gathered to point at the bust line.

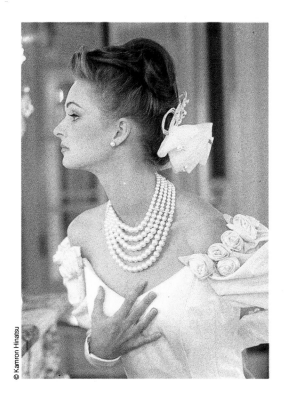

Every bride should, of course, carefully select a gown with flattering proportions. The neckline should be comfortable and complimentary, drawing attention to the face. **OPPOSITE PAGE:** *This gown by Yumi Katsura features a wedding band collar, a high neckline that allows support for full-figured women.* **ABOVE:** *Off-the-shoulder necklines, as in this dress by Catherine Rayner, demand a graceful shoulder and a secure foundation.*

An illusion neckline is a high neckline with either a scoop neck or a wedding band collar, but the bodice is sheer—made of net, point d'esprit, or chiffon—and may appear almost invisible. A bateau neckline has a shallow curve across the collarbone, and is cut the same front and back. Popular with French designers in the 1950s, the bateau works well in gowns cut to rekindle the 1950s spirit. The strapless neckline or bodice is sleeveless, boned, and molded to the chest. If this style seems too bare for a church wedding it can be modified for the ceremony with a removable bolero jacket or a stole of tulle to cover the shoulders. A jewel neckline is a high, rounded line without a collar or binding, originally designed as a simple background for jewels—such as a triple strand of "jawbreaker" pearls. A scoop neckline is a low, curved sweep extending to the shoulders or cut deep in the front or back or both. The scoop is a simple but handsome option for a woman with a beautiful neck and shoulders. A V-neckline couldn't be more straightforward in description. The V may be in front, back, or both, and may be shallow or deep. Some deep V-necklines extend to the waistline and are covered with illusion.

Selecting the right waistline option is critical in order to achieve a flattering shape. The waistline shapes the dress, bringing proportion to the silhouette. The basque waistline is the most popular waistline featured in traditional bridal gowns for one main reason: it looks great on everyone. The basque waist sits at the natural waist in the back but dips to a lower point in the front. The V-line of the basque point slenderizes the waist by pulling the eye forward. The point may be raised or lowered to make the most flattering silhouette. Frequently, the seam of the basque waistline is rolled for definition. A natural waistline sits at the waist and is a classic element of the ball gown. The natural waistline

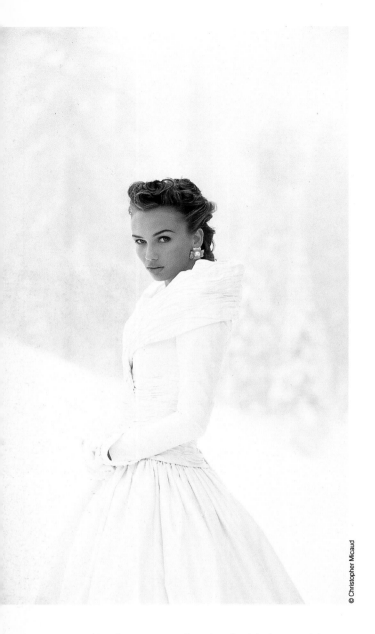

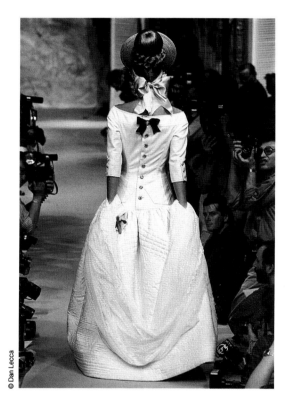

most closely linked to the season of the wedding—although the bride's preference for short or long is the deciding factor. A puff sleeve is a short sleeve gathered at the armhole or at the cuff or band of the sleeve, or both for a spherical shape, often small in dimension. A Juliet sleeve, named for Shakespeare's heroine, is a long, fitted sleeve with a short puff at the shoulder. Some brides opt for an opaque fabric for the puff with the rest of the sleeve a sheer lace. A cap sleeve covers just the top of the arm. Some off-the-shoulder gowns are finished with a cap sleeve. A bishop sleeve is a full sleeve set into a normal armhole and gathered into a band at the wrist; this style was extremely popular in the 1860s. The leg-o'-mutton, or gigot, sleeve is an exaggerated sleeve that is wide and rounded at the shoulder, tapering to a snug fit on the lower arm. This sleeve is common in gowns that echo Victorian fashions. A three-quarter sleeve ends just below the elbow and is often finished with a small cuff or band. A fitted sleeve is long and narrow, and usually has a snap, button, or row of buttons at the wrist. The wedding point is a V-shaped extension on a long, fitted sleeve that comes to a point, covering the top of the bride's hand.

Trains date from the Middle Ages, when the length of a train, worn only at court, indicated the wearer's rank. Today the train indicates differing degrees of formality and an attention to tradition. In the late nineteenth century, when it was typical for a bride to be presented at court soon after her marriage, the bride would rewear her bridal gown, changing a few details of the dress to meet court dictates—a lower neckline, shorter sleeves—and she always added a train. For modern brides, the length of the train and skirt determines the overall mood of the wedding and corresponds to the formality or informality of the event.

A knee-length or shorter gown is rarely seen in church and is often the choice of a bride who wants a nontraditional gown that is more in tune with her daily personal style. Short dresses are classified as informals, but this does not necessarily mean the dress is casual. Indeed, short dresses are often quite sophisticated. A minidress is a favorite for the second-time bride who does not necessarily feel comfortable surrounded by all the traditional pomp and circumstance; a mini is also perfect for the avant-garde bride with great legs.

The best design details are cut with an eye for elegance. **LEFT:** *A beguiling portrait neckline lends a demure charm to this gown by Antonio for Bergdorf Goodman.* **ABOVE:** *The rear view is riveting through even the longest ceremony when it is a reversed jacket with bateau neckline, three-quarter sleeves, and dropped waist by Karl Lagerfeld for Chanel.* **OPPOSITE PAGE:** *Anneliese Sharp's dress of silk dupioni sculpted into a universally flattering basque waistline features pastel embroidery garlanding a gentle scoop neckline.*

is often trimmed with a highlighting ribbon, cord, or sash. A dropped waistline falls below the natural waistline in the classic flapper style. The lower waistline can be defined by a seam or obscured with a blousoned bodice. Lightweight laces and cottons carry this drop-waisted line with grace. Dresses with low waistlines are flattering on women with thick waists and full bosoms, because they draw the eye down and away from the less-than-perfect feature. Many drop-waisted dresses are also tea length, following the style of the 1920s.

The sleeves give extra interest to the bodice and balance the skirt of the dress. Of all the traditional options, the sleeve choice is

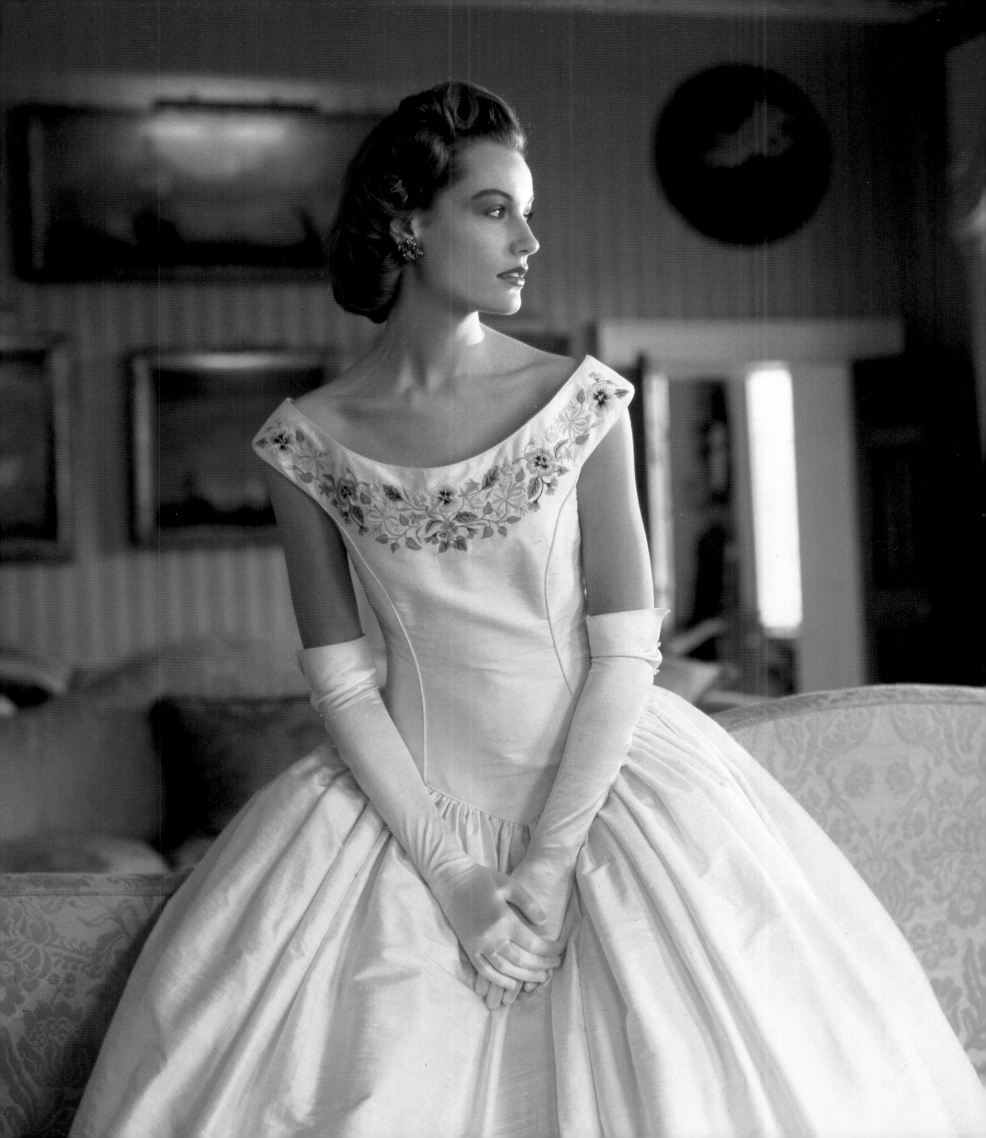

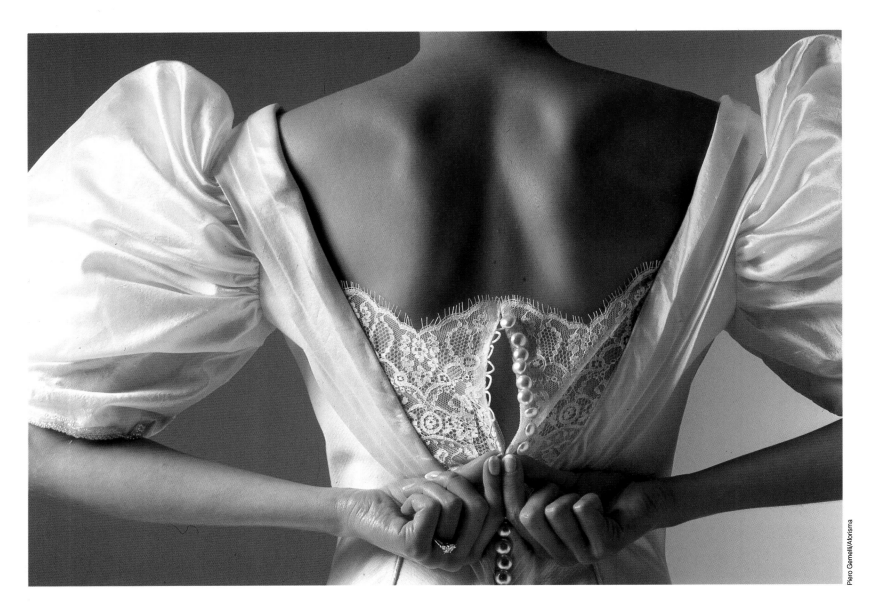

Piero Gemelli/Aforisma

Seductive drama is the natural result of a beautifully cut bridal gown. **ABOVE:** *The puff sleeve creates a soft but defined shoulder line on this Van Lear dress.* **OPPOSITE PAGE:** *The subtle glimpse of skin through sleeves and a bodice of lace are alluring without the revealing sheerness of illusion. The filigreed fabric also softens this fitted sheath by Yumi Katsura.*

Gowns that fall anywhere from the mid-calf to a sweep train are considered semi-formal, although most such dresses have many of the same elements as a formal gown, such as a big skirt and a long veil. Ballerina skirts, which reach to the center of the calf or a little lower, were popular for the 1950s bride. This skirt length is, of course, perfect in layers of tulle. A sweep train just brushes the floor, and is a trouble-free choice for brides who want the traditional effect of the train but none of the complications of manipulating the extra fabric.

Gowns with a chapel or cathedral train are considered formal and ultra-formal. A chapel-length train extends about one yard. A cathedral train is anything longer than a

yard and appropriate for only the most formal weddings, as that of Princess Diana, who opted for an amazing twenty-five-foot sweep. Cathedral and chapel trains must be bustled after the ceremony using a system of snaps, hooks, buttons, or hidden laces. It is presumed that a bride opting to wear a long train will have enough bridesmaids to see to it that every bit of lace or satin properly follows her. Designers understand the movement of fabric and often design a long train with embroidery and beading, the extra weight and proper placement of the ornamentation helping the train to fall properly.

Watteau and court trains, which cascade from the shoulders, are less common. The Watteau train is named for Antoine Watteau,

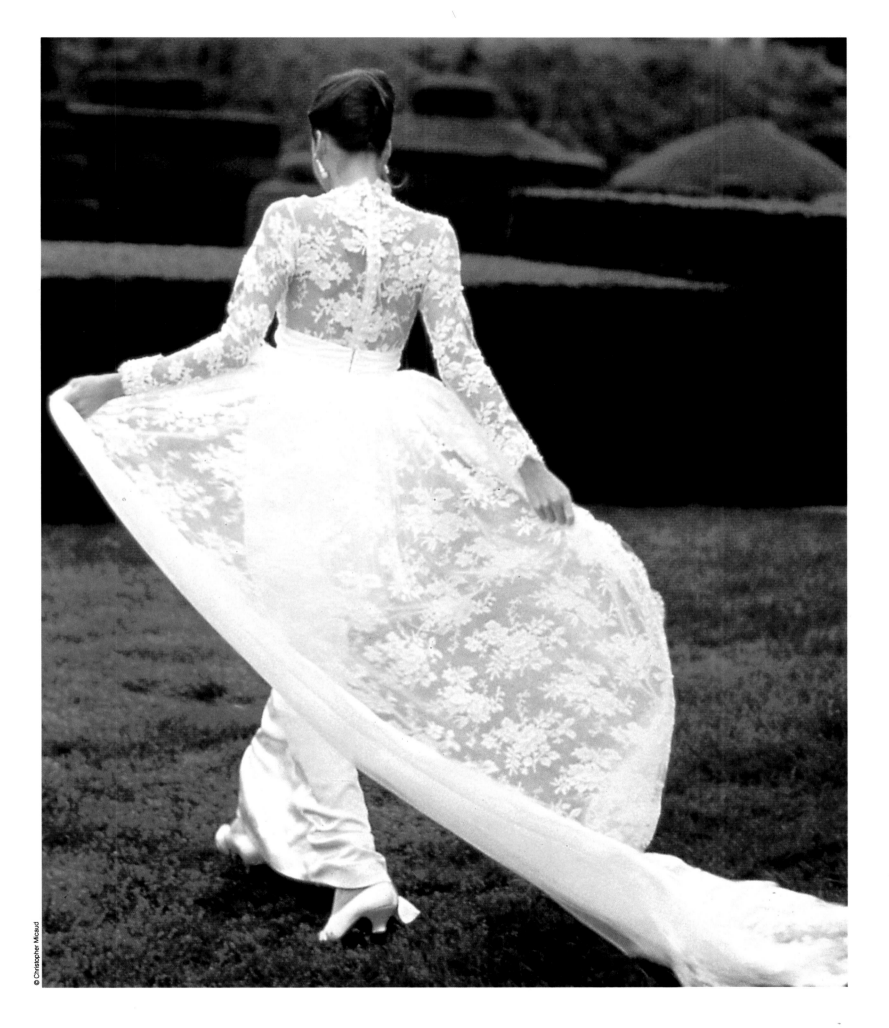

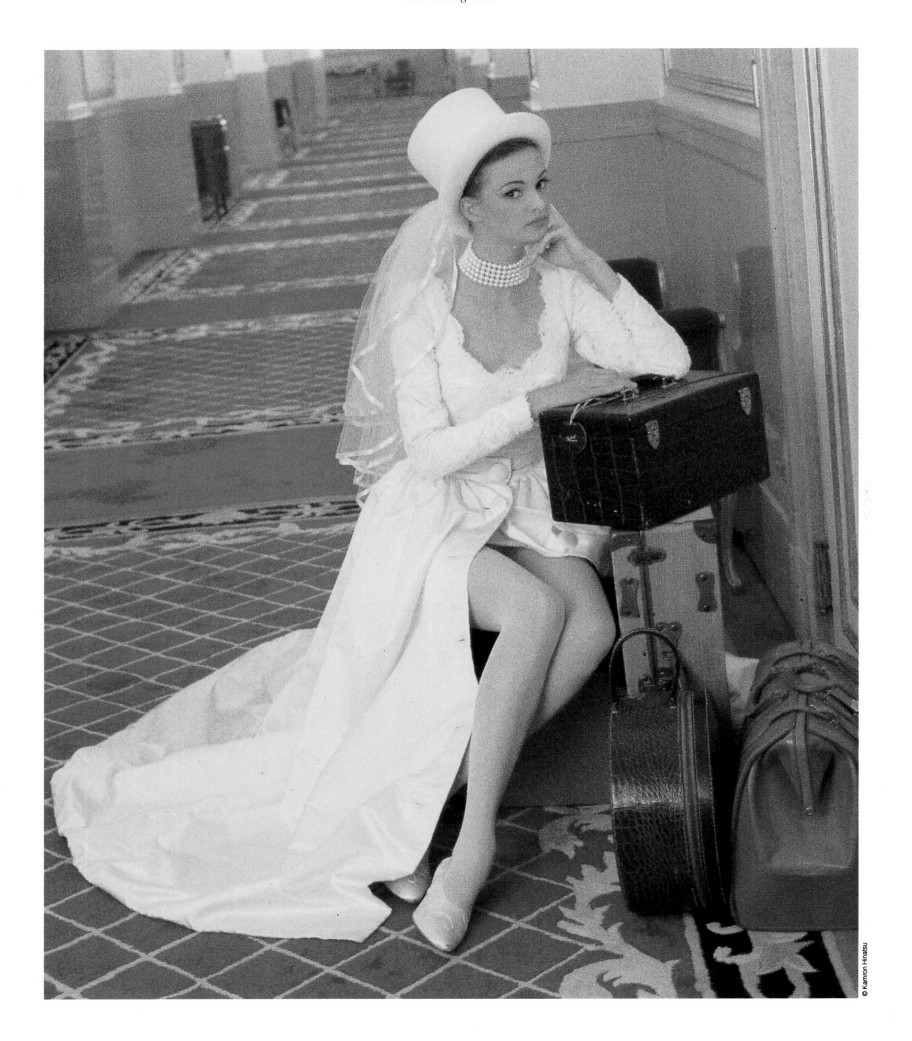

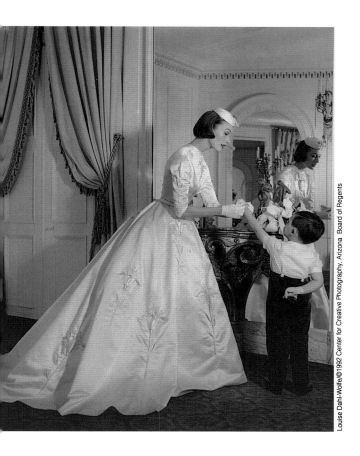

Louise Dahl-Wolfe/©1992 Center for Creative Photography, Arizona Board of Regents

course of the wedding day, from an antique kimono worn during the traditional Shinto ceremony, to a Western bridal gown worn for the wedding, to a ball gown worn for the reception, the bride who wears a detachable train maintains an aura of anticipation through all the stages of the wedding day. After the nuptial ceremony, the bride is freed from the cumbersome demands of a bustled or trailing skirt, and if the train is valuable— perhaps it is heirloom lace—it's protected from the rigors of celebration.

Formality and personal choice should determine the length of a bride's train. **OPPOSITE PAGE:** *A semiformal detachable train unveils a fabulously informal minidress of lace by Carmela Sutera.* **LEFT:** *Generally considered less formal, the chapel train is appropriate for very formal weddings when embroidered lilies are substituted for length, as in this Balmain gown.* **BELOW:** *The formal sweep of a cathedral train can be unwieldly unless bustled as in this gown by Rani for St. Pucchi.*

whose early eighteenth-century paintings depict women wearing elegant gowns with distinctive box pleats that sweep into a train. Watteau's paintings influenced the course of fashion in the 1700s, and the train is still found on some bridal gowns today. The court train, copied from regal fashions, is a separate sweep of fabric, but like the Watteau, it is attached to the shoulders of the gown. Finally, a detachable train is for the woman who wants it all—classic style and versatility. The detachable train can be any length. It is frequently attached to the back waist of the dress with hooks and buttons, but it may attach to the shoulders or wrap around the waist as a skirt. Once removed, the detachable train reveals a new look— perhaps a minidress under a swirl of tulle or a ball gown released from its court train. Without changing, the bride has two distinctive fashions for her wedding day, three if the ensemble is paired with a jacket. Like many modern Japanese brides who change their dress completely three times during the

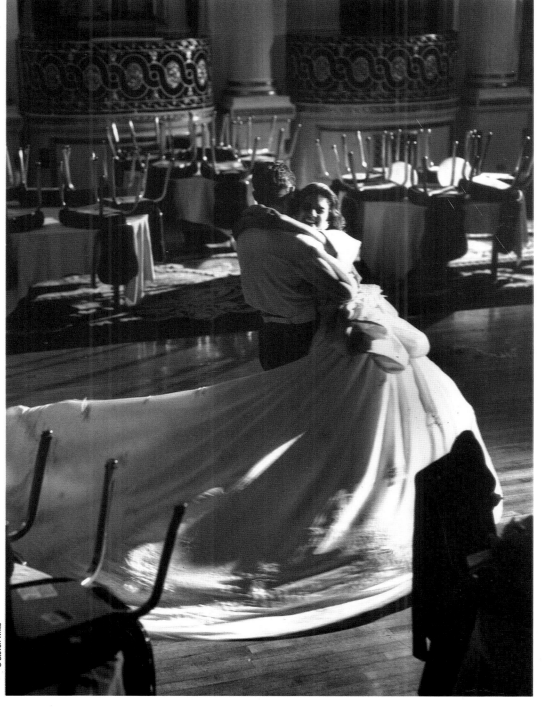

© Steven White

ROMANCE BY DESIGN

Today, almost every wedding dress is a unique masterpiece made exclusively for one woman. The best gowns blend timeless period details from fashion's most influential eras, with sumptuous fabrics and modern aesthetics. Design is an interactive venture, a dynamic combination of substance and imagination. Bridal designers meld fabric, cut, and style into gowns with impeccable balance, proportion, and workmanship that have as their final goal a beautiful bride.

Design is a process of distillation: from the chaotic mixture of trends, history, fantasy, textiles, notions, silhouettes, and personality the designer channels the right elements into a perfect gown. The designer must use a calculating eye and a discerning touch to create a gown that is not only fashionable but also stylish, or it risks being buried under the

weight of so much lace and beading. The ongoing debate of fashion versus style seems to suggest an either-or dichotomy. Coco Chanel applauded the endurance of style, noting "fashion fades, only style remains the same." But Yves Saint-Laurent recognized the value of fashion, noting at a retrospective of his designs: "Fashion is a kind of vitamin for style. It stimulates you, it gets you going. But there's a risk of overdose. It can destroy the balance of your personality—that goes for a designer and the woman who wears his clothes. Fashions pass quickly....Playing with fashion is an art." The designer is an arbiter of taste who must respect the delicate balance between fashion and style. A bridal designer must be especially conscious of this balance, because a bridal gown is an emotional investment that should continue to provide satisfaction long after the confetti has been swept away. Unlike ready-to-wear clothing, a bridal gown must have a distinctive style that nevertheless does not go out of style. A bridal gown is timeless when it borrows the best of contemporary and historic influences to exist outside of fashion as a pure, perfect entity unto itself. This kind of timelessness calls for a suspension of reality; it is not about the moment, it is about eternity—the ultimate fantasy.

An element of fantasy is an essential part of each bridal gown; indeed, fantasy gives the dress its romantic essence. Christian Dior once said, "Fashion comes from a dream." Bridal gowns represent the ultimate dream; in no sense is a bridal gown a utilitarian garment. To achieve the perfect combination of fantasy and style that is romance, the imagination of the designer must not only soar to inspired heights but also fulfill the fantasies and tastes of many different women.

A bridal gown may be the only dress you will ever own that will be custom-fitted to you. Unless you are opting for a vintage gown

(which often needs custom alterations), a ready-to-wear suit, or a discount bridal (a less expensive, off-the-rack dress), your gown will be made to order. The luxury of wearing a gown with a perfect, personal fit is a pleasure not often encountered in this ready-to-wear world. With the exception of Parisian haute couture, private designers, tailors, and seamstresses, only bridal gowns are made with old-fashioned custom labor.

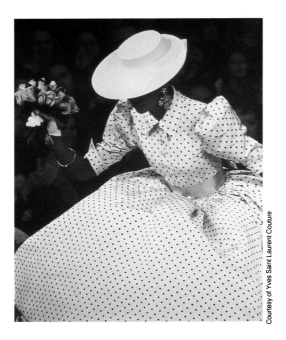

Courtesy of Yves Saint Laurent Couture

LEFT AND ABOVE: *Yves Saint-Laurent's imaginative collaborations of fabric and design and the elusive but critical advantage of elegance define the spirit of brilliant bridal design.*
OPPOSITE PAGE: *Richard Glasgow's designs show a diligent attention to detail and workmanship characteristic of the best gowns.*

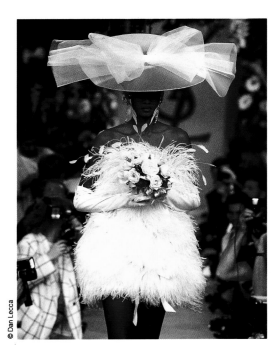

© Dan Lecca

Most fashion today is mass-produced and sold to stores that buy certain styles in a variety of sizes to offer their customers. Designers who are recognized as American couture manufacturers—Carolina Herrera, Geoffrey Beene, Isaac Mizrahi, Calvin Klein, Ralph Lauren, and others—are really premium-priced ready-to-wear designers—their clothes are beautifully made but they are not made to order. The breath-catching price tag of made-to-order designer clothes, the time-consuming process of fittings, and the delayed gratification of waiting for an outfit makes custom order a ridiculous proposition for the average consumer, particularly when ready-to-wear designers have so thoroughly thought out what every woman might want to wear for every moment in her life. But custom-ordered fashion does thrive in the bridal business, and it is the couture bridal designer—a bridal manufacturer or private designer of made-to-order dresses—who keeps alive a vanishing art: the hand-worked, custom-ordered gown.

Until the mid-nineteenth century, a woman who wanted a dress had to make it herself or hire a dressmaker. If the woman hired a dressmaker, the dressmaker followed the instructions of her client. Chances are the client copied the look she wanted from a ladies' magazine and even supplied the fabric herself. Dressmakers rarely originated styles, but rather followed the fashions of the times, which changed very slowly—a switch of trimming might be the big news for a season—the dressmaker's art was workmanship. In 1850, Charles Worth upset the status quo by being the first dressmaker to present fashion to his clients, beginning the now common practice of showing completed gowns on models to prospective customers. Worth also had the confidence to label huge, crinolined gowns passé by 1870, after which every fashion-conscious woman wanted to wear his bustled

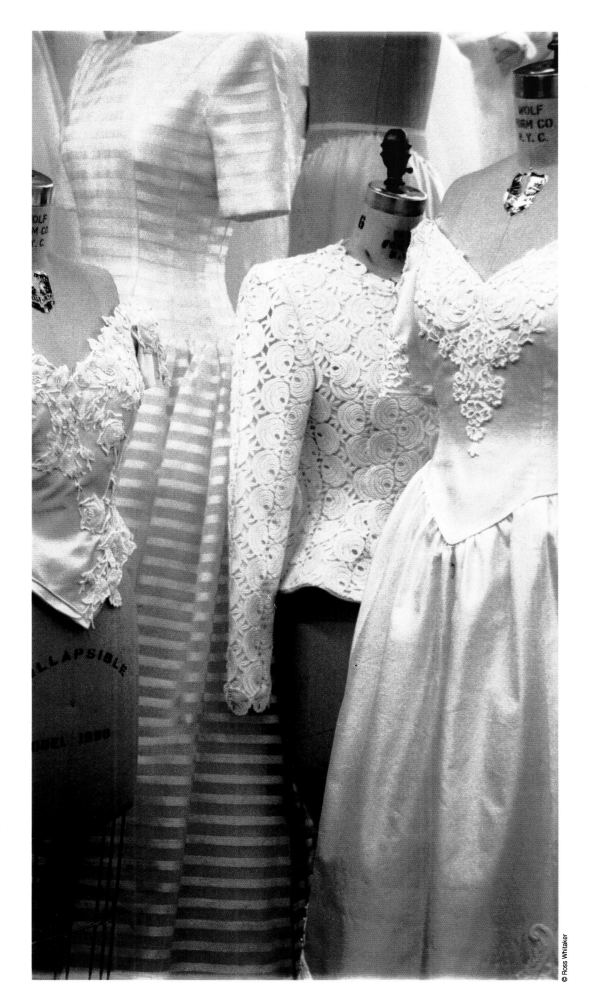

gowns. Worth made himself the world's first arbiter of style, setting the tone for couturiers to come with a lavishly decorated house that sold not only gowns, but also style—a style of dressing and a style of living—at a time when many were desperate for style direction. During Worth's era, status was no longer purely an inherited trait; it could be acquired. The nouveau riche, who were most anxious to show some style, needed help since they had no established family traditions to give them guidelines. Women of means flocked to Worth's door. For those who couldn't make the trip to Paris, ladies' magazines illustrated his lavish styles—often up to a year after they were introduced—for their readers to copy as best they could.

Worth's legacy was that by the twentieth century, the most important changes in fashion were initiated by influential designers. At the height of World War II, couture houses temporarily closed their doors and ready-to-wear finally gained a foothold with consumers as women bought what was available and affordable. After the war, spurred by explosive publicity about Dior and his "New Look," couture again became important, and eyes turned once again toward Paris for the latest fashion news. Although the ready-to-wear industry had become entrenched by the postwar era, fashion trends continued to be launched by couture designers.

Although the label "couture" traditionally applied only to those expensive Paris design establishments, members of the Chambre Syndicale de la Couture Parisienne, where clothes were made to order with several fittings for private clients, its meaning has evolved. Today most people think of couture as referring to a group of designers whose work is on the cutting edge of style, forecasting the direction of the industry as a whole—yet it is not design, but rather workmanship, that is the true foundation

of couture. Superior workmanship and exceptional fabrics mark the work of today's true couturiers, in addition to their ability to experiment and push the conventional limits of fashion design.

For today's women, well-made, fashionable, immediately wearable, and affordable (compared to five-figure-and-up price tags of haute couture), ready-to-wear clothes are the fashions of choice. *The New York Times* has recently suggested that the death of couture might be imminent, as couture designers themselves produce and introduce more and more ready-to-wear with their couture lines. Pierre Bergé, partner of Yves Saint-Laurent, declared in 1992 that "couture will be dead by the year 2000." Perhaps it will; perhaps the future of fashion is immediate accessibility, which is the keystone of ready-to-wear. But as Yves Saint-Laurent noted, couture is more than fashion: "Dior had taught me to love something other than fashion and style: the essential nobility of a couturier's craft." Couture will survive and remain true to its roots as long as fine workmanship remains valued. Most couturiers design an extravagant bridal gown as a finale to each show—not merely to embody a seasonal fantasy, but for a purely practical purpose—it is this gown that sells best. Fashion made-to-order is the foundation of the bridal business, which means that the bridal industry may well be the future of couture.

ART OF CONSTRUCTION

The majority of bridal gowns sold are designed and manufactured by bridal manufacturers that specialize in the production of wedding gowns. The bridal manufacturer's business is an endless June. All manufacturers market to bridal salons; the smallest firms may sell to only a few salons, the largest

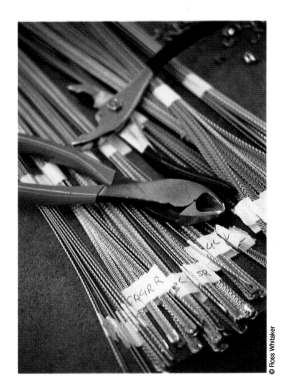

to hundreds. Whatever the size or focus of the manufacturer, the bare-bones process of designing and selling is the same. A sample line is produced and shown to salon buyers twice a year, when the buyers decide which styles to offer their brides. If the gown is manufactured by a custom bridal house, the sample can be used as a guide, and the bride's actual dress can be ordered with changes—a different neckline, waist, sleeve style or length, train, and sometimes even different fabrics or a particular bodice with a different skirt—for a fee. If a bride purchases a gown through a bridal salon, an order is then placed for the dress.

Bridal gowns are also created by appointment with private designers. Some designers have exclusive relationships with a salon that wants to offer as much choice as possible to the prospective bride who knows exactly what she wants but can't find it already sampled. The primary difference between a couture bridal manufacturer and a private designer is the relationship with the bride. A private designer has a personal relationship with a bride—the two work very closely together, designing and creating, from scratch, an individual gown. Based on the design selected and fabrics used, its price can vary dramatically. In contrast, it is the couture bridal manufacturer's business to make elaborate gowns to fit measurements of women he or she never sees, while the salon staff is responsible for the fitting and working with the customer.

Elaborate beading, tiny buttons, hidden zippers, and the intricate manipulation and placement of lace all require an overwhelming amount of hand sewing and cutting that is impossible to do by machine. Off-the-shoulder, thoroughly boned marvels of suspension require fastidious workmanship and impeccable construction. Whatever the style, the best gowns are as perfectly finished on the inside as they are on the outside. If a dress is privately designed, the designer will meet with the client, get to know her, understand how she dresses, visualize how she sees herself on her wedding day, discuss favorite fashions and inspirations, and measure her. Working from ideas, photos, sketches, swatches and drapings of fabric, samples of ribbons of lace and satin, a selection of buttons and bows, and assorted notions of nuptial splendor, the designer

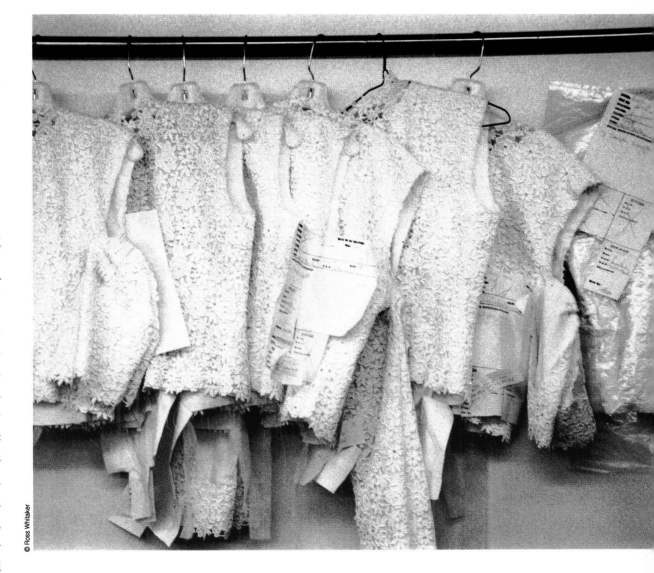

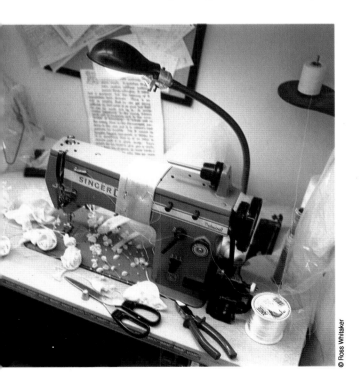

sketches the client's ultimate bridal gown. If a gown is created not for an individual customer but as a part of a season's first samples to be sold later to a bridal salon, the designer creates a series of gowns that best embodies his or her fantasy image of the bride. Following sketches, fabrics are draped on mannequins, then pinned and basted in place to reflect the actual finished lines of a gown.

Once a design is sold to a bride and ordered from a manufacturer, it takes an average of three to four months to finish a cut-to-measure gown. Private dressmakers are often small businesses and can usually produce a gown in half the time. At the workshop, gleaming bolts of assorted white fabrics rest untouched until a gown is actually ordered, for all gowns are cut to order and

ABOVE AND OPPOSITE PAGE: *Originally fashioned from whalebone or wood, today's boned bodices feature up to fifteen spiral metal bones, each able to twist in every direction to support the bride securely and comfortably.*
LEFT: *Elaborate workmanship is the foundation of the best wedding gowns, and a schedule of several months is needed to finish each gown perfectly.*

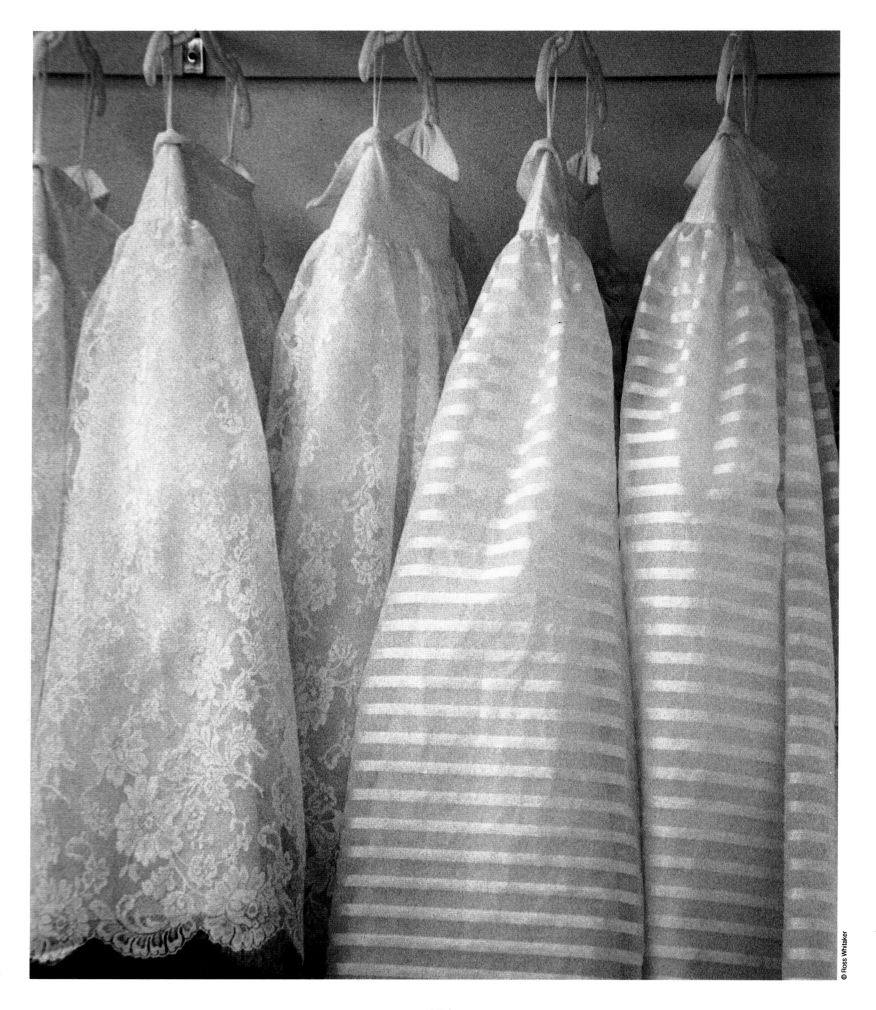

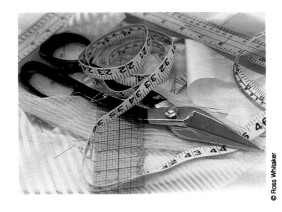

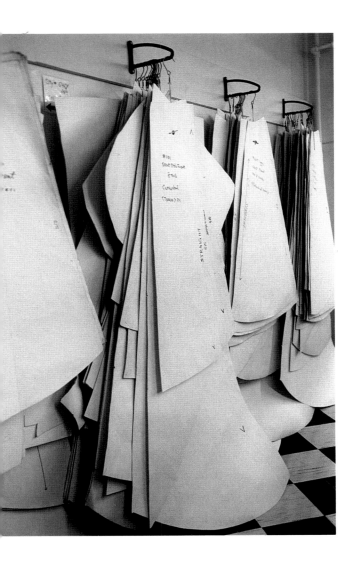

not before. Frequently, a muslin or canvas of the dress will be made first then fitted to the bride. Only when the canvas fits perfectly—two fittings are often required—and the details of decoration approved, is the outer layer of fabric cut. If a gown is individually designed, the canvas may actually be the pattern for the dress. Once cut, one precious layer at a time, the fabric is marked with a tag, listing all the measurements of the bride, her personal design requests or alterations from the basic design—such as a sleeve or train change—and when and where the gown is needed. This tag remains with the dress until the finished dress is presented to the bride.

The sewing begins when a seamstress sews the basic body of the dress. If the gown features a bodice with intricate pleating, for example, each pleat is pinned in place on a mannequin and stitched down by hand. The best gowns are made with both an inner and outer body. The inner body is the support system; it holds the boning, the facing, and the petticoat, which is often sewn directly into the best gowns. This inner body must fit like a glove. Each seam is hand-finished, the raw edges hidden between the inner and outer body. Lace motifs, if used, are cut by hand, pinned in place, and sewn. Lace bodices are molded, cut, and sewn by hand so that no seam or dart shows anywhere on the lace. Ribbon lace and silk flowers are rolled and sewn by hand; beads are carefully stitched in place so they won't pull off. During the sewing process, the gown is constantly pressed so that seams lie flat and lace is smooth. Zippers, buttons, hooks, and eyes are all sewn in by hand. The dress is fitted to a mannequin again, to inspect the gown for perfection of fit, finish, and draping. If the gown is privately ordered, it is then time for final fittings. At least three—and sometimes more—fittings are necessary throughout the design process for a perfect fit. If the gown is

ordered through a bridal salon, it is pressed, stuffed with tissue, and sent to the salon where the fittings will take place.

Couture bridal gowns are often priced starting at about $1,500 and climb quickly, but the exquisite designs, attention to personal requests, details, fabulous fabrics, and skilled workmanship make the price tag a relative bargain.

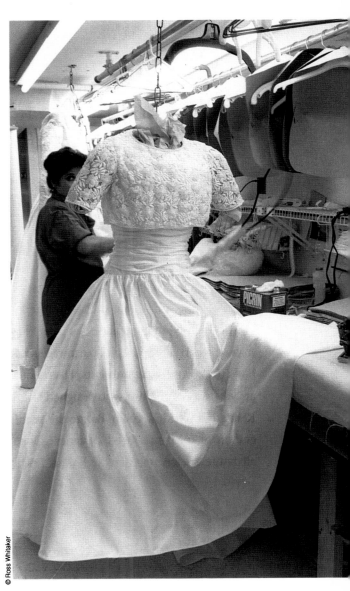

OPPOSITE PAGE: *A row of individually cut and sewn Richard Glasgow skirts are ready to be matched with their bodices.* **ABOVE:** *Although dozens of women may select the same style of gown, each dress is individually cut to the bride's size and measurements. Patterns for every size are kept handy for each order.* **RIGHT:** *The final task includes a thorough pressing and stuffing with tissue to preserve the shape of the gown, this one by Robert Legere for The Diamond Collection.*

THE DESIGNER'S VISION

Every designer has a specialty, a point of view that characterizes his or her line. There are over a hundred registered American bridal designers, untold private designers, a handful of American couture designers who offer limited bridal lines, dozens of ready-to-wear designers with an odd piece or two in their lines that would make interesting bridals, an antique gown specialist, numerous vintage bridal collectors, and European couture and ready-to-wear designers who also offer styles for the bride. It is virtually impossible to review them all, but there are a few designers worth highlighting. A sample follows, but these by no means constitute an inclusive list of the best. Look at their designs for ideas and inspiration. The great bridal designers offer beautifully made dresses with true style, even for the most traditional gowns. They are dedicated to producing the best dress—on time—for their bride, and they stand behind their product. The best dress for a bride is one that she treasures both at the time of the wedding and long afterward.

Couture bridal designers hark back to a bygone era when ladies of leisure had all their clothes made to order. Andrew Koval, who designs two lines—his own custom line, Endrius, and a couture bridal line for Galina—started in the business at Saks Fifth Avenue when all the finest department stores had custom-order departments. His mentor at Saks was Ann Lowe, who designed Jackie Kennedy's wedding gown. Before the proliferation of mass-produced designer gowns, all haute society women had their bridal gowns made to order at department stores. Koval acknowledges that custom work executed in the best tradition will always be expensive. Hand work is a time-consuming process for which few people are adequately

trained. The best fabrics are not inexpensive, and it takes a lot of time to design the gowns; if a gown is to be a couture masterpiece there is no other way to produce it. Both of Koval's lines are designed with updated, classic, traditional details (like his signature handmade ribbon lace and intricate, invisibly stitched pleated bodices).

The Dior bridal line, a licensee of Christian Dior, Paris, painstakingly recreates old Dior masterpieces, gorgeous ball gowns from the 1940s and 1950s that continue to inspire all bridal designers. The Dior bridal line is dedicated to maintaining the couturier's own

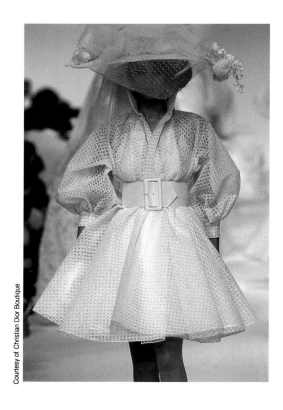

Courtesy of Christian Dior Dior Boutique

Equally influenced by fashion trends and historical details, every designer each season balances color, luxurious fabrics, fantastic embellishments, and perfectly coordinated accessories into one glorious gown with a very personal point of view. **ABOVE:** *An updated A-line coat dress by Gianfranco Ferre for Dior.* **OPPOSITE PAGE:** *A reinvented lace and satin sheath by Ronald Mann for Victoria Royal.*

standards of beauty and perfection, and a timeless quality of simplicity and construction is evident in every dress. To protect the integrity of original Dior designs, Dior bridals are one of the few couture lines that cannot be altered according to the bride's whim.

Unlike other Paris couturiers, Gianfranco Ferre, designer for the House of Christian Dior, does not design a bridal gown as the finale to his seasonal fashion show. However, any one of his gorgeous evening gowns may be easily reinterpreted as a bridal gown with just a switch of color or fabric. Ferre is convinced that the right bridal gown must evoke "emotions of happiness, joy, and excitement. In spite of all the changes, the wedding day is and will always be, for most women, a very important day, maybe experienced with more emotional involvement than the brides of past generations. When I create a bridal gown, I try to sum up the dreams and desires of the woman who is going to wear that dress." Almost ten percent of Ferre's yearly orders are for bridal gowns, and it can take up to a thousand hours to complete each glorious gown.

Norma Le Nain specializes in lace and beading; her gowns are incredibly detailed. Le Nain is dedicated to pleasing the bride, and to that end, any alteration is possible. She will work from a muslin to achieve a perfect fit, and she can even fax a detailed sketch to the bridal salon so the bride can see her gown with all the requested changes. She also custom-designs: "Like other designers, I have private customers who are looking for a special and unique design that is not already in the line."

Richard Glasgow designed his first bridal gown when he was fourteen; he considers it his destiny to design and refine the quintessential bridal gown. Glasgow's creations are meticulously built dresses that can literally stand up on their own: each dress has a pet-

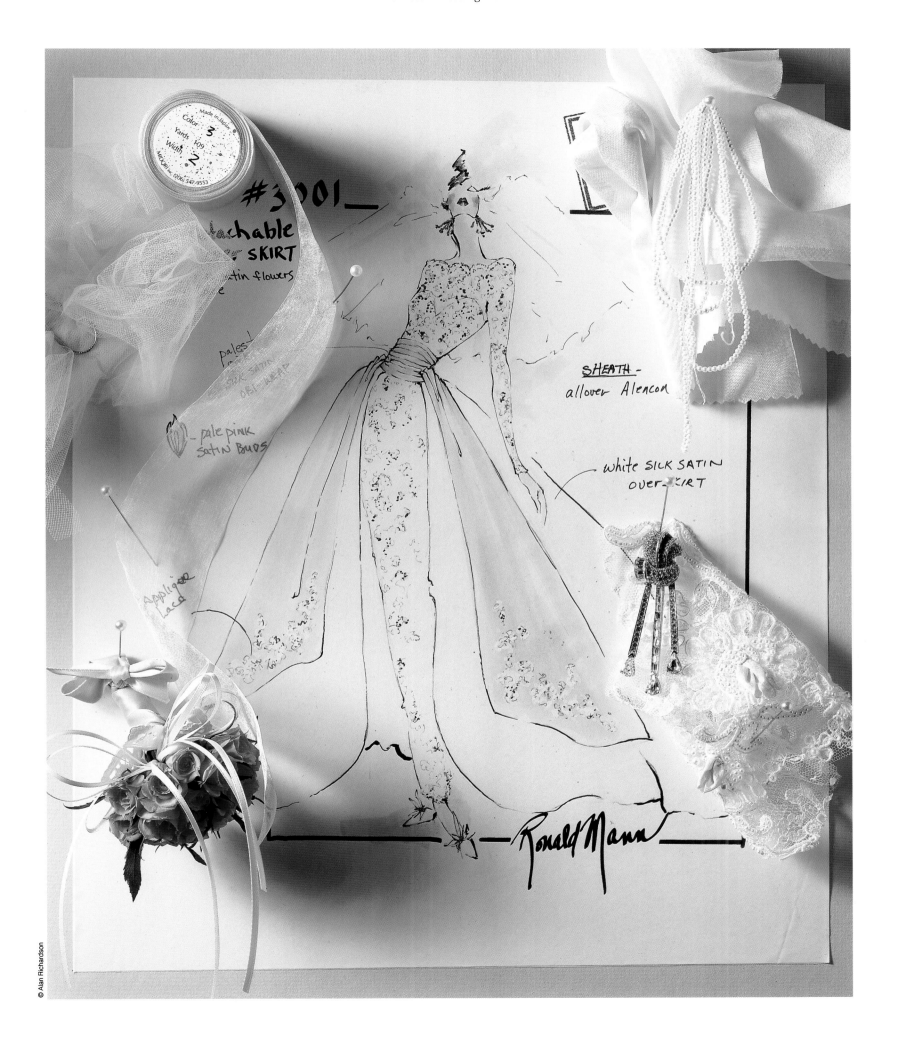

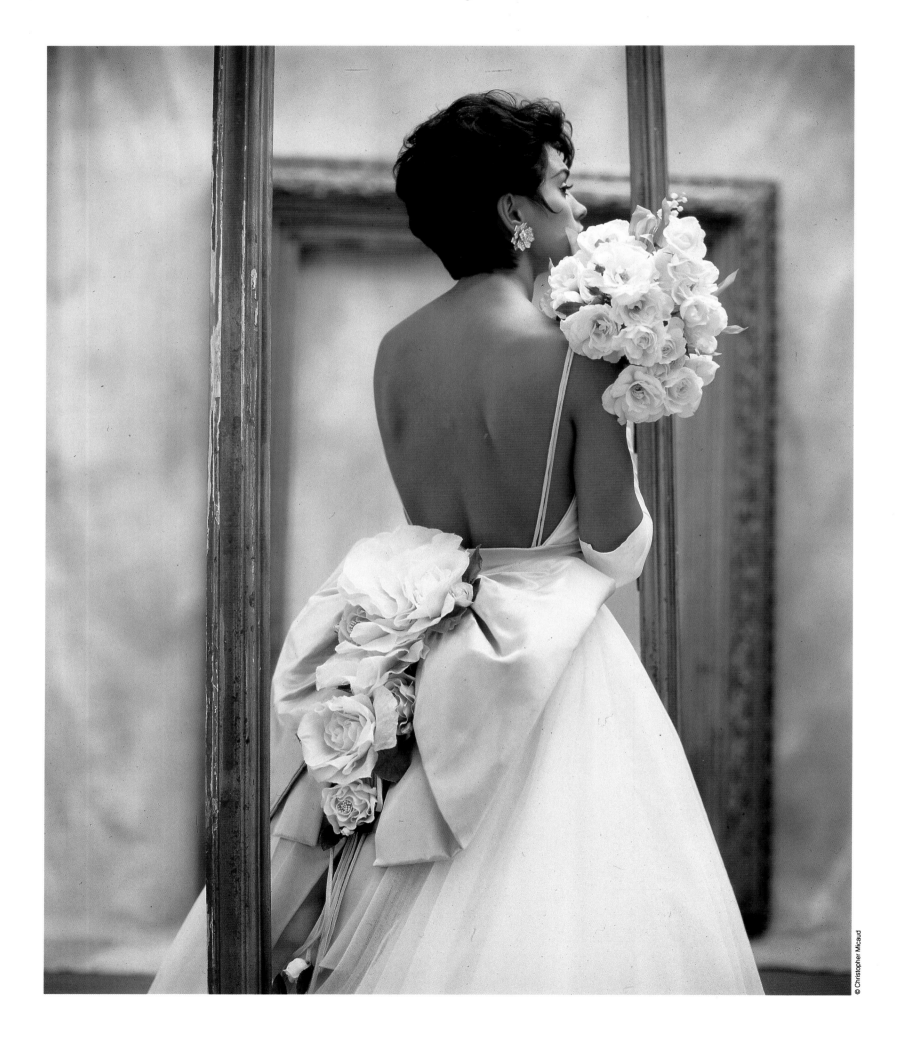

ticoat sewn in and a fully boned bodice (fifteen metal spiral bones that bend in every direction) as part of the inner body of the dress, which is sewn to fit perfectly. The "outer" dress is cut to fit just a bit looser so it never has wrinkles that pull at the waist. Glasgow "likes a dress to look on a hanger in a salon the way it will on the body—beautiful." He knows the key to a sale is to entice the bride to try it on. Flawlessly finished, Glasgow's gowns look as beautiful on the inside as they do on the outside. Indeed, because the inner lining is so solidly finished, the dresses are difficult to alter, and he demands thorough measurements to ensure that the gown needs very few—if any—alterations. Although his gowns offer a lot of fashionable touches—pleated tulle skirts and elongated Guipure lace bodices, fitted jackets over big skirts—the unmatched beauty of his dress is in its careful construction.

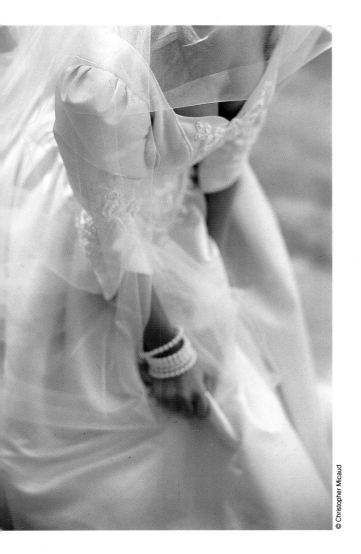

© Christopher Micaud

"What's fundamental is how each dress fits and moves; I'm always trying to improve the quality of the dress." The average Glasgow dress uses at least sixty yards of fabric. The designer is fastidious about every detail: the workroom is immaculately clean, with no open windows and no outdoor shoes allowed in (to protect the easily dirtied white gowns) and he keeps detailed, methodical records. Each dress is keyed to the bolt of fabric from which it was cut and the bolt is kept at least one year—this way, despite the extreme variations in tone from one bolt of white cloth to another, if alterations are necessary, the fabric can be perfectly matched.

Christos has designed bridal gowns since the 1960s. The times and the brides have changed, he reflects, but "not what the bride wants: a well-made, tradition-rooted gown that makes her look beautiful." Christos is noted for his unusual treatment of lace, which is cut and sewn by hand to give the illusion of embroidery. Christos believes that second to the perfect workmanship that must be the mark of every gown, his most important goal is a strong relationship with each bridal salon. Even though Christos rarely deals personally deal with each bride, his close link to the salons does ensure some interaction. If a bride orders a dress with changes that Christos believes to be unworkable, he calls the salon on the phone to work it out. Christos feels it is up to the designer to be a guide, to help the bride achieve the look she wants by generously sharing his skills and experience.

Pat Kerr felt she had to start designing bridal gowns because she had collected so much lace she didn't know what else to do. An avid collector of antique textiles, Kerr is recognized for her exquisite gowns made of one-of-a-kind pieces of lace. Kerr sympathizes with the common bridal dilemma of not being able to find the "right" gown,

Manifest in the most exquisite bridal gowns is a clear connection with history matched by a contemporary appeal. **OPPOSITE PAGE:** *Dior's classic ball gown.* **LEFT:** *Christos' gown with period sleeves awash in pink.* **BELOW:** *Pat Kerr's sumptuous creation of gilt lace, a favorite of queens.*

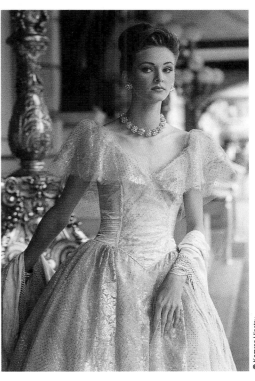

© Kamron Hinatsu

because she had the same experience as a bride: "I felt frustrated. I couldn't find a dress that was typical of my own style. Shopping for a wedding gown should be a thrilling experience, it shouldn't be a difficult one. I like to listen to brides; once I know what she has in her mind, I know that I can give my client what she wants. I have a small business and I'm very solution oriented!" A bride knows that when she wears a Pat Kerr gown, no other bride will ever wear anything just like it. "All my dresses are very simplistic in construction but the fabrication is complex."

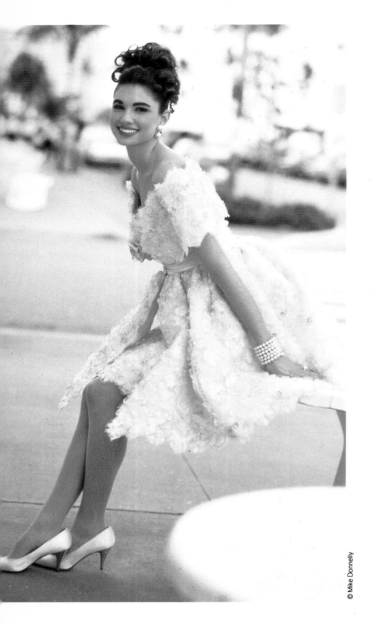

© Mike Donnelly

Kerr, who cuts all her own lace, likes to juxtapose lace and fabric, mixing antique with new, for a uniquely lavish "mix of countries and centuries." From time to time Kerr will meet a kindred spirit—a bride who truly appreciates museum-quality lace and understands the workmanship that went into these treasured pieces of old lace and fabric. For this bride Kerr will create a spectacular, priceless (actually about $30,000) gown using her finest antique laces. Kerr's gossamer gowns have a fairy-tale quality: they are typically off-the-shoulder with fitted bodices atop big, full, ball-gown skirts with detachable trains and the kind of period details that flatter the antique laces best.

Ron LoVece, an American designer who is known for his trademark silk rosebuds tucked into lace, describes his gowns as the epitome of sophisticated femininity. LoVece's clients, who as professionals are normally suited and tailored every day, love the sensation of wearing a thoroughly feminine wedding dress. Proud of all the detailed handwork that goes into every gown, LoVece describes his seamstresses as dressmakers. Each dressmaker takes one dress from start to finish and even inserts the zipper, because, as LoVece claims, "production-line sewing always shows." Lace is a LoVece specialty; each lace bodice is carefully, precisely molded—cut and stitched in place by hand, like a jigsaw puzzle—so that not one seam shows in the lace. LoVece offers a second line through the Diamond Collection. His couture gowns are designed to reach a broad market, with details that can be simplified to accommodate brides who want a couture gown but are unable to spend $4,500 and up.

Arnold Scaasi has been designing couture evening wear for women since 1964. His elaborate designs always capture the spirit of fashion at the moment, which is probably why his bridal line is one of the most popular. The bridal gown, although similar to many of his "timely but also timeless" evening clothes, is nevertheless "a completely different dress; bridal gowns have to be more exaggerated than evening dresses. Every bride I see, even if she's dressed in jeans and a T-shirt, wants to look like a fairy princess." It's this fantasy that guides the glamorous design of every Scaasi gown. "I like my brides to wear white, a full skirt, low décolletage, and long sleeves—very traditional," yet each dress is always true to his vision of the bride. Scaasi prefers gowns that are floor-length because they move more easily; instead of a train, he likes a very long veil that trails the floor. "I have never been afraid of the word *pretty.*"

Hanae Mori began designing thirty-five years ago as a costume designer for Japanese films: today she is a member of the haute couture. Mori characterizes her gowns as "elegant, romantic, and dreamy. Bridal gowns do not follow trends; however, fashion is a mirror which reflects the times, and only as the style of ceremonies changes will bridal designs change." Madame Mori feels her greatest strength in designing bridal gowns is that, like most brides today, she is a woman with a career who is able to share the same vision that appeals to her clients when designing a bridal gown.

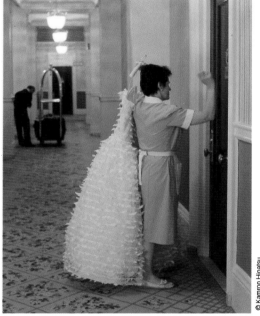

© Kamron Hinatsu

Even the most modern bridal incarnations generally feature some traditional element. **ABOVE LEFT:** *Ron LoVece's gilt-edged ribbon lace sheath worn under an overcoat is sprinkled with rosebuds.* **ABOVE:** *A strapless ball gown with a thousand tiny bows by Scaasi.*
OPPOSITE PAGE: *Hanae Mori's pearl-strapped fluid chiffon dress with a bustier bodice.* **FOLLOWING PAGE:** *Maestros of bridal design understand the compatible duality of tailored femininity. This modern expression of synergy is beautifully balanced by Carolina Herrera with a bodice of sleek silk crepe and skirt of swirling layers of point d'esprit.*

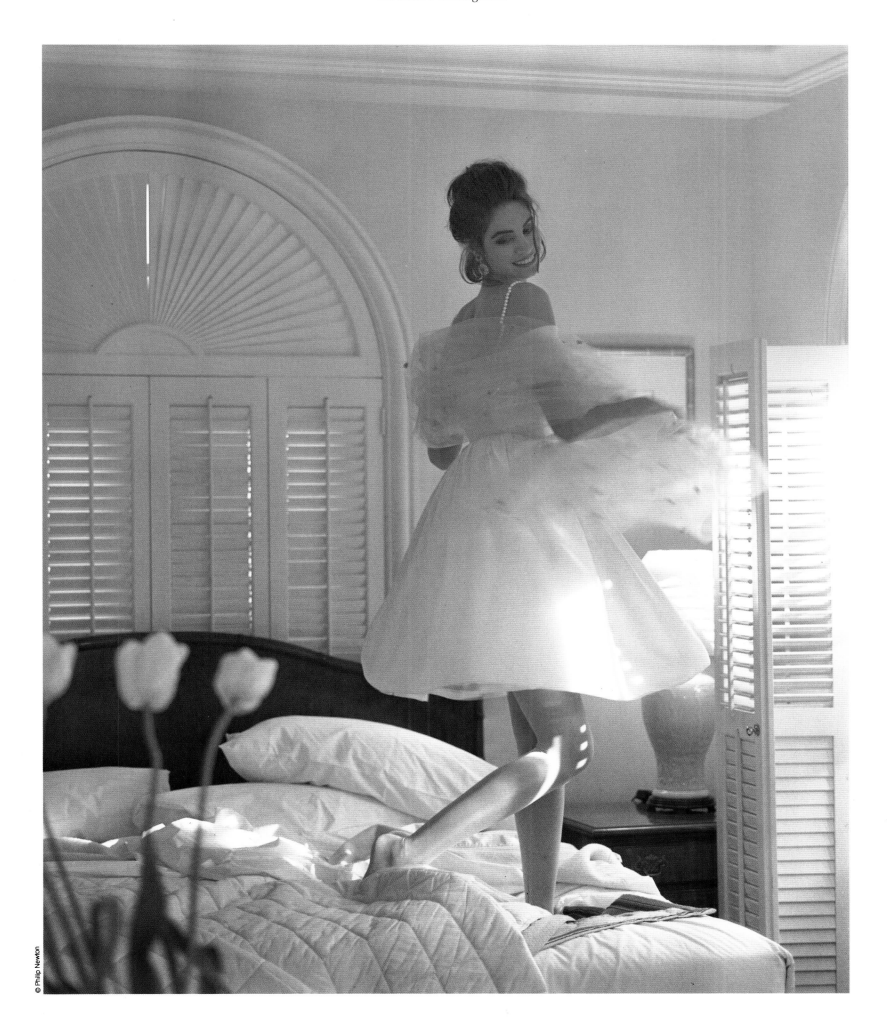

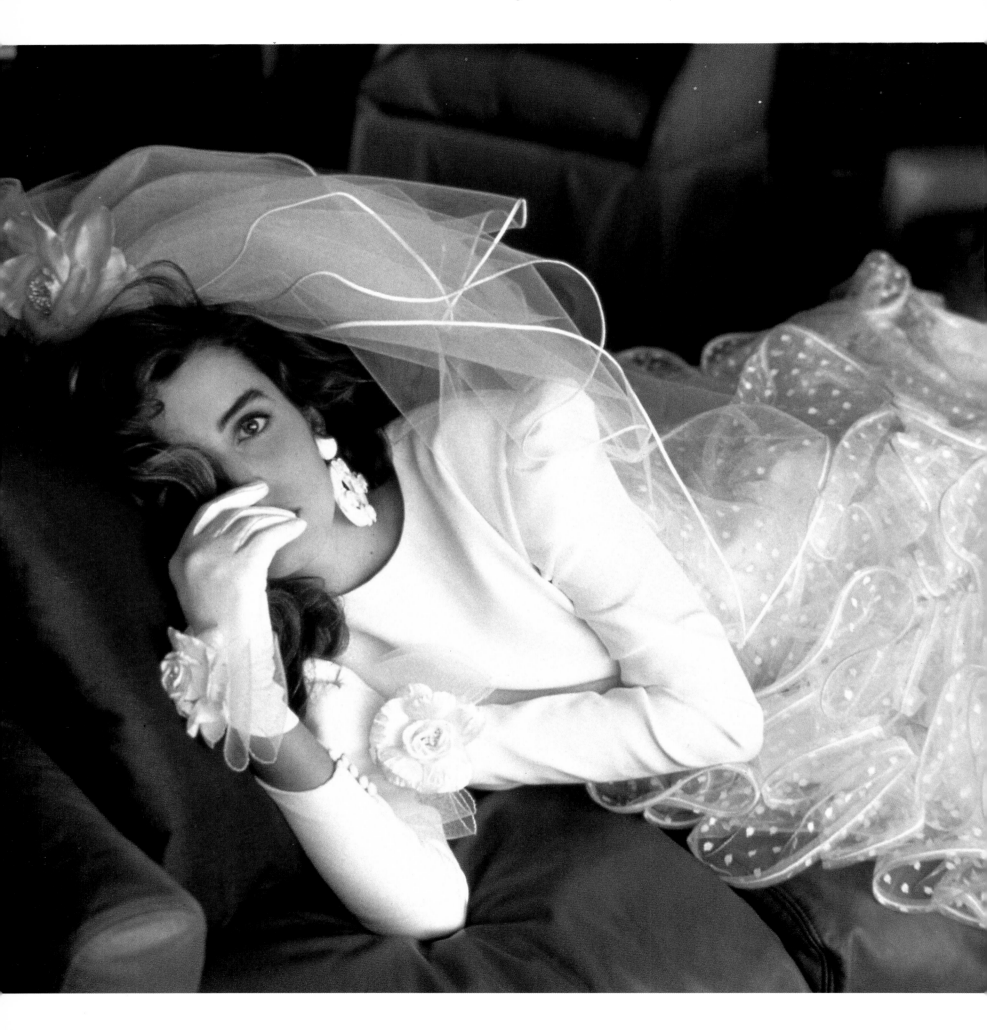

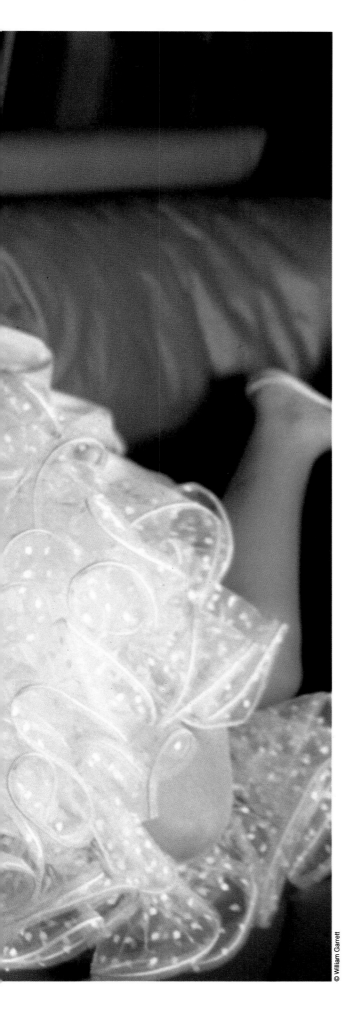

Carolina Herrera exploded onto the bridal scene with a refreshing line of classically elegant, supremely simple wedding gowns. Bringing to her bridal line the same aesthetics that inform her couture dress line, Herrera stresses, "Simplicity is the basis of elegance. What brides needed was a wedding gown with good lines; really, if there are too many elements you can't see the bride. Many dresses are just too fussy." Herrera began designing bridal gowns because "I wanted to design for the most important day in the life of a woman." Herrera loves to design dresses with tulle, as she did for her daughter's wedding gown ("it looks like a cloud"), and to incorporate details that have some personal significance for the bride. For Caroline Kennedy, Herrera entirely embroidered the dress with shamrocks. "A bride must feel good in her dress, her personality must shine through."

The Laura Ashley bridal collection has been a favorite of brides since 1968. Ashley recognized sooner than most designers that many brides desire something simple but feminine and nostalgic. These old-fashioned gowns tend to be more moderately priced, as well, a factor that contributes to their popularity. The style of a Laura Ashley gown is rooted in the Victorian and Edwardian eras— with tuckings, flounces, and poufs of lace typical of those times. Because of the unique period design of the gowns, custom design alterations are not available. The big design change over the years has been the inclusion of bridal suits in the Ashley line to meet the needs of nontraditional women marrying again.

Michelle Piccione designs for her family-owned business, Alfred Angelo, started by her father fifty years ago. Using the most advanced technology the fashion business has to offer, Alfred Angelo has become the largest bridal manufacturer in the world.

Michelle Piccione designs all the dresses herself. Each and every dress is custom-ordered and cut according to the bride's requested design alterations. Much of the detail work— such as cutting and pinning lace motifs—is done by hand, but because of the volume of production and the mechanized workshop, Alfred Angelo is a mass-market operation. Michelle Piccione notes, "Because of the amazing technical advances, we can produce a much better garment for better value." Alfred Angelo incorporates two major technological elements in production: mechanization, using cutting machines that can simultaneously cut 120 layers of fabric in three sizes—using 9,600 yards, they can cut 1,444 dresses an hour, and during their peak season Angelo can produce 8,000 dresses a day—and computerization, using computers to grade—that is, to calculate precise sizing differences within an individual style or pattern—and draw patterns. Alfred Angelo offers dozens of very different styles each season, because, as Michelle Piccione stresses, "over the last ten years, everything has opened up, and there is a great variety in choices. Some dresses are more ornate, others theatrical, others traditional, others very streamlined, some are short. We offer all of these choices to the bride. Women are learning to wear what's comfortable for themselves, to be more independent and wear what they want without worrying about following a trend. We don't believe in dictating a look— Angelo is large enough to have all the different looks in every style and price—it's the bride's choice, and her decision is top priority."

Until 1945 there were few designers catering exclusively to the bride. That year, sensing a void in the industry, Priscilla Kidder opened a bridal salon and launched her own bridal collection. For almost fifty years, since that day, thousands of women have exchanged "I dos" gowned in a Priscilla of

Boston creation. Few would dispute the legendary reputation of this grand dame of bridal design. Priscilla herself acknowledges that over the years, "there isn't a single trend in bridal design that I didn't introduce," including the use of bows, the addition of color, seasonless bridal gowns, elegant, streamlined designs, and lavish, regal confections. Priscilla's longevity and success are rooted in her ability to sense the needs and desires of the customer. She notes, "the bride herself always influences me; they tell me what they want and I listen. I blend a traditional look with beautiful body lines in exquisite fabrics to flatter the figures of real women, not models."

After decades of designing gowns for the most fashionable and influential women around the world, couturier Hubert de Givenchy continues to be inspired by the romantic image of the bride. He knows that "on her most important day she will wish to appear more beautiful than ever." Givenchy prefers to dress a bride according to her personality. "Some women prefer to wear a suit and others a more classic long gown, but

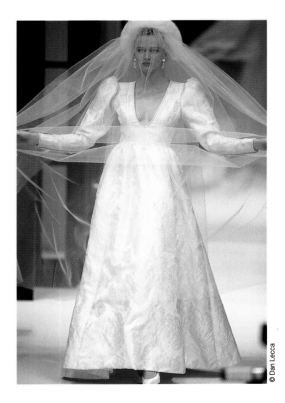

each wedding dress must represent purity— not only in the cut but in the details." Givenchy's clarity of design doesn't overshadow symbolic personal sentiment; indeed, "the seamstresses sew a colorful thread into the hem of each dress as a good luck charm for the bride." Every bride can use a bit of luck— even when dressed by the best.

Christian Lacroix is the modern couturier who will be remembered for his celebrated outrageous, witty, thoroughly feminine fashions that marked the end of the opulent 1980s. Few designers have created collections that have such startling impact—a single Lacroix season will offer dozens and dozens of luscious, imaginative designs that inspire legions of fellow designers. Lacroix always finishes his couture presentation with a grand bridal finale, a celebration both of "the unique moment of a woman's life and the unique moment in the history of fashion." Indeed, while Lacroix, like all couturiers, designs for every aspect of a woman's life, the bridal gown is especially important. Wedding gowns account for about 40 percent of Christian Lacroix Couture orders, and all bridals are sewn and designed in a separate studio. "All brides are touching and beautiful. They are young, happy, and live this period of their lives with intensity. Obviously the wedding dress plays a starring role in this event. For this reason, I prefer to design an exclusive original dress for each bride."

A connoisseur of fashion, Vera Wang was a fashion editor at *Vogue* magazine before opening the most elegant bridal salon in New York City and designing her own bridal collection. Wang describes her internationally known store as "an incredible lab. It offers a unique opportunity to not only see what sells, but what works. Everyone is not a model, although I style each bride following my own subtle, classic aesthetic. Fashion is

what I know." Wang finds excitement in the opportunity to offer the bride designs not found in every bridal salon, wedding dresses that are always "graceful and dignified with a fashion edge. I design gowns with pure lines in luxe fabrics, but the simplest dresses are the most difficult to design [because] every seam shows."

In addition to all the modern options for a new, customized wedding gown, the past is also a viable and unique source for every

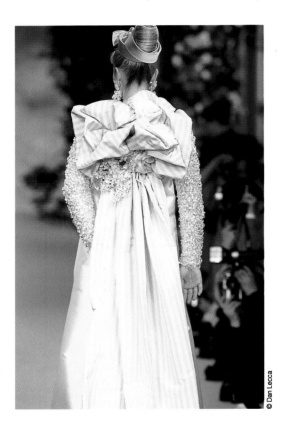

Legendary designers influence the direction of fashion trends. **LEFT:** *Hubert de Givenchy's ball gown with a deep-V neckline.* **ABOVE:** *Christian Lacroix's train bustled at the shoulder.* **OPPOSITE PAGE:** *Priscilla of Boston's spectacularly full ball gown.*

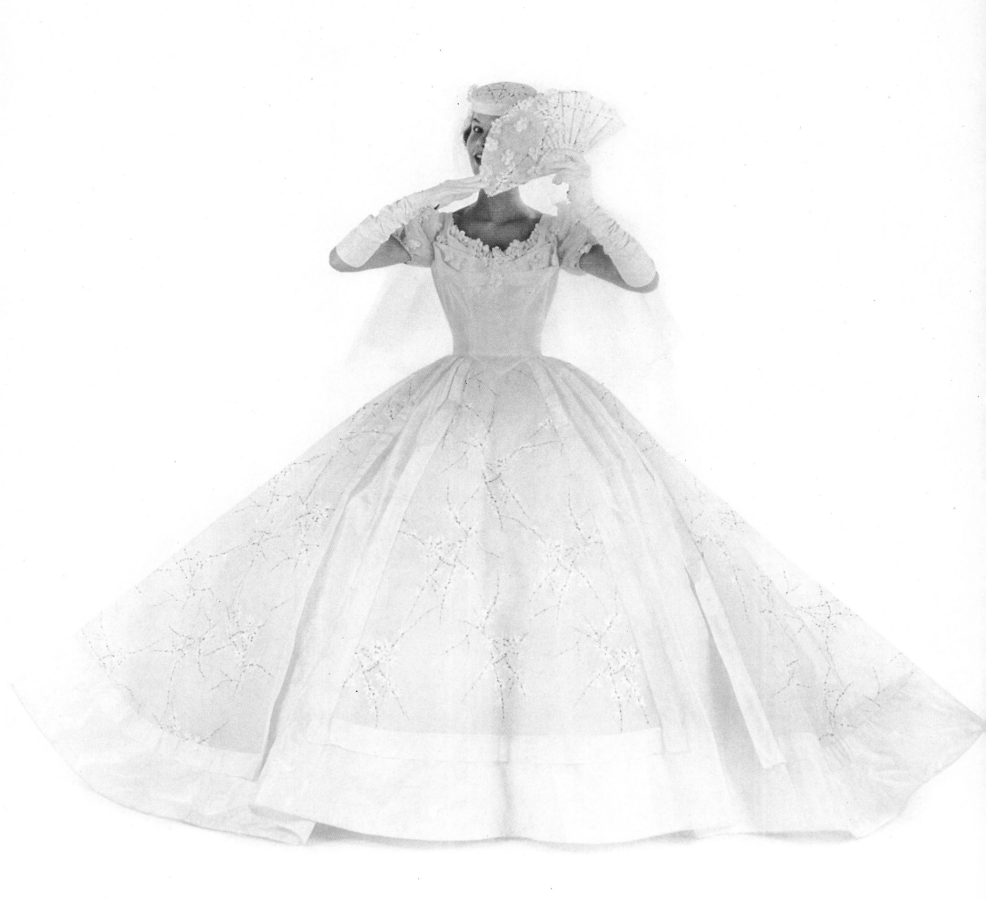

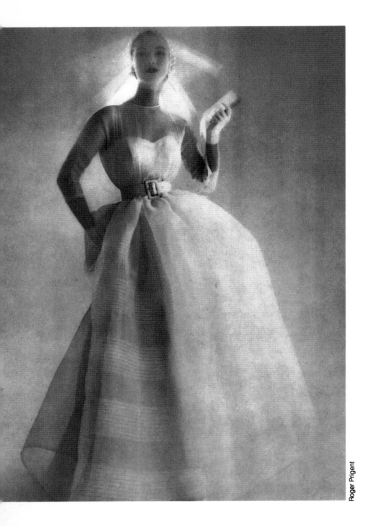

Roger Prigent

bride. All vintage gowns are one-of-a-kind. A host of vintage bridal salons have opened their doors in recent years, owned by avid lovers and collectors of antique dresses. These salons are dedicated to the bride with a nostalgic appreciation of clothing who considers vintage design to be wearable, not merely collectible. Vintage salons usually specialize in gowns from the turn of the century, featuring fine handmade cotton-lace dresses. They may also stock dresses from eras as recent as the 1960s, including lace and satin-coat dresses with three-quarter-length sleeves. Most collections include only natural-fiber gowns of silk and cotton. Cotton, which is the easiest fabric to restore and refresh, is durable and bleachable. Silk, on the other hand, doesn't release stains well and cannot be bleached. Even the best-quality vintage bridal gowns need to be restored and reworked, and a good vintage

salon can handle all of the necessary alterations. Jean Hoffman–Jana Starr Antiques stocks a tremendous collection of old lace to match and alter old gowns and will include the cost of cleaning and restoring a gown in the overall price. Alterations cost more because they require design changes to meet the individual whims of the bride. A typical alteration of a 1950s high-necked gown at Opal White, a New York City salon, might lower the back—not only would the bride's back look thinner, but the dress would fit a modern body better. Vintage salons have all the resources at hand to rework their gowns and also offer appropriate vintage accessories to completely outfit the bride. If, however, you already own an inherited heirloom gown or have found one at an auction or flea market, be sure to closely inspect the gown for its practical workability. Do you like the style? Can it be reworked? Does it need major restorations and alterations? Are the sleeves too small? Are there underarm stains that could be eliminated by opening up the armhole? Are there major holes in the fabric? Could any flaws be covered with lace or a flower? Will the repairs need to be handled by an expert? Some vintage salons refer brides to restoration specialists, and costume departments at museums and colleges can be sources of information, too.

Despite all of the versatile, affordable options for the modern bride, including rentals (which were a popular alternative during World War II, and have flourished again recently due to a trend toward multiple weddings and a recession), there are still a few brides who want to wear a gown they make themselves. Most savvy consultants will recommend that brides opt instead to have a gown made for them. The detailed planning process of every wedding can be so stressful that it is the rare bride who can also sew her own gown and not rue the decision.

Vintage gowns and private designers are resources worth consideration. You can update and refit a family heirloom with judicious cuts. **ABOVE:** *Create a strapless gown from a demure organdie ball gown.* **RIGHT:** *Pare away a dozen tiers of lace for a snappy minidress.* **OPPOSITE PAGE:** *Skilled tailors can immortalize any fantasy as in this romantic yet tailored combination.*

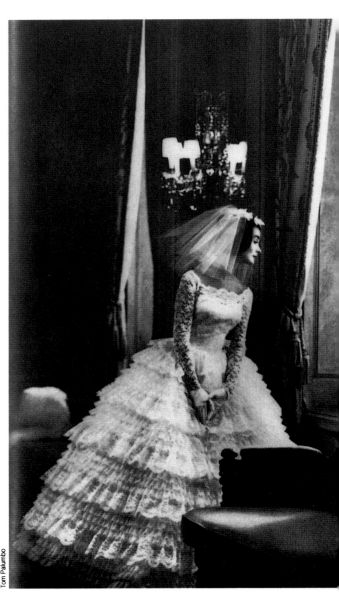

Tom Palumbo

The bride who wants a sense of doing it herself should consider working with a private designer or seamstress. In this relationship the bride must be intimately involved in the creative process of design, and it becomes a thoroughly satisfying, luxurious, and not necessarily expensive adventure—without the turmoil of personally laboring over every stitch. Designing and working with exquisite white fabrics is a delicate, exacting process that should not be undertaken by a novice. This is a dress that not only will be worn on a very special day but will also become an important memory that should not be sacrificed. With all of the effort involved in creating your own gown, when the final costs—financial and emotional—are calculated, it is rarely worth it to sew your own gown.

If you wisely decide to work with a private designer or seamstress, interview several people. Friends, some bridal salons, phone books, even occasional newspaper or magazine reviews can suggest or list qualified options. Based on your conversation with the designer and his or her references, you should have a strong sense of trust, not only that this person can handle the workmanship involved in a timely fashion but that this person will also respect your ideas and fantasies—after all, this is your wedding gown. The process of design should be a pleasure.

On the other hand, if you are still completely confident in your own dressmaking skills, be sure to allow plenty of time to design and create your gown so that the process is as stress-free as possible. Be meticulous and research the best techniques before cutting any fabric (fashion college libraries can be a great resource). Above all, follow in the tradition of the best custom designers—make a trial garment first to ensure a perfect fit, and with your savings, splurge on the best fabrics—it's your wedding gown and you deserve the best.

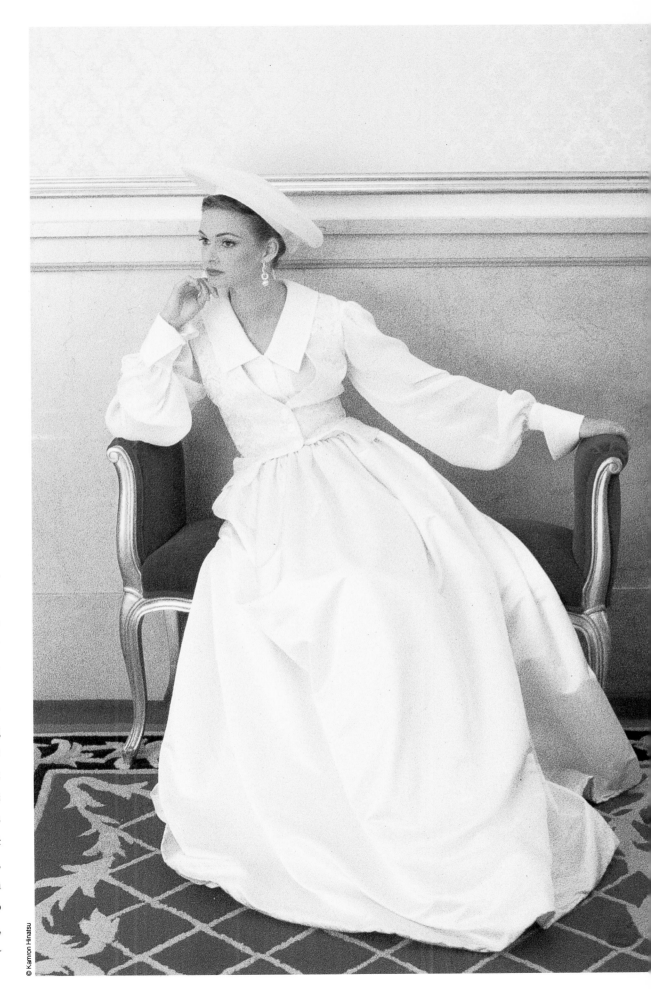

© Kamron Hinatsu

YOUR

WEDDING

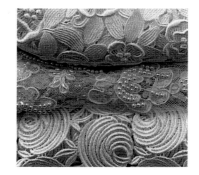

DRESS

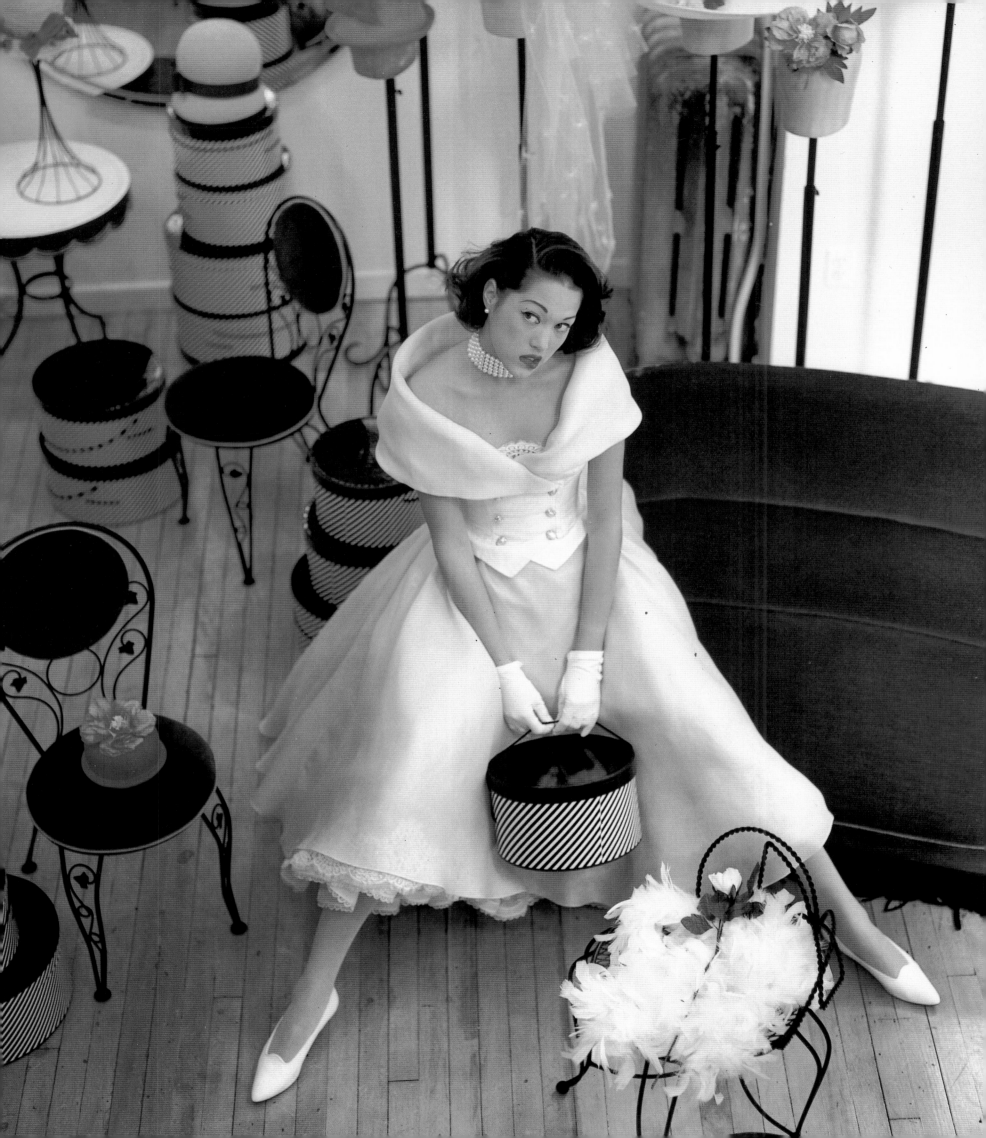

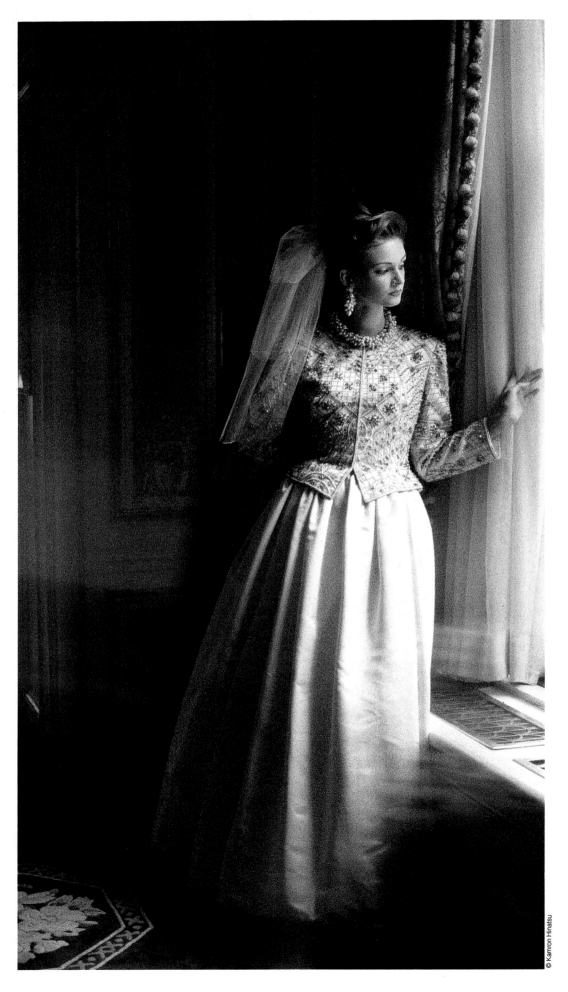

© Kamron Hinatsu

Choosing the right wedding gown is an intensely emotional, personal, and sentimental transaction—for even the most matter-of-fact bride. Trying on the right bridal gown evokes special feelings; even the most unflappable bride, once she has finally found the "perfect" gown, may find herself moved by the image in the mirror. Although her selection process will be at least partially based on practical considerations such as the season and theme of the wedding, there is no denying the emotional impact of this very significant purchase. For not only must this gown match the style of her wedding, it must also inspire and delight the bride. The right gown is one with which the bride feels an emotional connection; it makes her look and feel beautiful, it sets her apart from all other brides, it incorporates all of her bridal fantasies, and it satisfies a profound need to dress appropriately for an event of great personal significance. It seems almost impossible that several yards of satin, tulle, and lace could fulfill such tremendous expectations.

For many brides, the most difficult part of selecting the right wedding gown may be simply making a decision when so many choices abound. It may seem impossible to settle on one gown: "There are wedding dresses that look like evening dresses and evening dresses that look like wedding dresses," notes Barbara Tober, Editor-in-Chief of (the recently renamed) *Brides & Your New Home*. The diversity of choice should not be overwhelming; rather, it should be empowering. Given enough time and imagination, anything is possible. Remember that style need not be a function of finances; good taste is not dictated by money, but is a manifestation of smart choices. The key to making the right choices is starting with the right focus—choose the gown that's right for you.

THE RIGHT DRESS

How does one make the right choice? It's not by satisfying some outdated standard of suitability. There was a time when it wasn't socially acceptable to marry without the works: a full-trained skirt, luscious fabric, long veil, a dozen attendants, and a huge wedding reception. Today, appropriateness is not a matter of opting for the works, it's about making wise and thoroughly personal choices. The question of appropriateness often arises for second-time brides, who frequently struggle with their choice of wedding gowns. A "small ceremony, no attendants but one, no white gown, and no pretending it's the first time," was the advice of *Brides* in 1967. Acknowledging a dramatic rise in remarriages, *Brides* recommended freedom of choice in 1989, noting that brides who remarry can confidently "wear traditional styles—a floor-length gown, white lace or satin, which symbolizes the joy and hope of marriage. This may be just the look you want, particularly if it was not the style of your first wedding." At the most basic level, no wedding dress is right unless the bride loves it: the right wedding gown should look absolutely fabulous, be made well, and fit perfectly; feel entirely comfortable, reflect the bride's own style, and meld smartly with the wedding festivities. The right choice is one that works for you and brings all the different elements of your wedding day together.

"The bride is the central figure on this day of days. Everything around her is the frame that sets her off and enhances her. As the focal point in the picture, she must be at her loveliest. Her gown must be the most becoming she can get, and it must harmonize with the surroundings in which she is being married. Lucky is the girl marrying this autumn, for the bridal gowns are so beautiful that fifty years from now they will call forth the exclamation: 'How lovely!' Their classically simple lines will never lose their essential quality of beauty," exclaimed *So You're Getting Married,* in the 1934 inaugural issue. Elegance and simplicity are timeless qualities; gowns cut with this in mind are destined to be classics. The wise bride will recognize

Options exist for every bride. **PAGE 105:** *The right choice might be Bob Mackie's vested bodice with a portrait collar over a full, fifties-inspired skirt.* **OPPOSITE PAGE:** *For another bride, a satin suit with a jewel-encrusted "Fabergé" jacket by Ronald Mann for Victoria Royal might be perfect.* **BELOW:** *Audrey Hepburn in a gamine gown by Givenchy.*

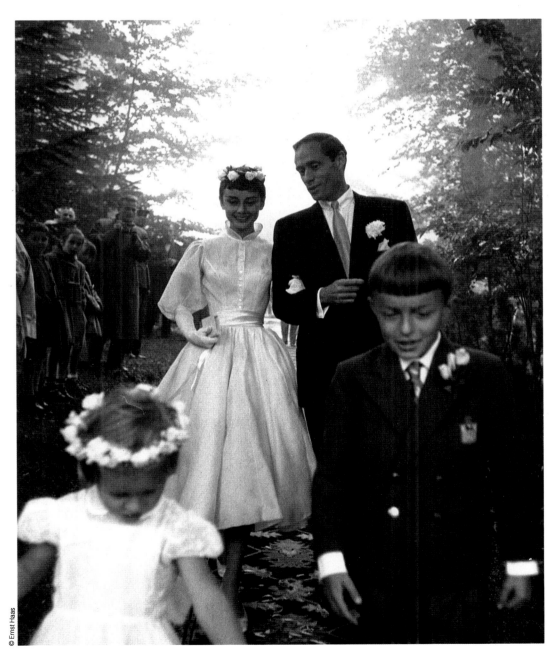

© Ernst Haas

that a beautifully understated gown is also the easiest to wear. "If there ever is any time in the life of a woman when her costume should be simple, it is at her bridal....Everything that will impede freedom of movement or thought should be banished, and, above all, whatever would make her conscious of how she was looking," noted *Godey's Lady's Book* in 1850. Although the time invested in carefully choosing the right dress is well spent, ultimately the bride wants to forget about the dress she's just spent months pon-

dering. If she has made the right choice, she can put it on, feel secure, look great, and have a good time.

The best gown flatters but never overpowers the bride; the gown should make the bride look beautiful without distracting from her own radiance. This wise axiom has been repeatedly heralded by authorities on style: in 1953, "At weddings, as always, *Vogue* likes a dress to become the woman...not to overcome her." And now: "Elegance is an understatement. The woman should stand out; the

est and one of the oldest bridal salons in the United States, stocks over a thousand gowns for a bride to try on, and easily serves around eight thousand brides a year. Fondly known as Miss Hedda and Mr. K, the Schacters have probably counseled more brides than a thousand marriage counselors combined. For an elegantly sexy silhouette, they suggest an off-the-shoulder neckline, deep-V bodice (possibly with an illusion neckline), a body-hugging sheath, a minidress, or a sheer or backless gown.

Before she tries on a single gown, a bride must already have made certain decisions regarding her wedding plans, so that she is able to answer some basic questions. When is the wedding to be held? Depending on the season in which she is going to be married, different fabrics and styles will be appropriate for the bride's gown. Spring and summer brides will select gowns of lighter fabric, such as eyelet, piqué, linen, chiffon, or chantilly lace; and simpler details, such as short sleeves, minimal beading, crochet gloves, floral wreaths, wide-brimmed hats, and contrasting pastel bows to sash the waist. Fall and winter brides will prefer dresses of heavier fabrics, such as velvet, duchesse satin, brocade, or even mohair; and more ornate details, such as fur trims and muffs, heavily beaded bodices, long sleeves, high necks, jeweled headbands, and lots of petticoats.

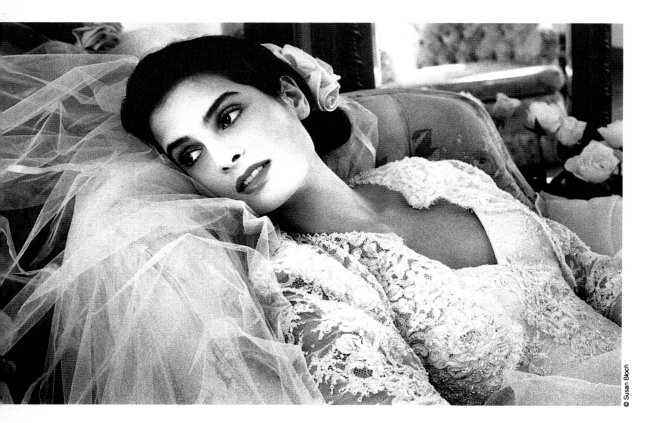

Impeccably correct gowns are styled to match the ceremony and are always elegant and flattering. **ABOVE:** *Classically reinterpreted lace and tulle by Candace Solomon.* **OPPOSITE PAGE:** *An avant-garde wrap of organza over a silk satin chemise by Flyte Ostell.*

clothes should not overtake her," philosophizes elegance guru Calvin Klein. The perfect dress enhances the bride's own beauty, so that all attention is centered on her, and her dress is just part of her overall loveliness.

Some brides are demure, while others are extroverted, but every bride wants to feel, be, and look sexy on her wedding day. So believes Hedda Schacter, who, with her husband was a founder and co-proprietor of the famous Kleinfeld's, a bustling Brooklyn, New York, bridal emporium. Kleinfeld's, the larg-

Where will the wedding be? The location decrees in part what style of gown will be appropriate. For example, for a garden wedding, a floor-length gown with a big romantic skirt made of a lightweight lace, and flowers in the hair without a veil would be perfect. Equally appropriate would be a shorter dress with a handkerchief hem in a floral print. For a civil ceremony and restaurant reception, a smart suit, floor or knee length, with a removable jacket and a tidy, small-brimmed hat is an ideal option.

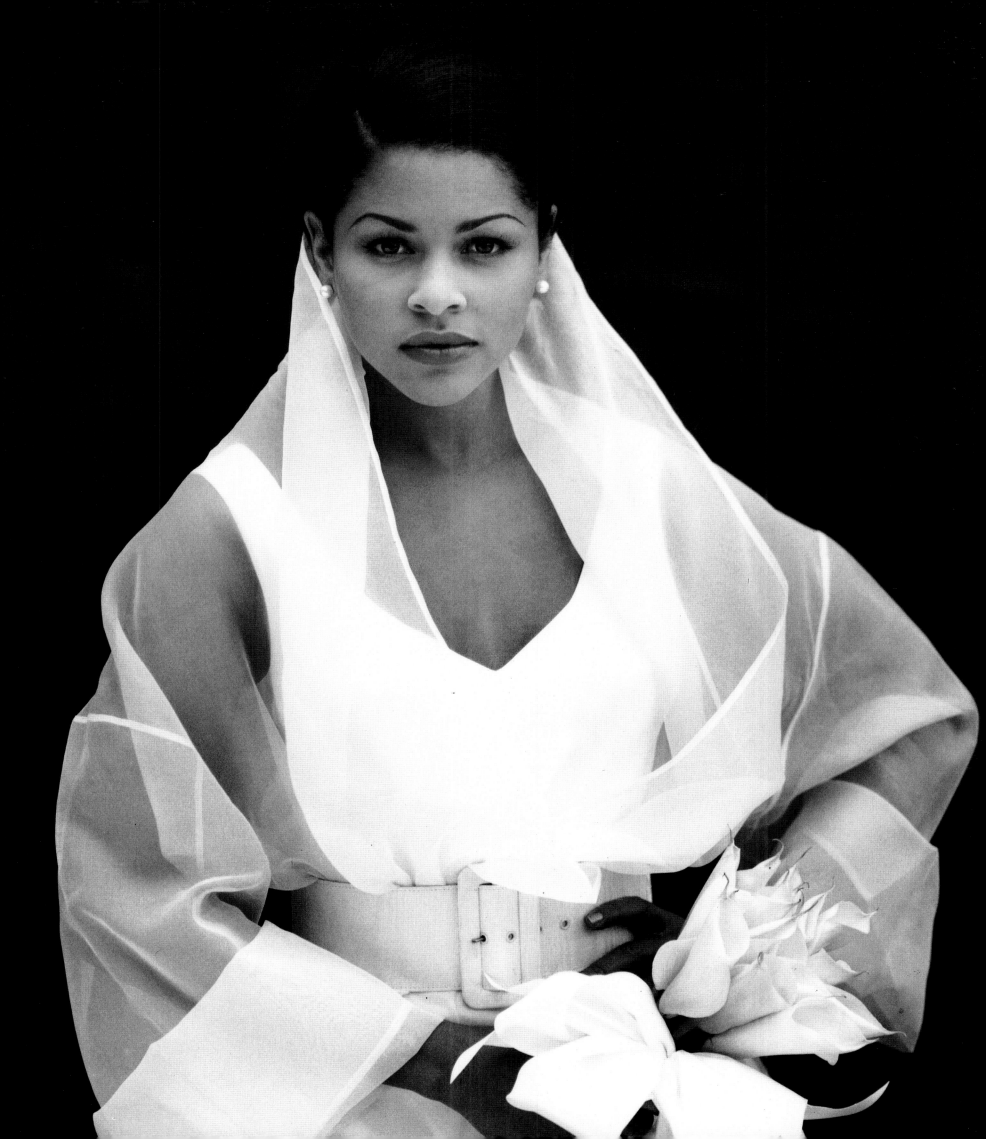

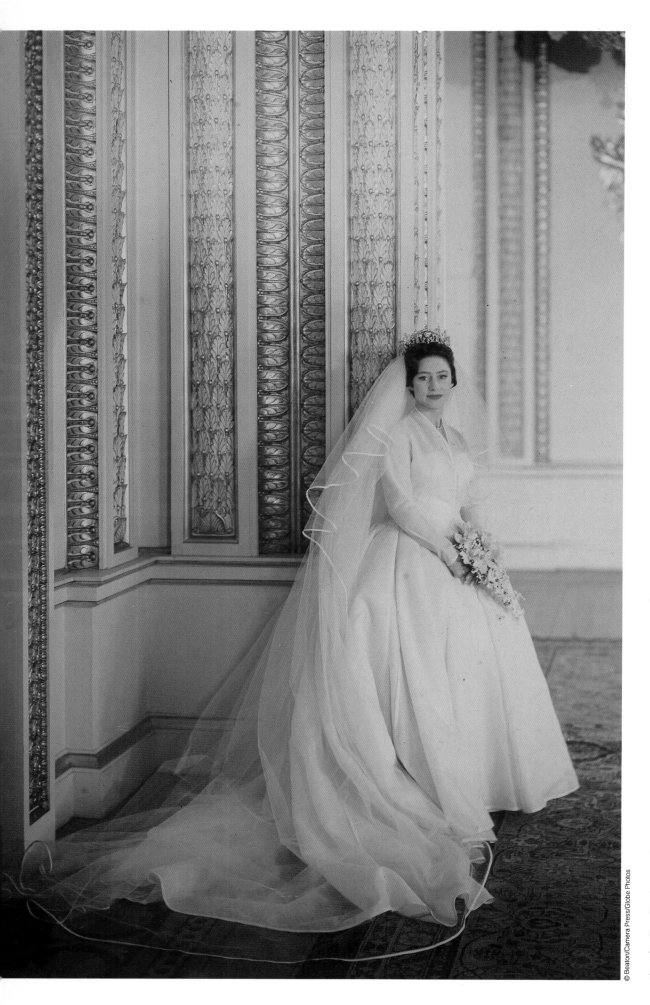

Finally, and most important, how formal is the wedding? Weddings are broadly classified according to their level of formality: ultraformal, formal, semiformal, or informal. The scope of the celebrations and the style of the wedding dress should be matched according to the formality of the event.

FORMALITY

An ultra-formal wedding is always a very grand affair. Every traditional ceremonial element of a wedding is included in the festivities and many are elaborately embellished. The guest list is large, with 250 or more receiving engraved invitations. An ultraformal wedding may take place in the evening or at noon. The setting may be a cathedral, synagogue, or elegant hotel. No fewer than six and no more than a dozen bridesmaids will escort the bride, all gowned in full-length dresses. For extra drama, they may also wear all white. The groom is attired in white tie and tails for evening or in a cutaway suit for a daytime ceremony. The bride generally opts for an all-white gown with a long, wide, opulent train (the basic rule of thumb for ultra-formal weddings is long aisle, long train; longer aisle, longer train) and a long veil. Her gown should vary according to her personal taste and the season of the wedding: a summer bride might choose an all-lace, princess-line gown, with a cathedral train, ornate beading edging every lace motif, a sheer tulle veil clasped to a coronet of pearls, and a bouquet of delicate lily of the valley ringed with starry stephanotis; a winter bride might prefer a very full ball gown of the finest satin fitted to the edge of the shoulder with short sleeves, graceful sixteen-button kid-leather gloves, a detachable tulle train, a triple-strand collar of pearls, a mantilla of lace, and a bouquet of miniature white calla lilies blooming from a mass of tender white sweet peas. Elaborate bouquets, carefully matched to the bridal gown would decorate the wedding site. A typically ultra-formal touch would be a canopy extending from the door of the church or synagogue to the curb. The wedding is always followed by a full reception. Live music, perhaps a chamber group or harpist, would entertain the gathering guests, who would then be served a full-course dinner with fine wine. Dancing, champagne, and a many-tiered wedding cake would complete the evening.

Formal weddings are less ostentatious, scaled-down versions of ultra-formal events, but still grand and sophisticated. Invitations, engraved cards, within envelopes inside envelopes, will be sent to seventy-five to two hundred fifty guests. The formal wedding may be a religious or secular ceremony. Often, the wedding and reception are both held in the same place—a stately mansion, country club, or hotel. For an outdoor wedding, large canvas marquees are set up to shelter guests from the weather. In the receiving line, at least six bridesmaids and ushers will join the bride and groom—he'll wear a stroller for day and a black or white dinner jacket for night. The reception will include a dinner that may be served by waiters or set out as a buffet; in either case, seating will be assigned to guests. At its simplest, a formal wedding combines a big, grand party with a big, grand dress. The dress is usually a ball gown; it may be white, off white, or even the palest blush pastel. The skirt traditionally had a chapel train, but today just as many brides are opting for the easier-to-manage sweep train. The length of the veil is based on proportion rather than formality. The bridal veil can be cut a bit longer than the train to sweep the floor or it can be fingertip in length; either way, the veil should match the dress. If the dress is a pale blush, the veil should also be blush toned; if

the dress is embellished with pearls, the veil could have a scattered shower of pearls, as well. Indeed, the entire bridal ensemble should be perfectly coordinated: in this instance, a string of pale pink pearls would be an exquisite complement to a blushing bridal palette, along with a nosegay of pale pink Serena roses.

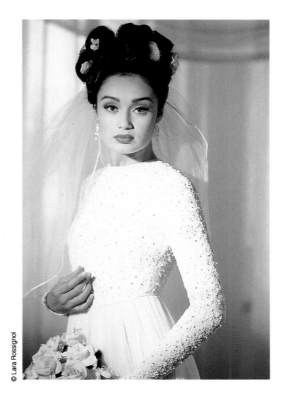

For a formal wedding, most brides choose a classic gown with a sweeping train. **OPPOSITE PAGE:** *A gown of organza and tulle by Norman Hartnell for Princess Margaret.* **ABOVE:** *Reembroidered beaded lace with pleated chiffon by Badgley Mischka. A formal gown must be complemented with elegant accessories, an elaborate hairstyle, and a lavish bouquet.*

Semiformal weddings are probably the most popular choice because of the comfortable mix of conventional ceremony and casual panache. The reception may be large, with up to a hundred fifty guests, or small, with as few as fifty guests. The semiformal wedding may take place at home, and the ceremony may be more intimate than at more formal affairs. A larger reception often follows the ceremony. Novel reception sites are also common: aboard a yacht, on the lawn of a lush botanical garden, under a canopy of oak at a charming country inn, or with scenic views atop a skyscraper. There are only a few bridesmaids, wearing very simple floor-length gowns or cocktail dresses, all echoing the bride's dress. The groom sports a classic dinner jacket or a suit: a summer choice might be a white linen jacket with oxford gray trousers or a navy blazer and white trousers; in winter, a solid dark suit. The bride's gown may be long or short; the details ornate or simple. For a garden wedding, for example, she might choose a full-skirted, short-sleeved gown of crisp organdy sashed at the waist with a voluminous contrasting bow of ivy green polka dots on white chiffon. This breezy silhouette could be completed with a broad-brimmed straw hat, its crown ringed with a wreath of tiny white roses and variegated ivy. The bridal bouquet could be a profuse nosegay of variegated ivy sprinkled with white roses. For a winter wedding at an elegant dinner club, a bride might wear a strapless gown of tulle under a beautifully cut golden brocade jacket. Golden pearls might encircle her throat, and in her hair a short veil would be attached with a golden comb, while she would carry a single white amaryllis with a gilded satin bow.

Informal receptions are perfectly suited to small weddings: indeed, they are frequently celebrated during the day after a civil ceremony. A good choice for imaginative couples

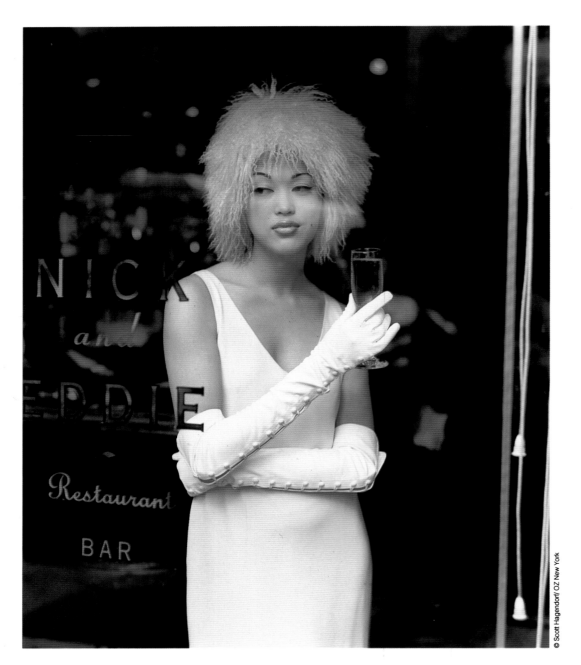

rings, and carry a posy of white violets. A weekend wedding at the family home or a beach resort is a wonderful way to celebrate with friends and family who live far away. For this wedding, the bridal gown might be a white Lycra maillot swimsuit under a short tulle skirt, topped with a white baseball cap instead of a veil—perfect for a post-nuptial splash in the pool. The bride would toss a posy of crisp white carnations.

The formality of your wedding, or lack of it, should comfortably harmonize with your personality. Seasoned outdoor types would chafe at the prospect of a "dressed-to-the-nines" wedding with all the trimmings. Urbane city folks would probably never consider marrying on a mountaintop wearing white ski suits, then schussing to the ski lodge for a fireside reception. Know yourself, know your options, then dress to thrill yourself and your groom.

Personal predilections for whimsy are best satisfied with informal bridal gowns. **ABOVE:** *Sylvia Heisel's sophisticated sleek chemise mated with a Mongolian fur hat.* **RIGHT:** *Ondyn Herschelle's fantastic cacophony of satin covered springs.* **OPPOSITE PAGE:** *Oscar de la Renta's insouciant pink silk gazar bubble dress.*

who want a less lavish celebration, these are weddings at which anything goes. The couple might exchange vows in late afternoon in a small hotel suite with a few close friends as witnesses. A short, simple reception—such as a champagne toast with wedding cake—would follow. A single bridesmaid stands up with the bride, and wears a fashionable, often short, dress or suit that clearly follows the bride's lead. The groom wears his favorite suit; similarly, the bride wears what pleases her best. For a hotel wedding, she might wear a short lace sheath with a high neck and long sleeves, pearl ear-

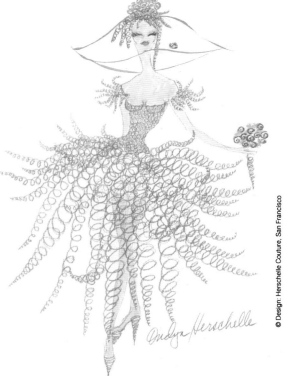

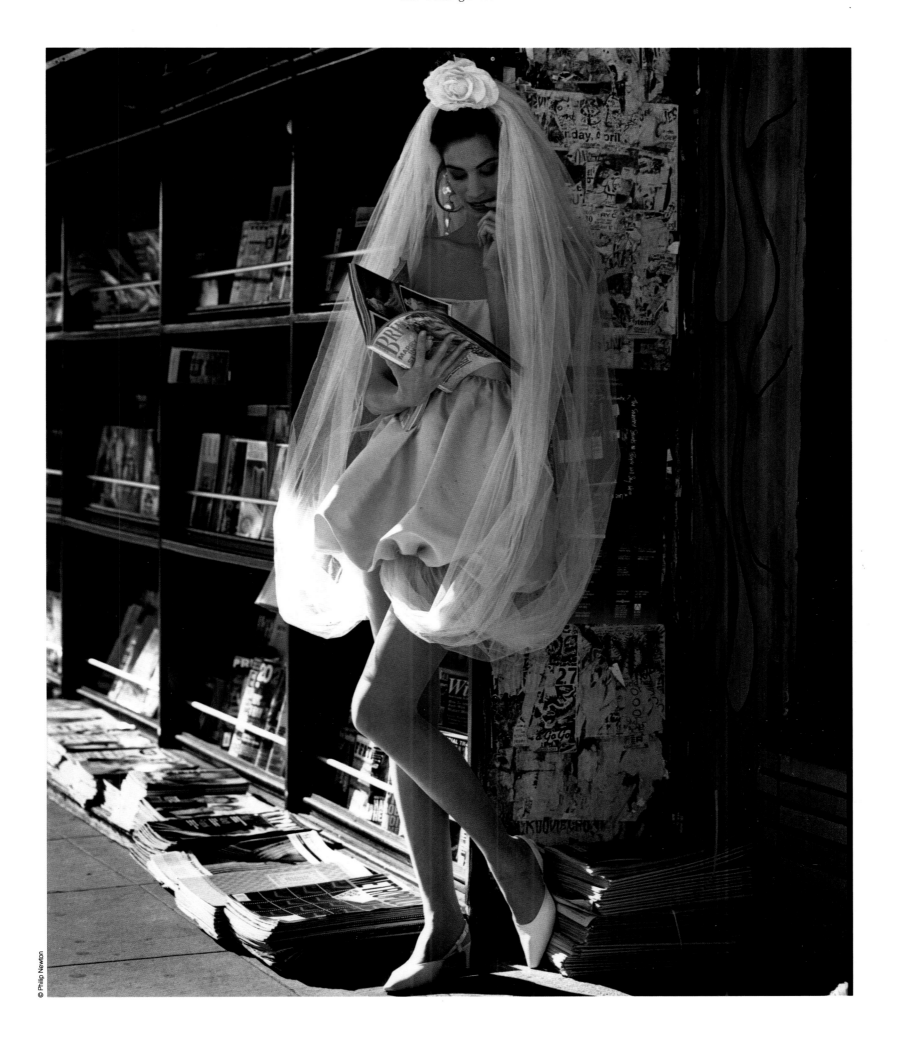

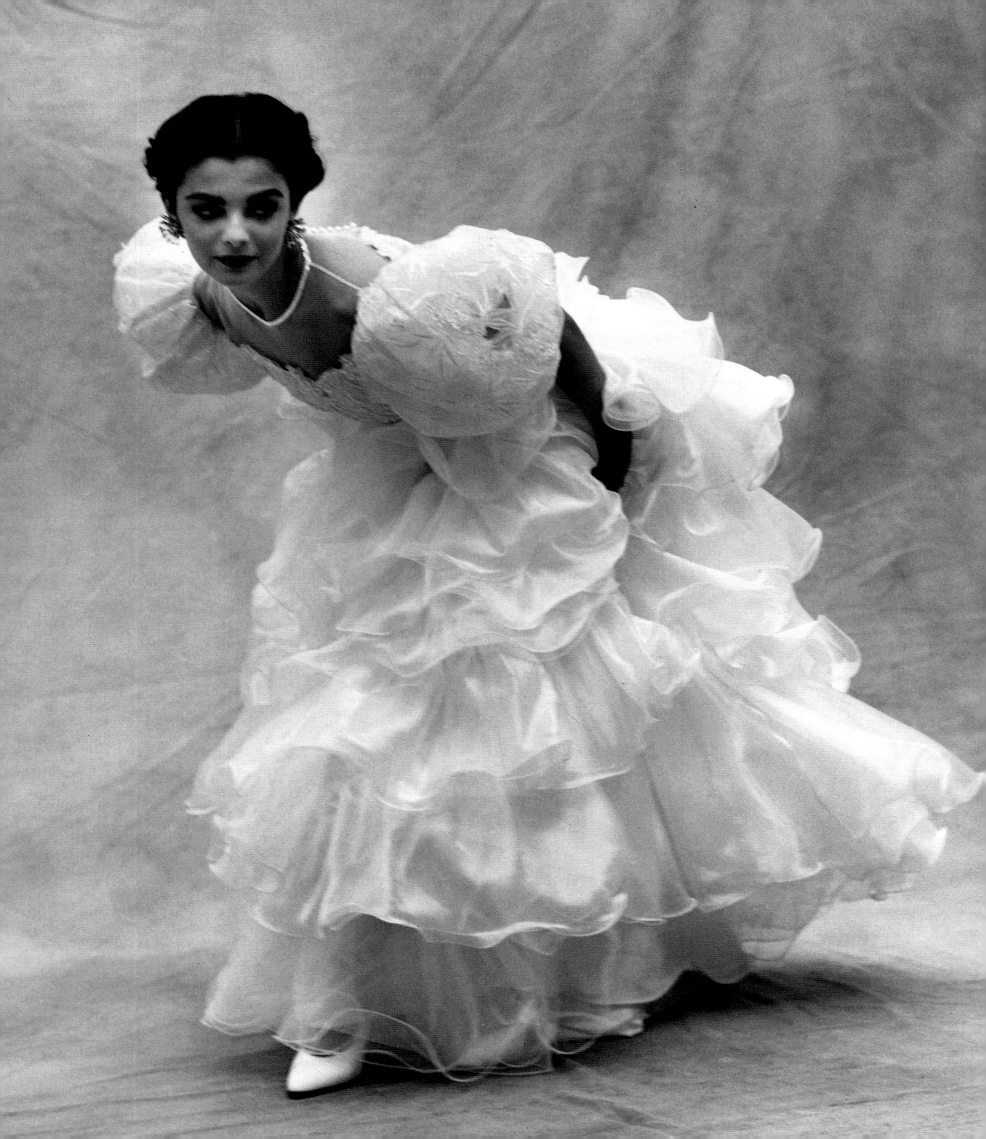

FIGURE BASICS

The best wedding gowns flatter a woman's best features, emphasizing a good figure or creating the illusion of a better shape. Every bride wants to look fabulous; luckily, most bridal gowns are designed to actively enhance a woman's figure. Fabric and silhouette are the key elements, as the cleverness of the cut and the drapability or firmness of fabric transform, conceal, and celebrate the feminine form. Some figure flaws—such as a small bust line or a full waist—are easily minimized with a little optical illusion, while other flaws—full hips or legs, or thin arms—are best camouflaged under a full skirt or long sleeves and a high neck. There is a wedding dress style to flatter every figure. Some suggestions follow; a good bridal salon will have others.

A very thin bride who wants to appear more curvaceous should choose a gown that adds shape to her figure, such as an off-the-shoulder gown trimmed with flowers or full sleeves—an exaggerated puff or leg-o'-mutton shape, for example—matched with a basque waistline and full skirt to create an instant hourglass figure.

Waistlines can be minimized with slimming shapes like the princess-line gown, cut and seamed so that it narrows at the waist; the basque waist, which slenderizes with its V-shape point; or a low-waisted gown topped with a short bolero jacket—the two-piece combination brings the eye in and out, from shoulder to hem, for a leaner silhouette. Short-waisted women should try gowns with elongated waists, which camouflage the natural waistline. Long-waisted brides can de-emphasize the waistline with an empire-style gown—seamed under the bosom, it falls straight down, completely camouflaging the figure dilemma.

In general, larger brides should avoid big bows at the back waist, which emphasize the rear end. A full-figured woman looks svelte under a simple, full skirt with a defined waistline. Ornate embellishments should be kept near the neckline, drawing the eye up and away from the hip and waistline, while tiny, delicate elements, such as a scattering of pearls or a textured fabric like point d'esprit may be used more liberally.

The bride with a very full bust should avoid off-the-shoulder gowns, as these accentuate the bust line; a clean, simple bodice and neckline, such as a high-necked smooth lace or a scoop neckline of shantung silk, is a better choice. Put any embellishments on the skirt, drawing the attention downward. The small-busted woman should opt for a gown with an embellished bodice—a profusion of flowers or a big satin bow across the front of a bateau neckline. These big flourishes give the illusion of size. Avoid plain bodices or deep-V necklines that focus on the bust line. Small breast pads are commonly added and can even be sewn into the dress by the salon.

Petites should avoid overwhelming dresses that have fussy details, which only make the bride appear more diminutive. Opt instead for simple details and elongating silhouettes such as sheaths and princess lines. For the most options, both petite and very full-figured women should work with salons that sell gowns dedicated to their special sizes. For example, Priscilla of Boston has a true petite line proportionally cut for smaller women, while Alfred Angelo can cut any dress from size four to forty-four.

The right dress disguises problem spots but emphasizes your best features: a beautiful neckline, magnificent shoulders, a perfect back, great legs, exquisitely shaped arms, an all-around sensational figure. Bridal salons have the expertise to help you select the dress that is the most flattering to your figure, and to suggest alterations where necessary.

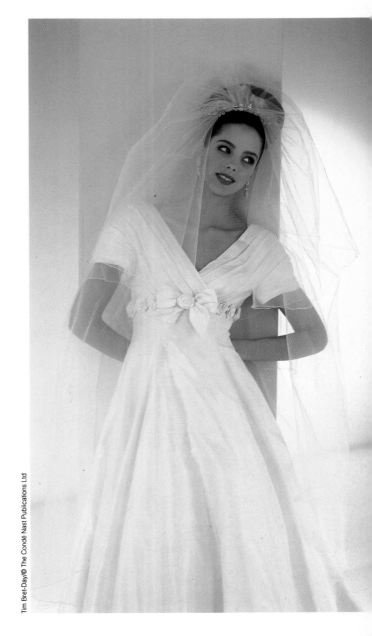

Curvaceous lines, defined bodices, architectural sleeves, and massive skirts with narrow waists refine every figure. **OPPOSITE PAGE:** *This gown by Lori features full puff sleeves, a shaped bodice, and a full skirt to create an hourglass silhouette.* **ABOVE:** *A Lyn Ashworth dress has embellishments that edge the bust line to maximize a minimal endowment.*

What you wear under the dress is also important; every gown will look its best, and so will you if you're wearing the proper undergarments. A salon will recommend a strapless longline bra for most women, not exclusively but especially for full-figured women and women wearing off-the-shoulder gowns. A longline bra makes for a clean, smooth line under the gowns and it lifts and flatters every figure. The best bras even have tiny slits over the breast area so that pads can be added, if necessary. Since wedding gowns, unlike other garments, are cut and designed specifically to flatter a woman's figure, with a little attention to problem areas, every bride can look sensational.

THE RIGHT WHITE

As every professional colorist and makeup artist knows, not every woman looks great in every shade of white; however, not all whites are the same. Commonly regarded as a neutral, white is really a broad spectrum of tones. Classic white bridal hues range from a crisp bright white to a pearlized, almost blue white, to a warm creamy white; soft pastels and deep ivory gowns are also popular. A white gown may also have colored elements, such as a neckline of colorful flowers or gold embroidered lace, or even a bodice of a bold color like red. The trick is to choose a color or hue that is most flattering for your skin tone.

The first step is to understand your skin tones. All skins have undertones—pink, blue, peach, or yellow are the most common —and many women have a mix of undertones that determines the overall skin color. If, like most women, you're unclear about your predominant skin tone, it's worthwhile to take the time and money to have a professional evaluation and makeup lesson. A consultant not only will help you understand which shade of white will look best on you, but will give you a makeup lesson as a great

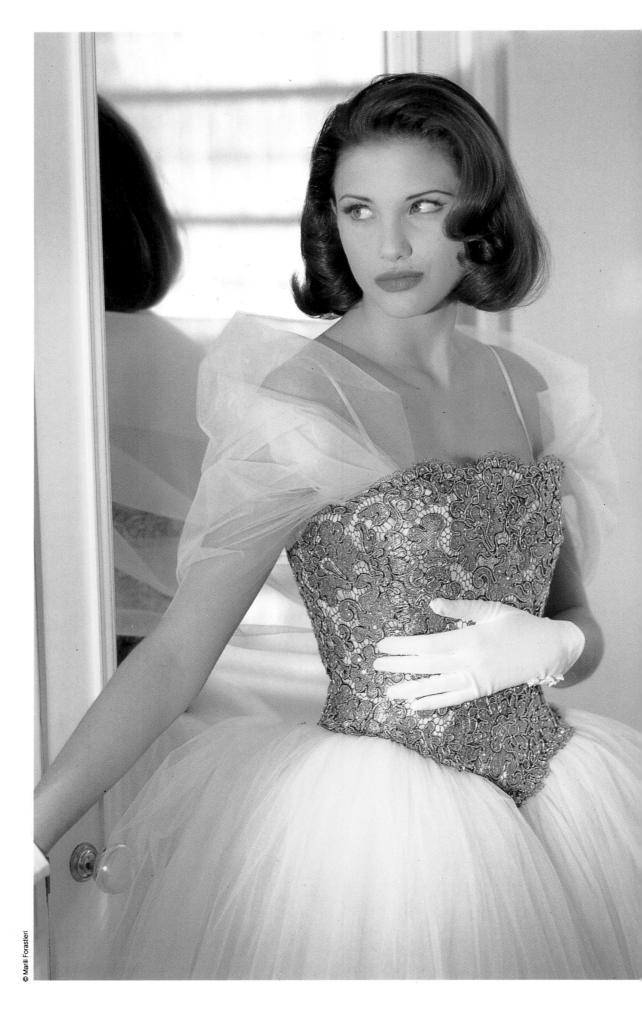

© Marili Forastieri

dress rehearsal for your wedding day. In general, women with dark hair and skin look beautiful in bright whites; blondes are flattered by pale ivory; women with dark hair and fair skin look best in pearlized, blue whites; and redheads are favored by deep, golden ivory. Because women have more than one undertone in their skin, it's wise to try on dresses in several different hues of white to judge your best option. If possible, try to evaluate the color in natural light, because fluorescent lights distort the true value of the tones. It's smart to wear some makeup for your try-ons, but keep it simple, avoid bright distracting colors, and wear a foundation that closely matches your skin tone. If you find a dress you love but it's sampled in the wrong white for you, remember that most gowns are available in white or ivory. Ultimately, the right white is the one that looks best on you.

PERSONAL PRIORITIES

No wedding gown is exactly right unless it is personally significant; after all, it's your wedding. Of course, your wedding gown will be personally flattering, compatible with your personal style, and fitted only to you. But for a more personalized and memorable dress, you may wish to add some cultural, heirloom, or other personal detail that gives originality and historical continuity to your gown, and thus to your wedding day, making it an intensely personal and individual occasion. Research your own family and ethnic history for significant wedding traditions. Most cultures have unique customs that are easy to incorporate or blend with modern rituals.

Historically, the Chinese considered red a very lucky color, a symbol of happiness and permanence. It was customary for the bride to wear a red jacket with an elaborately decorated collar, a red veil, and red shoes. The bride also had to wear four or six items of clothing, and the groom three or five, to conform to the perfect union of the ancient Chinese principles of yin and yang. Today's bride might consider wearing a little red for luck, too—a red floral wreath with a tulle veil edged with red ribbon, a bouquet of red flowers, or tiny red roses trimming the toe of a shoe. For a stronger look, she might wear a crimson faille jacket edged with pearls and finished with pearl buttons over a strapless satin gown.

The ancient Israelites bordered their wedding robes with blue ribbons as emblems of fidelity, purity, and love. This may be the root of the bridal adage to wear "something blue." A bride who wants to continue this tradition might add blue ribbons to her bouquet, wear a blue garter, edge her petticoat with blue ribbons, or even design a gown with blue ribbon lace on the bodice or skirt. Traditionally, Russian and Greek Orthodox couples were married under a pair of crowns united with a ribbon, with the bride and groom representing the king and queen of Creation. A modern bride might opt for a crown as a headpiece or have a pair of crowns embroidered on a pair of handkerchiefs for herself and her groom. Hindu brides and grooms would traditionally exchange necklaces of flowers during the ceremony, a touching, fragrant tradition that's easy to re-create. Whether you include a little symbolism or a lot, share the meaning of the tradition with your guests by asking someone to explain the symbolism during the ceremony or by adding a note to your wedding program.

The personal touch can also be achieved by wearing an heirloom gown, lace, or jewelry. Brides with a keen interest in family traditions often opt to wear heirloom gowns. With time and expertise, many old gowns are restorable—even if the size is wrong or the fabric is stained. Specialists in restoration

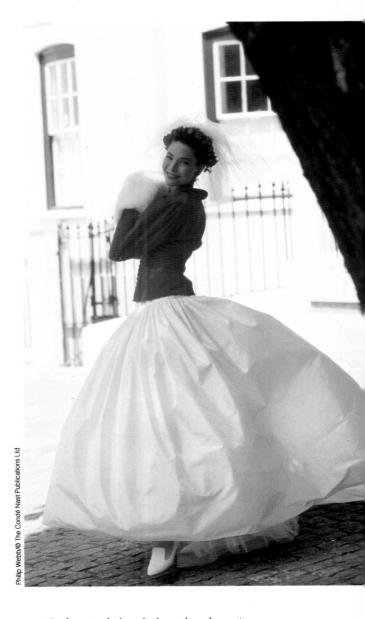

Philip Webb/© The Condé Nast Publications Ltd

*Exuberant splashes of color make a dramatic statement for the bride with an independent, but sentimental, streak—brides of yore usually wed in vibrant threads. Celebrate Chinese roots by wearing lucky red (**ABOVE,** by Anneliese Sharp) or lay claim to a regal pedigree in a gown of tulle and gilt lace (**OPPOSITE PAGE,** by Vera Wang).*

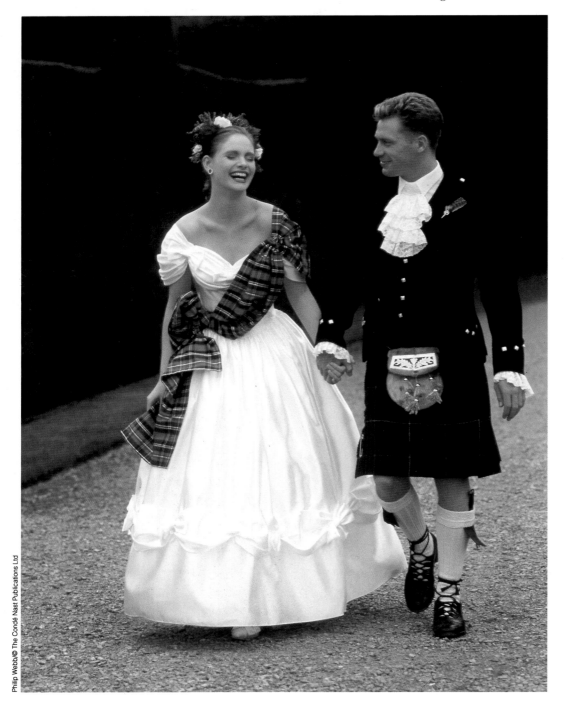

Philip Webb/© The Condé Nast Publications Ltd

For an extra-personal touch, incorporate symbolic elements of family roots or ancestral treasures into your gown. **ABOVE:** *A tartan sash adds a family tradition to a simple gown by Berketex.* **OPPOSITE PAGE:** *Estate jewels look beautiful with Eva Haynal Forsyth's elaborately beaded gown.*

can be found through historical societies, museums, costume departments, vintage clothing stores, and seamstresses. Restorers will clean and repair the fabric, and they should also be able to refit and rework the gown. Seams can be opened for resizing and reinforced at stress points (like shoulders, elbows, and seat), compatible fabrics and laces can be dyed with tea to match the gown's hue, and can then be used to cover or alter sections of the gown. Sleeves can be removed, backs lowered, dresses shortened or lengthened. Silk and satin will never look

brand new, but with cleaning and freshening they can look beautiful. Cottons, linens, and lace (but not silk) are bleachable, and when restored can look very bright and fresh. Silk lace should be hand-washed in soapy water with gentle powdered soap flakes and left out to dry.

For the bride who is lucky enough to have an heirloom gown or veil but wants to wear a new gown, some of the more interesting or unique bits of the gown might be added to the new gown to wonderful effect. A good seamstress could edge the new petticoat with lace from the old gown, make a detachable train from the heirloom fabric or lace, have ruffled cuffs made from the antique lace, or design a lustrous patchwork skirt with swatches of old and new satin and lace. An heirloom veil can look lovely with a new dress, or a new veil can be trimmed with an old veil's lace. If only small pieces of the old fabrics are in good shape, they can be used to make a garter or handkerchief. If there is no heirloom gown, but there is heirloom jewelry, wear it for luck. An antique ring that's too small can be slipped on a gold chain and worn around the neck for a unique and meaningful necklace.

It's not necessary to study your family history or inherit an heirloom in order to add some symbolism to your wedding; with a little creativity, you can create your own. Embroider your own and your husband's initials inside your gown with the date of the wedding and a pair of intertwined hearts. Design your gown with lace or a fabric that originated in your family homeland. Have your gown embroidered with a favorite symbol of your heritage, such as Irish shamrocks or Japanese butterflies. Use the language of flowers to express your creativity: the classic lily of the valley symbolizes a return to happiness, or choose a sentimental bloom, like the first flower your fiancé gave you.

© Horst

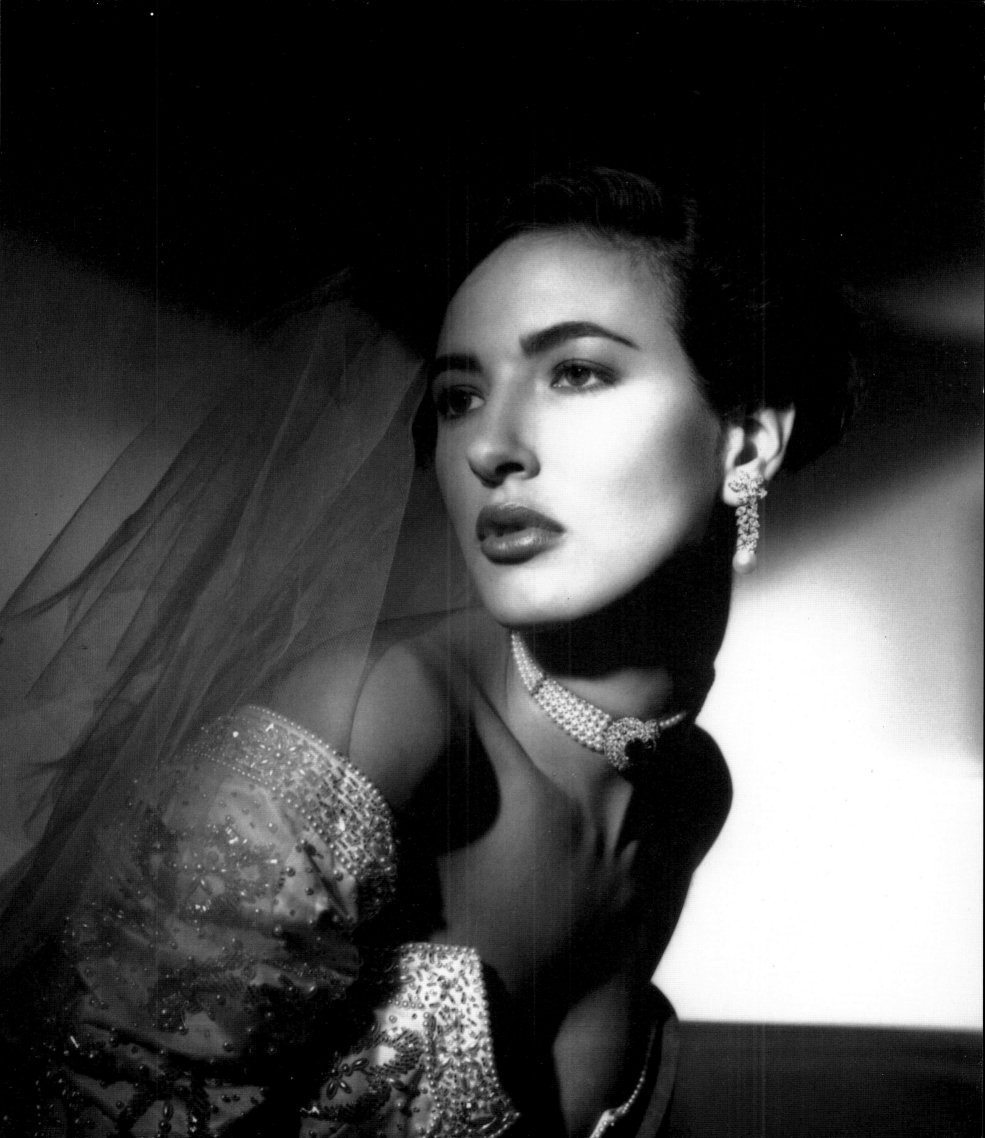

THE SALON EXPERIENCE

Decisions, decisions, decisions: for some women shopping is a sport, but for others, it's pure torture. With planning and the support of a good salon, however, shopping for your wedding gown should be an exciting, enjoyable, satisfying experience. Once you step into a bridal salon you're entering a world that celebrates a time when business, especially fashion merchandising, was extremely service-oriented. The first bridal salons originated in department stores. Carson, Pirie, Scott and Company, of Chicago, claims to have been the first department store to feature a bridal salon in 1935; by 1936 all major department stores across the country had bridal salons. New York's Lord & Taylor, in addition to designing and producing a bridal gown, proudly oversaw the ordering of flowers, bridesmaids' dresses, and a bridal trousseau, plus the hiring of photographers. Bonwit Teller would arrange for a wedding portrait in the store's own studio on the final day of fitting. For the cost-conscious, Best and Company advertised a budget bridal, which undertook to outfit a bride from head to toe for under one hundred dollars. All these companies flourished in the late 1930s but really proliferated after World War II, when surging marital rates unleashed a competitive frenzy between department stores, each trying to surpass the

other in service. Advertising created the impression that being married by the right store was as important as marrying the right man. Saks Fifth Avenue boasted of its superior, unflappable, resourceful bridal consultants: "When the groom shaved off half his mustache, she glued it back on. When a bride spilled nail polish on her lace wedding train, our consultant pinned a handful of orange blossoms over it." Service was such an important aspect of the bridal salon that most sales consultants also attended the bride on her wedding day. In the 1960s, consultants at Hess Brothers, a department store based in Allentown, Pennsylvania, would attend weddings with "happy bags" that contained their wedding emergency kits: needles, a dozen colors of thread, bobby pins, bandages, nail polish, pins, cleaning fluid, scissors, tissues, makeup, and sedatives, plus white flowers to cover sudden rips, fuses for home weddings, and, of course, smelling salts. Although a handful of major department stores continue to feature full-service bridal salons, today the bridal salon is frequently limited to the flagship store.

Most bridal gowns today are sold through smaller, independent bridal boutiques, but there are many other outlets for wedding gowns, including full-service bridal salons, department store salons, discount warehouses, renters, and vintage specialists. With so many options, it's important to do a little homework before making an appointment. Ask recently married friends for referrals: Were they happy with the service? Was the selection sufficient? Was the dress fitted properly? Local newspapers often run biannual bridal supplements; if one store is repeatedly singled out for interviews, chances are it is a reputable salon with a long-standing involvement in the bridal business. Although new bridal businesses are often ethical, expert, and successful, it

usually takes years to build a solid, service-oriented business with a knowledgeable, talented staff, and it makes sense to seek out established businesses with good reputations. Bridal magazines feature advertisements and articles that showcase wedding

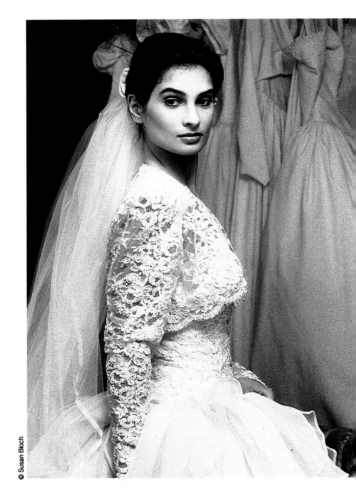

© Susan Bloch

Step inside a bridal salon and go back to a time when pampering was the norm. **ABOVE:** *At One of a Kind Bride, Candace Solomon provides dedicated personal attention, guiding each bride through the process of selection. Here, a lace bolero jacket adds a special touch to a lace and tulle ball gown.* **OPPOSITE PAGE:** *Racks at The Vera Wang Bridal House are laden with gowns cut to evoke fashions from eras past.*

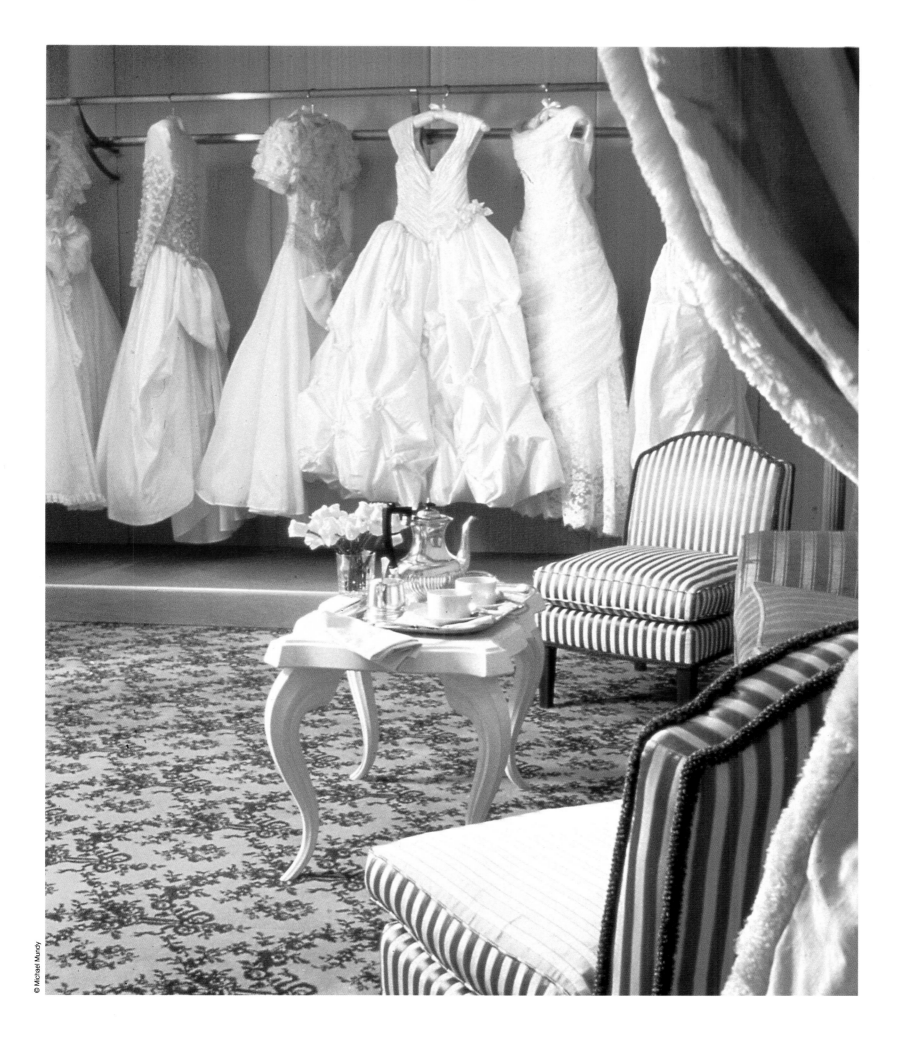

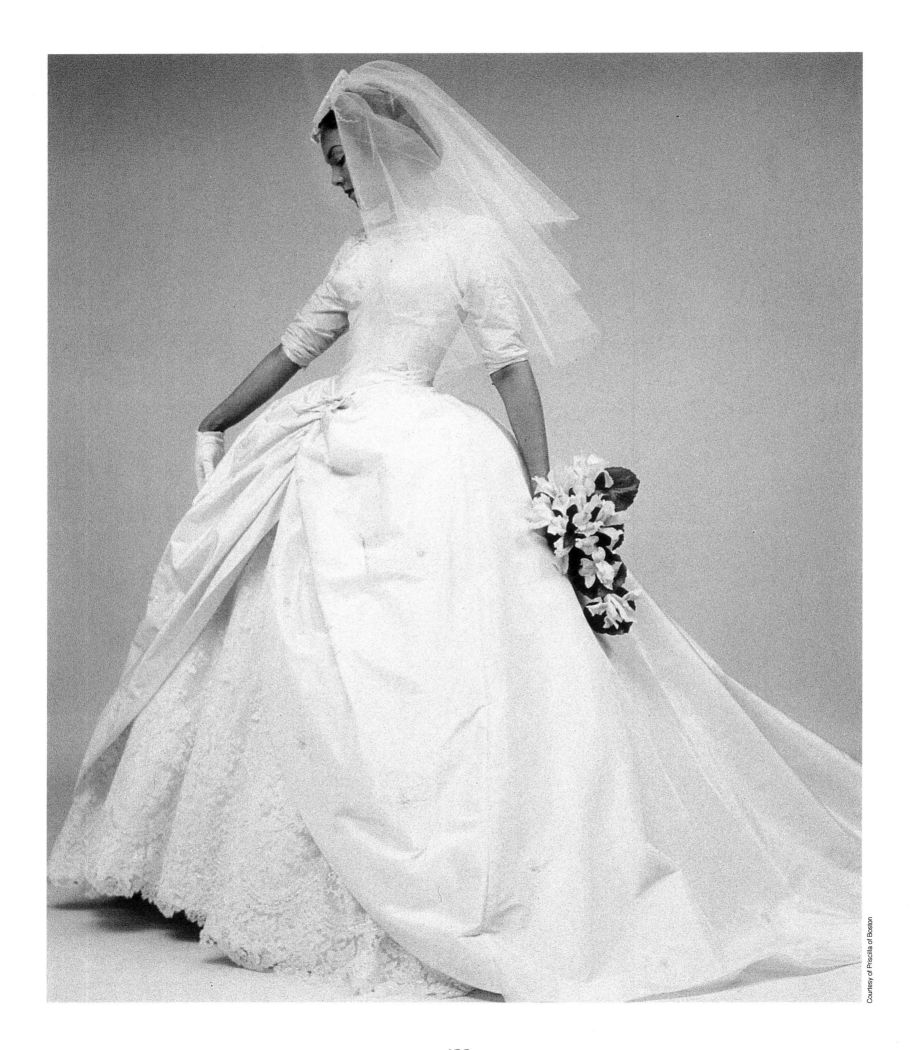

designers' best gowns, and a list of stores where the dresses are sold. Bridal salons that are cross-listed on several different better designers' advertisements are probably the best. Highly respected by many bridal manufacturers, these salons offer a wide selection of gowns and provide excellent service, so that the bride may feel confident patronizing these boutiques. Although the best bridal salons are judged on their service, it's worth noting a prospective salon's appearance, as this provides a good indication of its commitment to quality. The salon should be comfortable and clean (after all, it is selling white dresses) with spacious, tidy dressing rooms (there should be room to try on big gowns, with space for at least one companion), and the sample bridal gowns should be in good condition, not crammed together in a sloppy, wrinkled mess. If the samples are treated poorly, chances are the salon won't do much better with your finished gown.

A good bridal salon has a good reputation for good reasons. A good salon doesn't just sell a dress, it markets old-fashioned service: start-to-finish dedicated assistance, expert advice, quality products, and careful attention to the smallest details. The staff of a top-quality full-service salon is its backbone, and a good sales consultant "must have a good disposition, a lot of compassion, and good taste. And she must be discreet," insists designer–salon owner Priscilla Kidder. Originally a bridal consultant in the early 1940s for the department store R. H. White, Priscilla Kidder established her own bridal salon in 1945, Priscilla of Boston. Eventually, Kidder was not only the proprietor of her own salon, but its only designer, and today she owns five bridal salons in the United States. The sales consultant must be able to empathize with each bride, understand and respect the paramount importance of this emotional event. Brides need lots of reassur-ance and assistance in selecting this most important of dresses. An effective sales consultant will determine what the bride wants, guide her toward her dream dress, and ensure that the bride does not make an impractical choice. The consultant can be an invaluable resource in helping the bride select a gown that's best for her figure, appropriate for her style of wedding, and easy for her to manage.

All bridal salons operate in a similar manner. Each salon purchases and stocks a selection of wedding dress samples from different

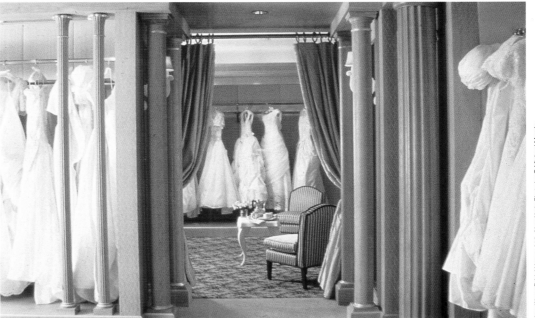

bridal manufacturers. The customer tries on these sample dresses and makes her choice from among them; orders are then placed with the manufacturer. The primary difference from one salon to another is the range of gowns sold and the extent of service offered. Many salons stock a variety of gowns in different price categories to offer something for almost everyone, but they usually specialize in a range of prices, either high-end (seven hundred dollars and up) or low-end (three hundred to a thousand dollars). Large bridal salons stock close to five hundred or more gowns. Naturally, these salons offer the greatest options in prices and styles, often attracting customers from out of town. The average salon is much smaller, stocking no more than one hundred fifty to three hundred gowns, with a narrower, more focused selection. It's unwise to choose a salon or a gown based on price alone; remember the old adage, "you get what you pay for." Of course, it makes no sense to purchase a budget-busting gown, but it is equally foolish to economize on the price of the gown by skimping on service. Prices vary; look for a quality bridal salon that

The first bridal salons, such as Priscilla of Boston, catered to the bride's every need, even arranging for official bridal portraits. Taking a cue from the past, contemporary salons often offer referrals for many important wedding services. **OPPOSITE PAGE:** *A 1954 Priscilla of Boston creation.* **ABOVE:** *The best bridal salons have an elegant and calming atmosphere.*

stocks dresses in your price range. You'll want to order your gown from a salon that can provide expert alterations and handle any emergency that might arise with your order. It pays to select a gown from a dependable, full-service bridal salon; who else sells wedding gowns every day, who else knows the intricacies of bustling and fitting an elaborate wedding gown, who else can meet all your requirements?

Reputable bridal salons have strong links with their designers and they are dedicated to satisfying customers. Not only do salons carry a designer's dresses, but each season most designers do trunk shows at better salons. Trunk shows, attended by invitation only, include personal appearances by the designer in a salon. Not only is a trunk show an opportunity for each customer to meet the designers and benefit from their advice, it improves the salon's management of the wedding dresses. The salon staff learns from the designer the best way to fit and order the designer's dresses, and the lessons improve the store's overall customer service. Stores with solid designer relationships can work miracles—a quick call to a designer by a salon can avert and solve almost any dilemma, from pushing through a late order to correcting an order error. A good salon is conscious of its reputation and is determined to satisfy every bride. Some unscrupulous salons and discount warehouses claim to have relationships with the option to order from any designer, but this is simply not true. Most designers, especially the better manufacturers, carefully control the placement of their gowns to only the most reputable salons who can handle their precious designs in just the right manner. If a bridal salon does not carry a single dress by a particular designer but promises that it will be no problem to get it, be wary. It's wiser and safer to order from a salon that has an actual

sample of a designer's gown in stock, which is a clue to a viable relationship between the store and that designer—ultimately, that is the best insurance.

Discount warehouses, which feature discontinued styles, samples from out-of-business salons, and overstock from mass-producing importers for sale off the rack, are popular with the budget-conscious brides. But beware, they offer no extra service: if the gown needs any fitting, the bride will have to arrange for it herself, often at an exorbitant cost and with no guarantees. Because of the savings at a warehouse, the cost of the gown must usually be paid for, in full, in advance. Be careful if you choose this option that the dress fits well and needs no alterations—otherwise, the dress may be no bargain. For peace of mind, service, and the rare pleasure of being catered to, a full-service salon is recommended. If your budget is limited, you may consider buying a sample gown from a salon. The sample has been tried on by other shoppers but the salon will clean and tailor it to your measurements. This allows you to enjoy the salon experience and get a wonderful gown—at a fraction of the cost.

"Never shop with a preconceived notion of what you want. Be open to lots of styles and try on lots of gowns. And don't listen to others' opinions. Let your heart be your guide. When you see the right reflection in the mirror, you'll know—you'll be radiant," advises bridal grande dame Priscilla Kidder. Even if you have no experience buying a gown, the bottom line is that you do know what feels good and looks good. "Each bride owes it to herself to try on a range of gowns; some women still go with tailored dresses if that's their style, but some are shocked that they fell for the frills," acknowledges designer Ron LoVece. Even though you may be older and less impulsive, even though you have a

preconceived notion of what style and level of formality you want—you've done thorough research through dozens of bridal magazines, you've attended many weddings, you've fantasized about your wedding day for months, maybe years—until you actually step into the gown, button it up, and look in the mirror, you can't know for sure which dress is right for you.

No matter how many gowns a bride considers, she almost always buys one of the first gowns she tries on. "If you see a dress you love and have shopped a bit, don't torture yourself, order the dress," recommends designer Christos, acknowledging that once requested, some gowns have taken up to six

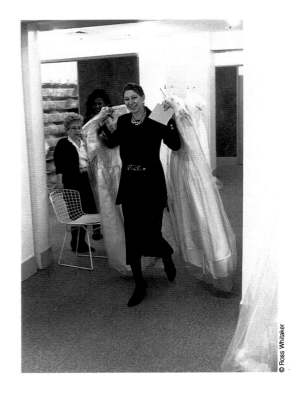

ABOVE: *Established salons such as Kleinfeld in New York know the key to a satisfied bride: the opportunity to try on a wide range of gowns from around the world and an expert staff who can alter or redesign any gown as necessary.* **OPPOSITE PAGE, RIGHT:** *Wear a white, strapless bra to try on dresses.* **OPPOSITE PAGE, LEFT:** *A good bridal salon will supply petticoats to fill out a skirt.*

months to be completed. Special lace may have to be ordered, specific alterations may take a long time. Natural and political disasters have even been known to cause problems: a recent volcanic eruption suspended production of embroidered fabrics from the Philippines, while an embargo made Haitian beaded laces and fabrics unobtainable—since these nations supply a majority of the specialty fabrics consumed by bridal manufacturers, delays were unavoidable. For a traditional bridal gown, most bridal salons recommend shopping at least six months before the wedding. Although it takes a bridal designer an average of three or four months to complete each gown and deliver it to the salon, time is needed for fittings and as a safety margin against delays and problems. Don't despair if you have less planning time, however; if necessary, some designers can rush orders or a salon may have a cancellation order or a sample it can sell you.

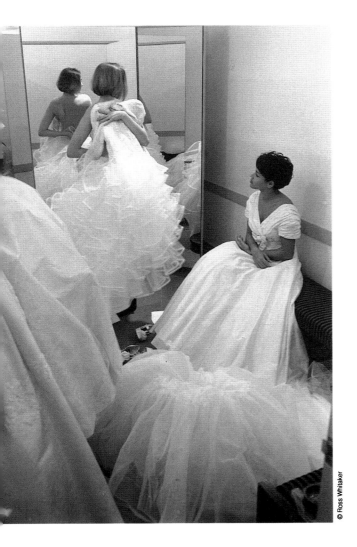

Always make an appointment before visiting a bridal salon; some salons are booked weeks in advance at the busiest times of the year. Plan to spend about two and a half hours per shopping appointment. If you take longer—some brides have been known to try on gowns for five hours at a stretch—the salon won't throw you out, but you'll be inconveniencing other anxious brides who booked appointments later that day. If possible, avoid the busiest periods, which are traditionally six months before June and September, after work, and on Saturdays. If you make an off-peak appointment you'll luxuriate in the calm atmosphere and enjoy the sales process all the more.

SELECTING THE DRESS

Be prepared on the day of your appointment. Know the big details of your wedding: the date, the size, the level of formality, the religious details, the location—outdoors or in—the time of day, and so on. All these elements will influence your choice of dress. Have a sense of styles you prefer—or absolutely can't stand—because even though you'll want to try on a range of dresses, you'll need a starting point. Be realistic about your budget: there will be many extras, and there's no use torturing yourself or wasting time trying on gowns that are absolutely out of the question. A good salon will have a range of styles in different price categories.

For shopping, always dress to undress: wear high-cut white underwear and a strapless bra, so you can judge each gown accurately without panty lines or shadows, distracting bra straps, or sagging bust lines. Bring along or wear shoes that are similar in height to those you'll want to wear on your wedding day, to give you a better idea of the right fit and length. Don't wear sneakers or boots, because you'll stand differently in the

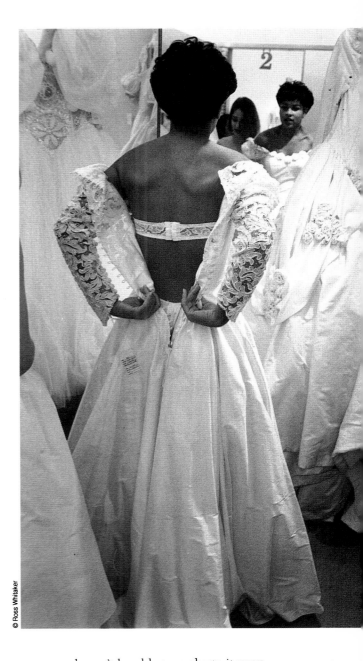

gown and won't be able to evaluate it properly. Also, wedding gowns are made of delicate laces and fabrics that are apt to be damaged by the wrong footwear. If you plan to wear your hair up on your wedding day, wear it up when shopping as well, so you'll be able to judge the right neckline. You'll get a better sense of your finished appearance if you also wear some makeup, but keep it sheer and muted, because you'll want to carefully determine the color of the gown that's best for you without being misled by makeup. Choose your dress before you consider headpieces, but if you're wearing an heirloom veil, bring it along so you can

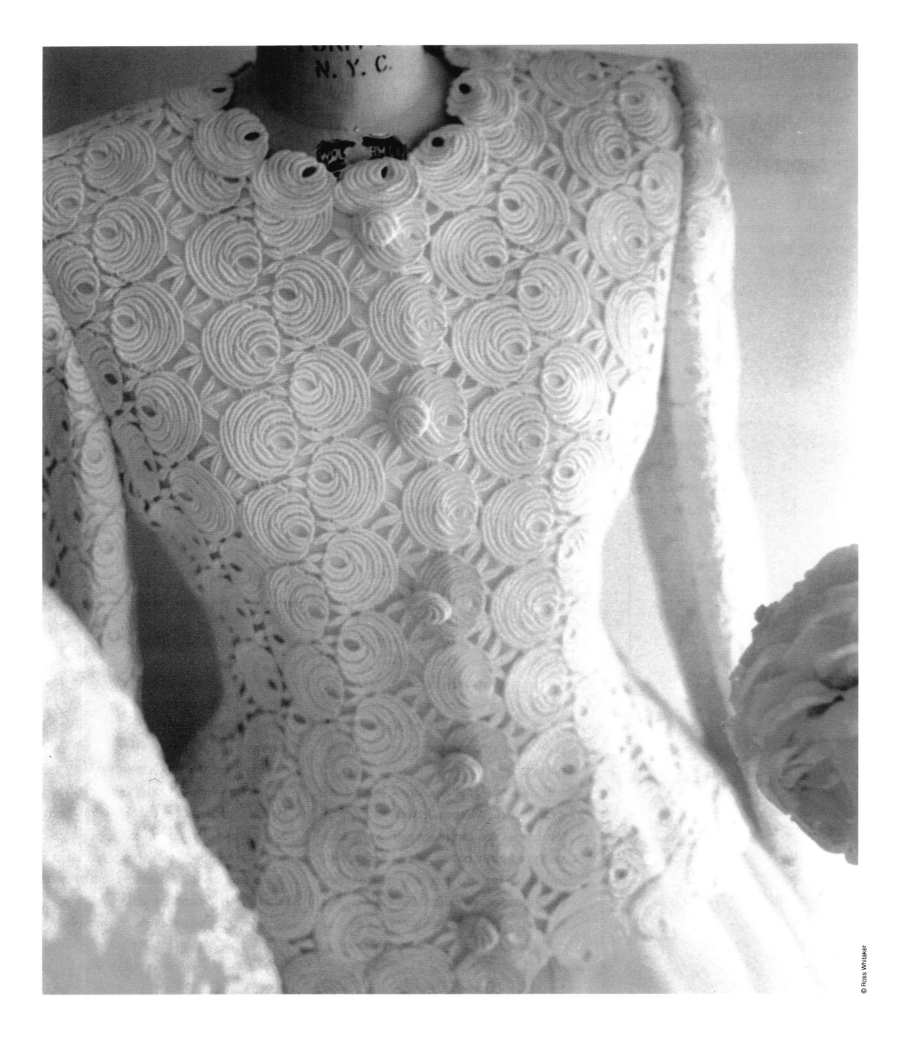

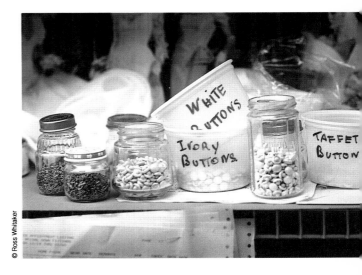

choose a gown that complements it best. Bring one friend, or your mother or sister, for security, but leave everyone else at home—too many opinions make it difficult for you to decide what you really want.

Evaluate each wedding gown you like according to several criteria: Style—do you love it? Comfort—can you sit, stand, and move in the dress with no discomfort? Practicality—does it fit the mood or season of your wedding? Finally, quality—how well is it made? Be sure to move around in the dress so you can truly evaluate its comfort level. Your reflection may be absolutely breathtaking as you pose carefully before a full-length mirror, but remember that you'll want to appear graceful and comfortable as you walk, dance, and sit as well. Above all, it should never appear awkward. Remember also that the back of the gown is nearly as important as the front, especially for a religious ceremony, when the bride is seen mostly from the back.

When evaluating a gown with a detachable train, make sure that the dress looks equally fabulous front and back, with and without the train; long trains that will need to be bustled should also be carefully reviewed—up and down. Before you make a final decision, study your reflection in three-way mirrors, walk, even dance a bit in the dress—imagine you're momentarily at your reception. If the dress has an overly complicated train, is uncomfortably tight, or is insecurely fastened, and cannot be altered to fit perfectly, reject it; it makes no sense to pick a gown that is difficult to wear. Distracted by your dress, you'll never properly enjoy your reception. A good bridal salon will not only help you to make the right choice, it will also make the dress right for you.

Expect your finished dress to differ from the sample in only two ways: freshness—each sample has been tried on dozens and dozens of times—and fit—it will be cut and adjusted to your specific measurements and requests. Do not expect your dress to be of substantially different quality than the sample. If anything, the sample should always be the best quality the manufacturer can produce, because it is the sample that clinches the sale.

The best gowns will be finished beautifully inside the dress, as well as outside—no raw seams should be apparent. A good dress should have enough layers and sufficient lining so the foundation garments do not show through the fabric. Working buttons should

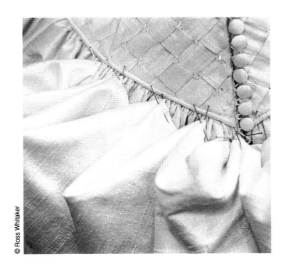

ABOVE and **RIGHT:** *Opt for your favorite gown, but carefully examine your choice: it should be made well. Samples may be well worn—after all, dozens of brides try on each gown—but a reputable salon will replace buttons and refinish seams as necessary so that the quality of workmanship in every gown will be evident.* **OPPOSITE PAGE:** *This Richard Glasgow creation shows the attention to detail that defines a top quality dress.*

be covered in the same fabric as the dress, fastening loops should be well stitched, and if buttons close the dress down the back, a long zipper should be hidden beneath them for security. Beading should be secure, with each bead individually stitched, so that one loose bead doesn't lead to a string of loose beads. In lace bodices, seams should be concealed and the lace should overlap itself like a jigsaw puzzle. The dress should have a lining that is lighter in weight than the outer dress fabric so that the lining doesn't change the character of the dress, and be faced with fabric to conceal seam allowances, boning, and finishing stitches. Interfacing should not be fused to the outer fabric of the dress or it will show through. Extra hooks and eyes should be added to common stress points—the back, waist, and neck—for support. A horsehair braid should be sewn inside the hem to push out the skirt and keep it from appearing limp. If the dress has an illusion yoke, it should be smoothly finished, with no bumps along the seam. The dress should feel secure, especially if it is off the shoulder. All off-the-shoulder and strapless gowns should have boned bodices for support. The best dresses have an inner bodice or corset sewn inside for a superior fit. The dress should feel great: the correctness of construction is something you can sense when the dress is on your body, and a well-made dress should actually be sensual to wear.

Gowns that cost over one thousand dollars should be made of pure silk. If lace is featured, it should be imported, and any beading should be done by hand. In addition, the gown should be perfectly finished. Marks of poor quality: all layers of the dress are sewn together in the same seam at one time—they'll never press properly or lay flat, and will always look like major body wrinkles; entire strings of missing or loose beading; glue marks; threads that show through the seams, cheap fabric, or lace—"fibers of undetermined origin"; unrestrained use of embellishments—too many ruffles, sequins, beads, and ribbons add up to quantity, not quality; no inner lining. If cost is a consideration, opt for a less expensive dress as opposed to a cheap dress. Your best choice is a quality dress with simple lines and mini-

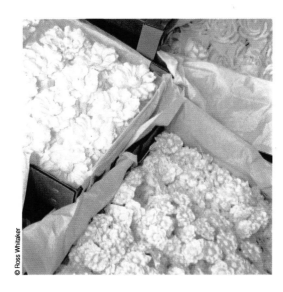

Superb emporiums of bridal finery offer customized design for the bride with an elusive but tangible fantasy. Many gowns can be redesigned on request—for an extra fee—by the bridal designer. **OPPOSITE PAGE:** *Lorenzo Riva's gown with an embellishment of lily of the valley along the hem.*

mal details—this look will echo the style of the most expensive dresses, which are minimally adorned and marked by a judicious use of extras.

If you have tried on a range of gowns that come close to what you want, but are not exactly right, consider custom alterations. Almost every manufacturer will allow basic changes to a dress: from white to ivory fabric or vice versa, shortening or lengthening the train or sleeves. A range of other changes can be made, depending on the designer's specific intentions or the price of the gown, since many gowns are designed to meet a certain price point. As a rule of thumb, the more expensive the gown, the more design alterations are allowed. Pearls can be changed to sequins, beading can be removed or added, sleeve and neckline designs can be altered, fabrics can be changed, white flowers can become colorful, or colorful flowers can turn white. The key for the best results is to choose one designer and work within his or her repertoire. For example, match the bodice from one dress with a skirt from another dress in the same designer's line. Some designers never retire a gown from their collection; Richard Glasgow considers his collection "a library" and allows any gown to be interchanged with a past or present design. If you suggest a questionable alteration, the salon will confer with the designer, maybe even while you wait. The designers know every stitch of their gowns and can determine right away whether or not a change will work or they will often suggest workable alternatives.

Remember that every design change to a gown will cost extra. If you find yourself requesting dozens of changes, consider a complete custom order. Many salons provide this service or can make a referral. Chances are the cost of a custom-made dress will be the same or negligibly different. Because of

the tremendous range of dress choices within each salon, custom design is rarely necessary and may be a better option for women with experience ordering dresses designed to order. Sketches are not dimensional and there is nothing to try on until a canvas is sewn. The canvas is not the actual fabric of the finished gown; it is for fitting purposes only, and it takes a woman with imagination, understanding, and experience to be comfortable, not nervous, with custom design.

Once you decide on your dress, the salon will carefully measure you and write up a sales order. The sales order will outline your measurements, your design specifications, the color of the gown, the date it is due, and your wedding date. The total price of your order will include the basic cost of the dress, extra fees for any design alterations, a bustling fee (if necessary), a fitting charge (sometimes the most expensive gowns include a fitting for no extra fee), the cost of your headpieces, petticoat costs (if necessary), and any other accessories you order from the salon. Most salons require a 50 percent nonrefundable deposit before they will order a dress. Deposits are forfeitable because each dress is cut to order. If you change your mind, you may be able to recover your deposit if the dress has not yet been cut for you. The balance of the dress payment, depending on store policy, is due either before the fittings or when the fittings are complete. You'll be on cloud nine after deciding on your wedding gown, but keep your feet on the ground until your order is complete, and be certain that you know exactly what you've ordered, what you will and won't receive. Every salon has a different policy, so make sure you understand your options. Some key questions to ask (and make a note of the answers): Is there a cancellation policy? What are the alteration fees? Are the alterations done on the prem-

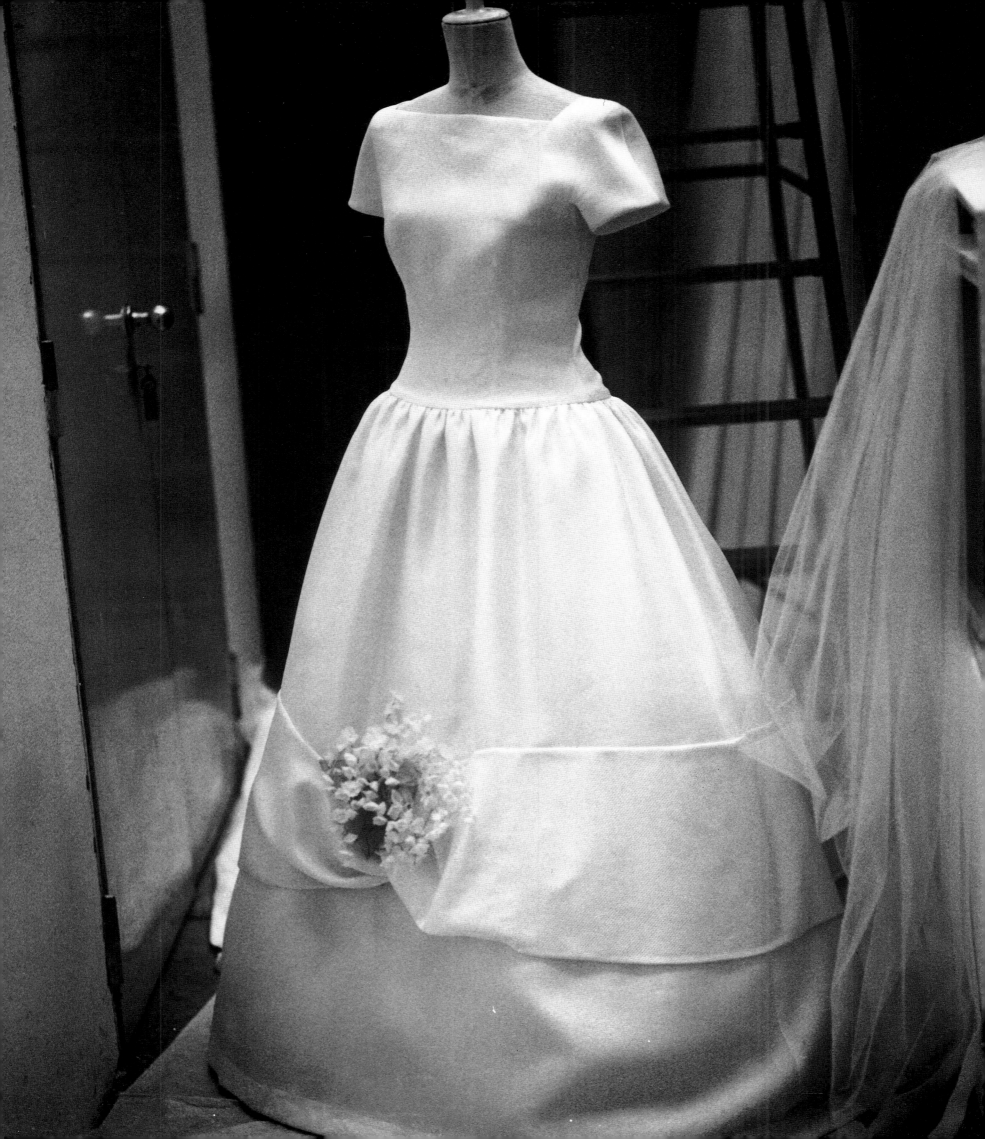

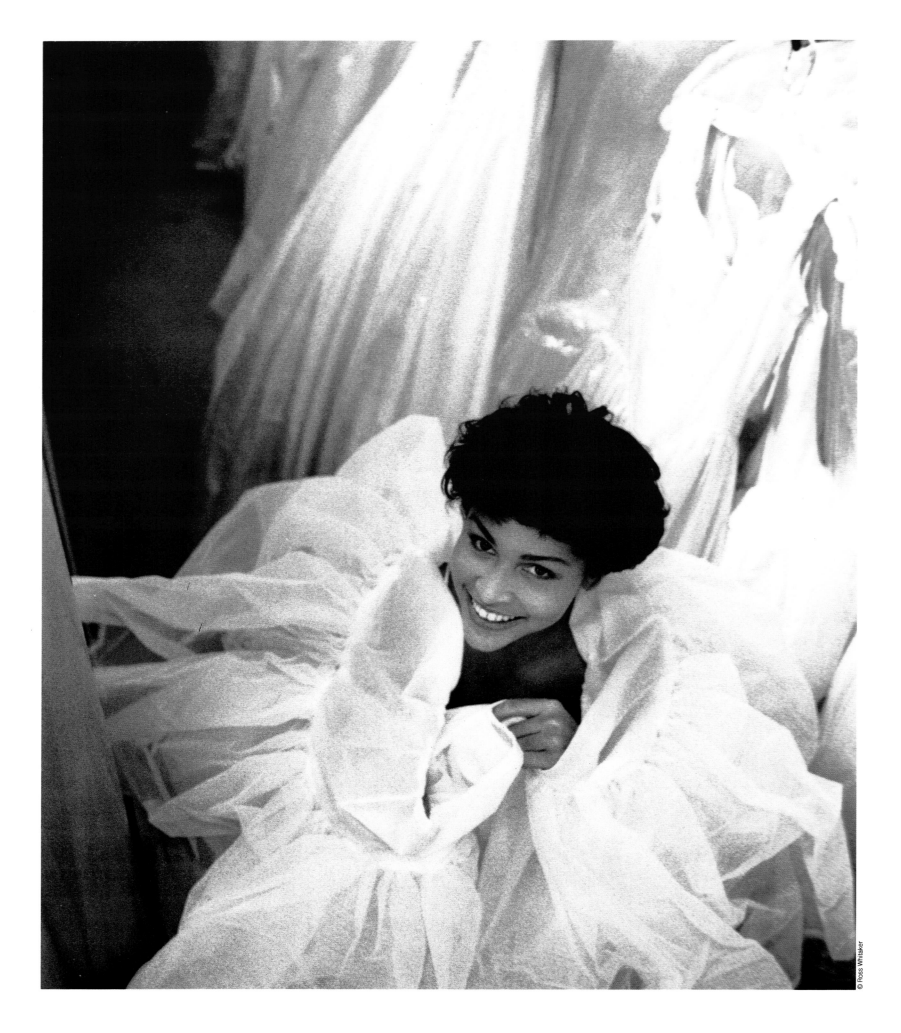

© Ross Whitaker

ises? Is there an extra length or size change? Is there a custom-fitting charge? Is there a bustling charge? Does this dress need a petticoat? Will the dress be pressed and stuffed with tissue on completion? Are there any delivery charges?

THE FITTING

Every woman experiences a giddy sensation when she finally tries on her own wedding gown; suddenly the wedding she's been dreaming of seems very real and exciting. Three to four months after the dress is ordered, it will arrive at the bridal salon and the bride will be contacted to arrange a series of fittings. At least two and frequently three fittings are necessary to precisely alter a wedding gown. Every wedding gown should be altered, because its true beauty is most apparent when it fits perfectly. Bridal salons are particularly proud of their fitting regimes, for it is then that the true artistry and talent of the salon shines. Large and small salons differ in the lead time they request to fit a dress. During the very busy prime marrying months, large salons prefer that their clients begin the fitting process three months before the wedding, while smaller salons schedule first fittings about four weeks before the wedding date. In each case, depending on a salon's business, fittings are scheduled as close as possible to the wedding day to eliminate extra fittings due to additional weight loss or gain. Fitting fees are either standard, one sum for any gown, or individually calculated according to the work necessary per dress; for example, the numbers of seams needed to be opened. The fees should be determined at the first fitting or earlier, and there are no extra fees for additional visits—it is the salon's job to make the dress fit just right, no matter how long it takes. Typical alterations include sizing the bodice to fit, taking the dress one size up or down. shortening

the hem, and lowering or raising the waistline and sleeves. Don't expect major design changes during this process; it is a fitting, not a redesign. But if you are unhappy with your dress and want major reworking done to the gown you chose, a good full-service salon should be able to handle this work.

Expect your first fitting to last at least one hour, possibly two, depending on how much work needs to be done. Gowns that are made precisely to your measurements may need very moderate amounts of fitting. Most gowns are made to the size closest to your measurements and require only fine tuning, but every gown will need some fitting, and to be done properly it must be done on the body. Always bring the right undergarments to your fitting; invest in a good, strapless, longline bra. Your bridal salon may sell them or can recommend the best place to find one. If you need a petticoat—and unless it is built into your gown or you are wearing a sheath, you'll need one—you can buy one or more, if necessary, from your salon.

The first part of the fitting is a process of evaluation: how does the dress look and feel? Has your figure changed dramatically since you ordered the gown and do you expect more changes? What bothers you about the way the dress looks, if anything? Is the petticoat full enough? Most wedding gowns that are ball gown in shape need very full petticoats to look their best, so you should always try on the fullest available petticoat with your gown—you may even need to layer two petticoats. All bridal gowns, especially sheaths, should have extra-long zippers that extend all the way to the hip line to facilitate getting in and out of the dress without stressing the fabric of the gown. Does it scratch anywhere? The fit of the bodice is critical, because this is the part of the dress most people will notice, and it is also the part of the dress that supports the remainder of the gown. Do darts

need to be altered? Is the bodice too large? If so, each seam should be opened for sizing, and the extra fabric should be evenly distributed. If the bodice is beaded, beads should not be sewn in the seams, but removed so it is not lumpy.

Do not forget to bring your wedding shoes to the fitting, too. The hem should be measured all the way around to fall at least three-quarters of an inch above the floor. This clearance will allow you to dance without

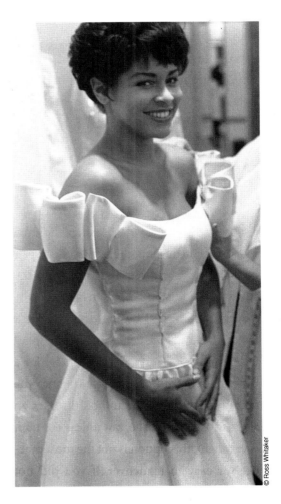

OPPOSITE PAGE *and* **ABOVE:** *Selecting the right gown is, of course, important, but the fitting process is critical. The best salons will know how to alter any bridal gown to fit perfectly, layering the dress first with all the correct undergarments.* **PAGE 133:** *The finished gown should never reveal any sign of alteration; it should simply look and feel marvelous, like this example by David Fielden.*

tripping on the hem. Marcy Blum, a Manhattan wedding consultant, likes skirts hemmed at least a full inch over the floor: "I remember taking a pair of shears to a $10,000 dress when the bride finally had one too many dancing partners step on her gown. Most men who come within ten feet of a bridal gown will step on it. Contrary to popular opinion, a wedding is not a sedate, genteel gathering. I recommend that my brides not just walk around in the dress but do a little dance and swing a little—that's a better test of the length." Once the hem length is established, a decision must be made about what to do with any train longer than a sweep train. Bustling is a practical, carefree solution; once the train has been bustled, the bride's hands are free. When bustled, even the longest train should clear the floor by at least an inch. A series of buttons, hooks, and snaps, often hidden by lace, bows, or flowers, are sewn into the gown to gather the train into a graceful bustle at the back waist. A pair of drawstrings can also be sewn into the gown as the bustling mechanism. Critically inspect the finished bustle: does the dress look as beautiful bustled as it does undone? Does the bustle rest and fall properly for a flattering rear end? A loop sewn onto the train to allow the bride to hold it up is an alternative to the bustle, but unless the train is very light, this option is not the most practical or easy to maneuver. If you did not choose a headpiece at the time you ordered your gown—women who order their gowns a year in advance often wait—do it now, so it will be available by the second fitting.

The second fitting, two to six weeks later, about ten days to four weeks before your wedding day, is to ensure time to complete all alterations properly. If you did not have your wedding shoes for the first fitting, you'll absolutely need them now—the bridal salon will not alter your hem until you have your shoes because even the slightest difference in heel height will affect the finished hem. If there are any weight changes, there will be further sizing adjustments. Are there any changes for the headpiece? Do you want a blusher added or removed? Should there be more or less beading? Is there any loose beading? Are the buttons and hooks secure? Are more or fewer flowers needed? Is the bow at the back waist of the gown too big or too small? Does the waistline sit properly? If the length of the sleeve or the hem of a lace gown was altered, did the seamstress maintain the beautiful, scalloped edge of the lace? It should never be turned under and lost in a hem. Unless your gown has a plain tulle skirt, which can simply be cut, the hem is actually shortened by raising the fabric at the waistline. If you had shoes for your first fitting, your dress will have been shortened by your second fitting, sewn delicately in place at the waist. Once the hem is double-checked for correctness, the waist seams will be reinforced or resewn if not correct; bridal skirts are very heavy and must be sewn well and then reinforced to support the weight.

If necessary, a final fitting may take place the week of or ten days before the wedding. Many salons prefer that clients pick up their dresses as close to the wedding as possible, because the dress will look freshest when newly pressed. Make sure your maid of honor, mother, or wedding consultant comes to your last fitting, so that she understands how to bustle or help you with your gown and headpiece. If you want an expert to help you dress on your wedding day, to guard against any last-minute problems, and to make sure that the gown is perfectly pressed, ask your fitter if she will service your wedding. Many will for a reasonable fee. If you're managing your dress on your own, be certain to get pressing instructions in case of an emergency. After a final try-on and check, you'll wait while your dress is pressed and packed with tissue to guard against any wrinkling. Tissue is stuffed everywhere: inside the arms, under the skirt, between every fold in the bustle, inside bows, and around flowers before the dress is packed in a garment bag.

When you take the dress home, salons recommend leaving the gown on its hanger and in its bag so you'll have less wrestling to do when it is time to transport the gown on your wedding day. Suspend the dress from the back of a door, a secure curtain rod, or any spot that is high enough to keep the dress from resting on the floor. Simply unzip the bag to keep the gown from getting musty and to release any moisture that may have accumulated from the final steam pressing at the salon. On the wedding day, or earlier, if you're dressing at home, remove the garment bag from around the dress, and place a clean sheet or piece of plastic under the dress to keep it clean. Remove the train from its hanger so any wrinkles that may have resulted from moving can "hang" out with the weight of the dress.

If you're extremely busy, some salons, like Kleinfeld, offer a one-day fitting. Arrive at eight for your first try-on, go out for lunch, return for a second fitting. Return again at the end of the afternoon for a final fitting and then wait for your gown to be packed to go. This option is particularly popular with out-of-town brides.

For consistency, most bridal salons assign one fitter to work with you for every fitting. If she has been exceptionally helpful, it is not unusual to want to offer a tip. Inquire with the salon's management as to their policy. Some salons discourage the practice, while others leave it up to the client's discretion. A satisfactory tip would vary from twenty to one hundred dollars, depending on the miracle rendered.

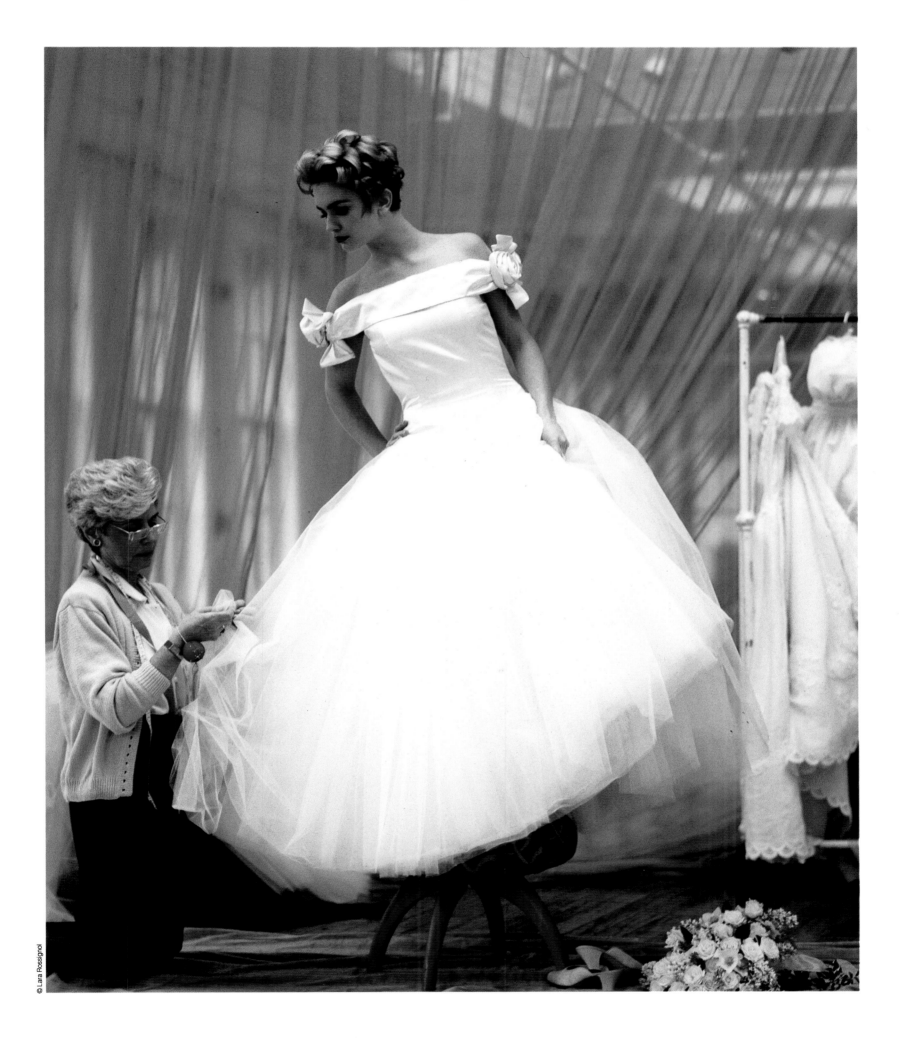

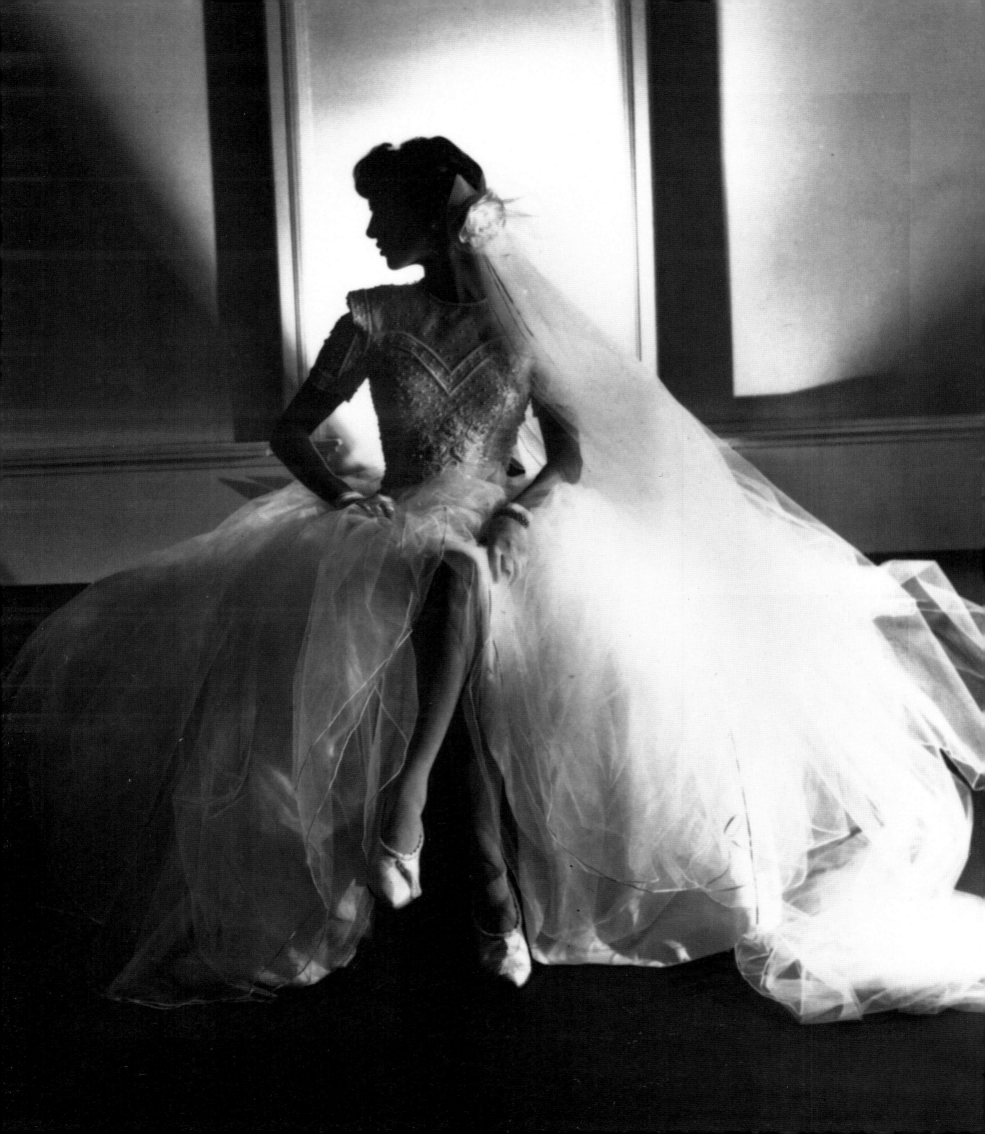

FINISHING DETAILS

Personal adornment has been a popular method of self-expression since ancient times. The oldest bridal vestments were actually accessories, with the dress itself having less significance. Over the centuries certain hallmarks of the bride—the veil, the flowers, the jewelry—were imbued with fanciful meanings and became integral elements of the bridal ensemble.

PERFECT TOPPINGS

The first bridal veils were worn to protect the bride from evil spirits. Today, some cultures veil women completely as a form of subjugation. The Victorians, however, viewed the veil as the perfect testament to feminine purity. Notwithstanding the veil's strong link with tradition, it is worn by today's bride largely because of its ethereal beauty, its perfect synergy with her dress, and its flattering appearance. Cut from fine net, veils have a gossamer, diaphanous texture that makes a romantic impression.

Poetry aside, choosing a veil and headpiece should be a practical decision. Head-to-toe evaluations should focus on proportion and balance. Bridal veils vary in length and suitability. A flyaway veil has multiple layers, brushes the shoulders, and is well paired with informal, ankle-length gowns or those with dramatic back details. A bird cage veil is cut to fall just below the chin, with the veiling covering the face, and is often worn attached to a small hat. A cathedral-length veil falls three and one half yards from the headpiece, and is worn with a formal gown, which also sports a cathedral train. A chapel-length veil is a yard shorter and is often worn with a floor-length dress or a dress with a sweep train, giving the illusion of a longer train. The most popular length is fingertip, which is perfect for any but the most formal gowns. The blusher covers the bride's face; her father or groom raises it from her face during the ceremony, and from this moment, it is never to shade her face again. The right length of veil is not so much a matter of tradition but proportion and what looks best with the dress. For example, a busy wedding dress needs a simple veil. Tall brides are better off refraining from poufs or other height-producing touches. Second-time brides who may choose to wear traditional, white gowns are counseled only against the maiden veil. Most veils are made of tulle or illusion, but a mantilla of lace is also an option. A tulle veil may have an unfinished edge to maximize its gossamer nature or be defined with a rolled edge, a ribbon edge, lace, or even with pearls. Pearls, flowers, crystals, lace motifs, silk or fresh flowers, even petals are frequently scattered over the veil. Veils are commonly removed after the beginning of the reception, usually after the bride's first dances or her introduction. Velcro fastenings and snaps detach the veil from the headpiece, freeing the bride for the remainder of the reception.

The headpieces are anchored to the veil as an extra measure of bridal regalia. The earliest headpieces were floral and herbal wreaths, which continue to be popular because of the enduring beauty and symbolism of flowers. Wreaths, among the easiest shapes to wear, can also be created from pearls or silk flowers. Wear a wreath over the forehead or nestled in the hair. The tiara, a regal emblem, is a full or half-crown constructed of pearls, crystals, or lace that rests atop the head. Big satin or tulle bows that clasp the bride's hair at the nape are good options for brides with long hair who want a simple headpiece. Jeweled, satin, or floral headbands are fuss-free, slightly tailored options for brides with very fine hair.

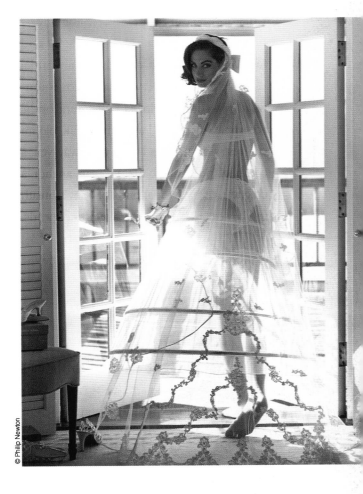

OPPOSITE PAGE: *Carolina Herrera's gown with a lavishly beaded bodice is worn with a cathedral-length train and tasseled satin slippers.* **ABOVE:** *What is worn under the gown is as important as the final wrappings. Here, a hooped petticoat is seen under a floor-length embroidered veil.*

Hats of every variety are appropriate bridal wear. Careful attention must be paid to the choice of hats, and proportion is the key: large hats work best with full gowns, while small-brimmed boaters and pillboxes are better with tailored dresses. A creative bride might want to sport a whimsical miniature white top hat and a pouf of veiling with a tuxedo-cut bodice or a full-size derby and Russian veiling with an Edwardian bridal jacket. Straw hats are worn only for warm-weather weddings. Flowers are natural bridal accompaniments: a large single silk bloom can rest atop the head with a flyaway veil, a comb of porcelain blossoms can anchor a chignon, or individual buds of baby's breath can be scattered in the hair like dots of pearls. All headpieces work well with a little or a lot of tulle. Every headpiece should also echo the style or a detail from the wedding dress.

The best headpieces, because they are worn close to the face, are simple. Fussy, overwhelming headpieces are too theatrical and distract from the bride's own beauty. When selecting a headpiece, try it on with your gown and experiment with different placements. Test its security and comfort by

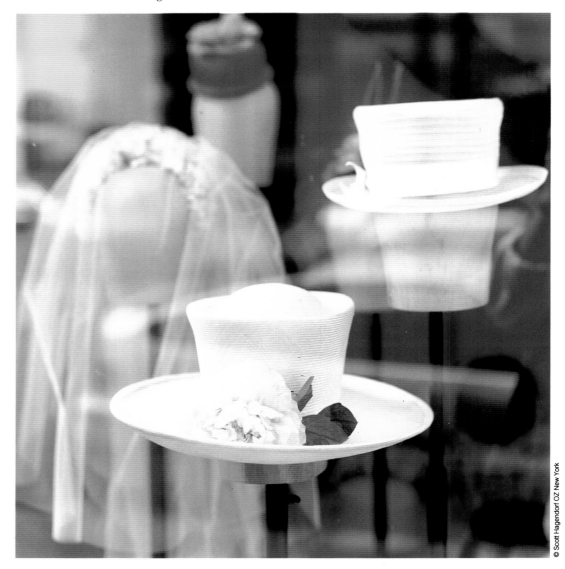

moving your head, then examine it from every angle—you'll want to be sure it looks great from every side. A combination of combs and bobby pin loops are the best way to anchor most headpieces securely. If there are no loops on the headpiece, request that your bridal salon insert them. If you're wearing an heirloom veil, have your salon seamstress inspect it and sew in the necessary anchors. Pick up your headpiece early and practice styling your hair. As *Harper's Bazar* noted in 1895, the headpiece "is a thing of beauty, but it is not easy to put on." As with the headpiece, the hairstyling should not be too fussy. Even if you normally avoid hair spray, use it to set your hair, particularly if the hair is worn up or pulled back. When it is held securely, chances are you can then forget it for the rest of the day.

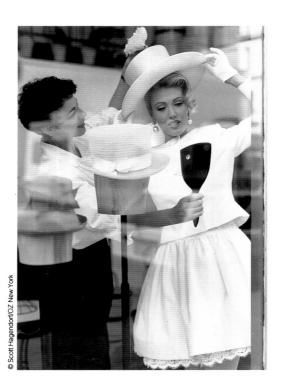

Blushing brides have said "I do" crowned with a wreath of flowers, layered under gossamer veils, or looking out from beneath a dashing brim. **ABOVE:** *Hats by Lola Millinery.* **LEFT:** *Choose the right topping to flatter your face, but also to balance the proportion of your dress. Lavishly trimmed broad-brimmed haberdashery makes a smart accent to a snappy piqué suit by Vera Wang.* **OPPOSITE PAGE:** *A veiled hat covered in cascades of blooms tops a coatdress by Norma Kamali.*

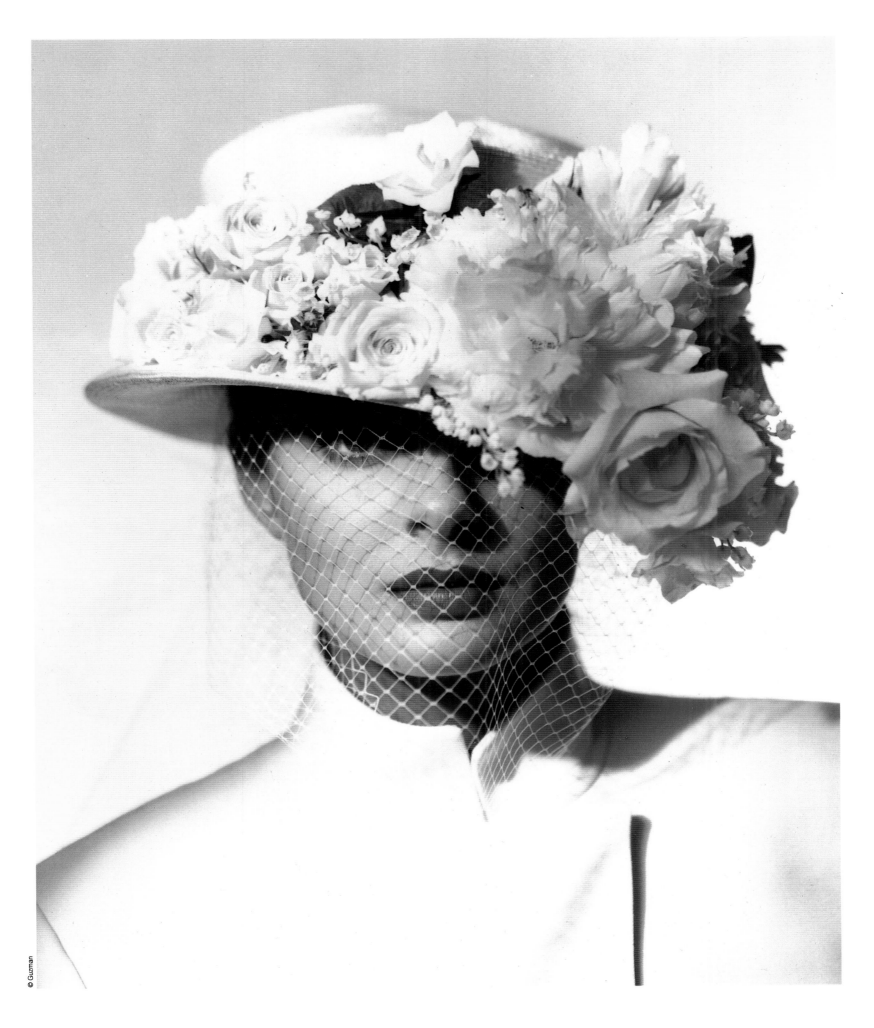

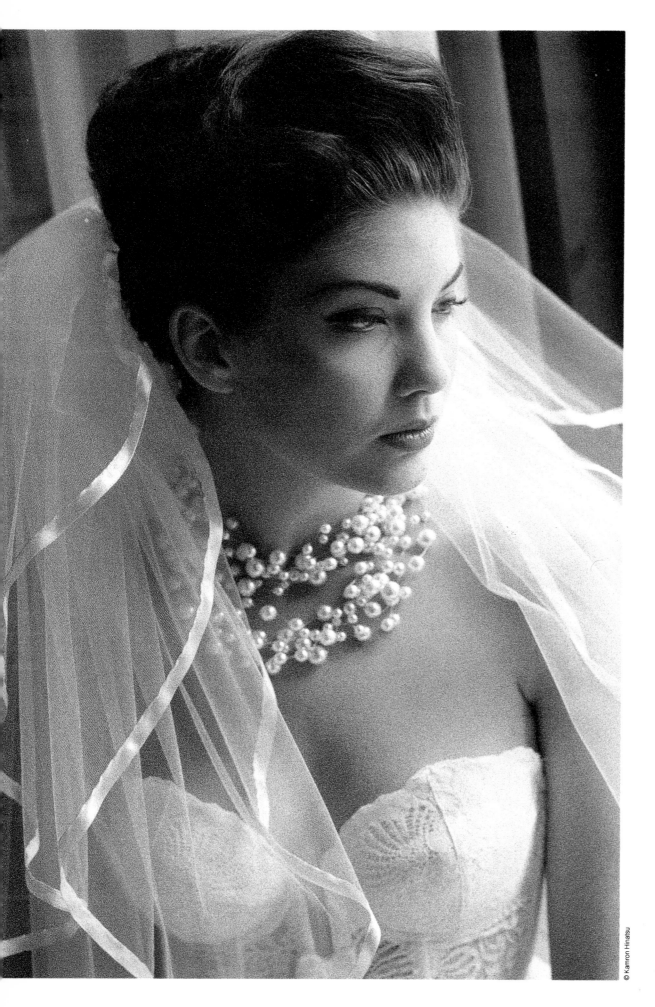

© Kamron Hinatsu

THE BEST FOUNDATIONS

Under all the layers of lace and tulle there are important underpinnings that improve the fit and silhouette of every wedding gown. In addition to its utilitarian advantages, bridal lingerie is also the foundation of any wedding-day fantasies. Functionality and allure are perfectly wed in frilly bustiers and petticoats. Bridal lingerie should be chosen first for comfort—it is worn close to the body all day, and pinching is a most unpleasant sensation—and secondly, for its effectiveness—the style of your wedding gown will dictate your choices, as will your figure needs. Finally, lingerie should be chosen for its beauty—even bras built for maximum support can be very pretty.

Virtually every traditional gown needs the support of a petticoat. Some designers, including Richard Glasgow, are so conscientious about the structure and shape of their wedding gowns that they prefer to build all the necessary petticoats into their dresses. Thus, there is no guessing game about which fullness is just right and no forgetting to add an important layer. Petticoats are designed to match the standard bridal gown silhouettes —they come in ball-gown shape, A-line, princess-line, tiered, basque-waisted, and hooped—every gown looks better with a little lift from underneath. Gowns cut from heavy fabrics like satin will benefit from slightly fuller and stiffer petticoats. Always experiment with more than one petticoat shape—some even have wide elastic waists for a smoother fit—and always try the fullest petticoat available before you start your fittings, because most gowns look best with extra fullness. You'll need to wear the same petticoat for every fitting, as the underlayers influence the fit of your gown. Your fitter

should also closely inspect the length of the petticoat you choose; unless it is designed to show, you'll want the petticoat hemmed two or three inches shorter than your gown. A less traditional gown shape—sheath, cocktail dress, chemise—may need only a simple slip. With heirloom and vintage gowns, you'll frequently find that the linings have disintegrated. If the gown is simple, such as a

elongated bra also creates a smooth, well-shaped, fluid line under a bridal gown. Fitters can also augment the bust line with pads, if necessary. Some bras are designed with extra padding or have hidden pockets to slide in just a bit more, and padding can even be sewn into some gowns.

Since medieval times, the garter toss has been a popular, festive element of many weddings. Garters, which were actually silk sashes tied below the bride's knees, were loosened and torn off by guests— supposedly to hasten the couple's consummation. "When bed-time is came, the bride-men pull off the bride's garters, which she had before unty'd that they might hang down and so prevent a curious hand from coming too near her knee. This done, and the garters being fastened to the hats of the gallants, the bridesmaids carry the bride into the bride-chamber, where they undress her and lay her in the bed," observed French writer Henri Misson in 1698. Garters were usually blue, the color associated with the Virgin Mary. Today the garter is frequently "something blue," but it is often worn at the sexier height of mid-thigh and, like its counterpart, the

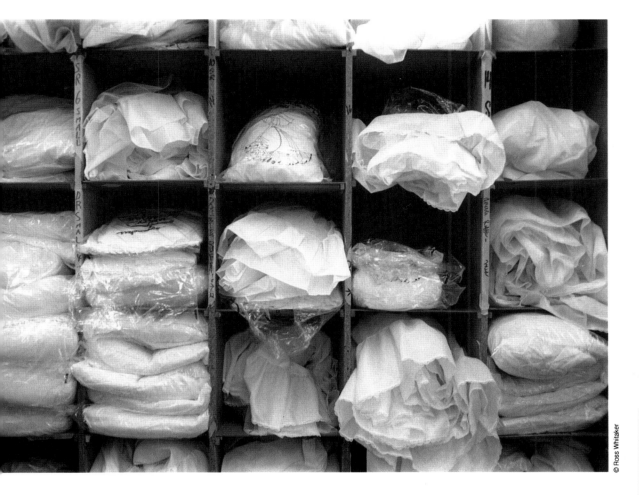

© Ross Whitaker

Essential, graceful deportment relies on a solid foundation. **OPPOSITE PAGE:** *The right underpinnings may include a sensual yet supportive strapless bra.* **ABOVE AND RIGHT:** *The proper petticoat will enhance your figure and your dress.*

princess-line lace dress from the Edwardian era, consider wearing a beautifully made slip in lieu of a lining.

Most women, even those with the best figures, look better with the right bra under their gown. The lift and shape even the simplest bra adds is significant, and as any lingerie fanatic can tell you, wearing the right finery provides a sensual thrill. Longline corsets—with vertical boning to prevent rolling —are proven shape enhancers. Besides a bra's fundamental effect on the bust line, the

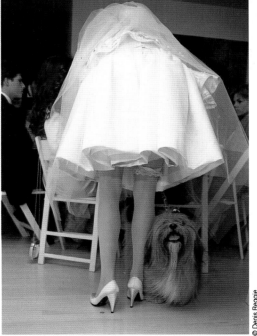

© Denis Reggie

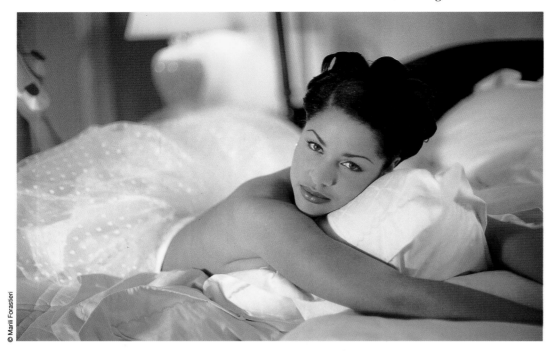

ALL THE EXTRAS

In days of yore, royal brides typically adorned themselves with every important jewel they owned. Many brides of Middle Eastern and Asian cultures would do the same, in effect wearing their dowry. Today, however, less is considered best. "A bride's desire to accessorize gains momentum with every fitting—when the bride first arrives she's even afraid of bridal veils—by the end, she wants everything," notes Vera Wang. "To me, it's equally important to style the bride as well as sell her the right dress." Although there are a lot of jewelry choices, not every dress needs jewelry. The busier the dress, the more understated or even nonexistent the jewelry should be. Beaded, ornate bodices are bejeweled spectacles in themselves and need no further ornamentation. Even off-the-shoulder gowns can be spared a necklace, as the clean neckline only accentuates the beautiful cut of the gown. If a headpiece is worn close to the face, chances are earrings can be eliminated or be merely delicate, simple pearl studs. The object is not to wear jewelry, the object is to present a beautifully coordinated bridal image. Bring a variety of jewelry options to your fitting, because not all bridal salons carry jewelry. Pearls are natural favorites for brides, and they come in a variety of lengths, sizes, and colors. Great costume options are pink or gold chunky faux pearls, and a double- or triple-strand choker is a wonderful modern alternative. Make a decision: either important earrings or an important necklace, but not both. Chances are, if

bouquet, it is definitely a prize catch of the wedding day. Make it even more symbolic by having one specially made using lace from your dress or embroidered with your initials and wedding date.

Every bride who marries in a traditional gown should wear hosiery, even on the warmest days of the year. Unless you're marrying barefoot on the beach, tradition demands that you adhere to all the right finishing touches. If you're to be married on an extremely hot day, consider stockings and garters (cooler than pantyhose). A hooped petticoat is an option that frees your legs from all the clingy, hot layers of crinoline under your skirt. If your gown is long, sheer hoisery is best, since there are already so many different fashion elements at work in your ensemble. Control line hosiery smooths the body and provides the sleekest line under your gown. Most short gowns are also best accessorized with sheer hose, which make the legs look leaner without distracting patterns and lets the attention stay where it belongs—on you. Always buy two or three pairs of hosiery as insurance for your wedding day; you may ruin a pair while dressing. Some consultants recommend that their most nervous clients stock five pairs of

hose for the wedding day. And if you're dressing somewhere other than the reception space, make sure there is an extra pair on hand until the end of the reception.

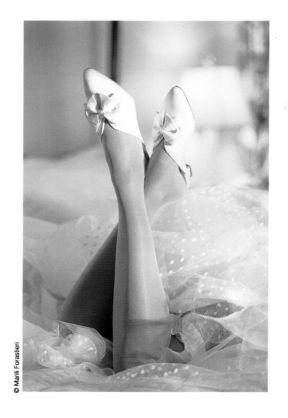

*Exquisite embellishments are expected bridal regalia—the majesty of the wedding event demands a special flourish. Subtle touches—a dotted tulle petticoat (**ABOVE LEFT**, Cross & Spellan), a bowed shoe and a satin garter (**ABOVE**), and opalescent pearls (**OPPOSITE PAGE**)—are the elegant mode.*

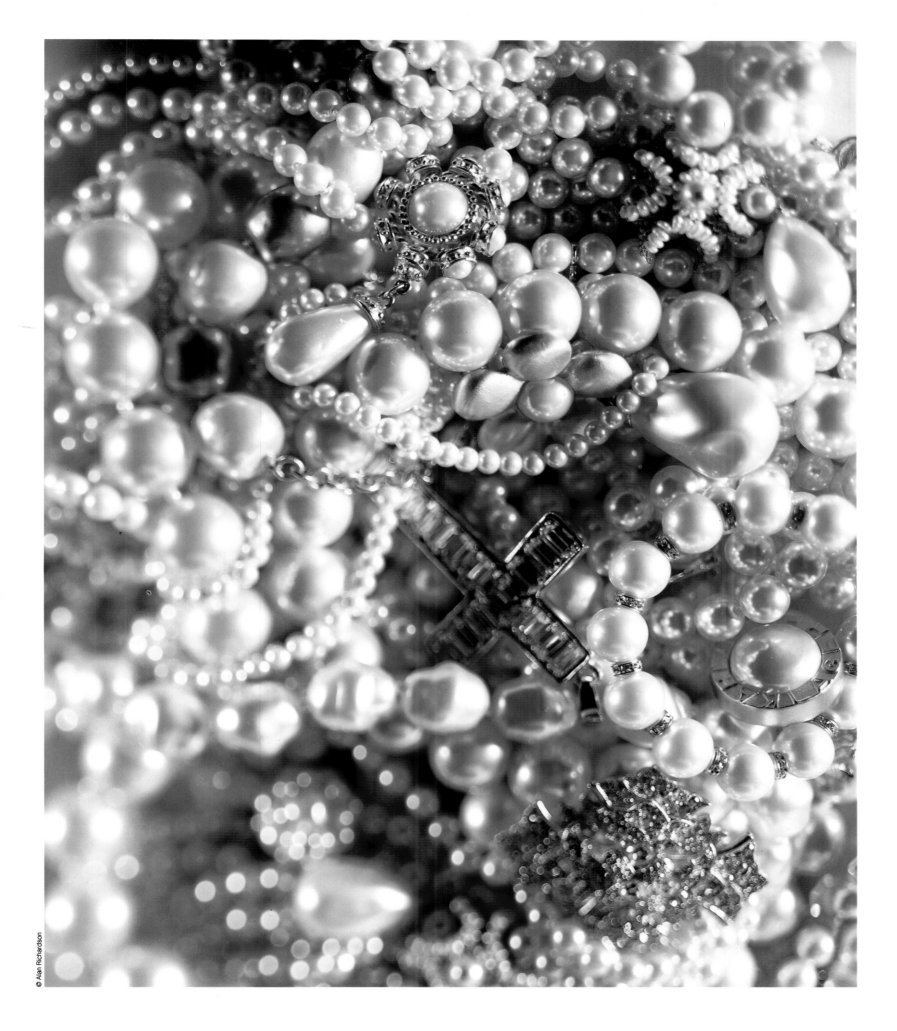

141

glove along the seam of your ring finger; at
the right time, pull the single finger out of

considered the foot a powerful fertility symbol, and thus shoes were often tossed after

may feel glamorous, when they are worn under all the layers of a bridal gown there is tremendous potential for tripping, not to mention the fact that feet and legs tire more easily in high heels. In addition, if you're celebrating outdoors, thin heels stick easily in the earth. Bridal shoes should be made of silk or satin; these fabrics may not be as lucky as leather, but to wear leather shoes is definitely an error in styling—they cheapen the finished look of the bride. Closed-toe shoes are the most elegant option for every bride—save the sandals for casual affairs. Consider sling-back pumps or an elegant side vent if you prefer an open shoe. Comfortable, affordable satin shoes are easy to find and they are dyeable to match the exact hue of your gown. Your salon may even sell shoes; if not, they will know where to find them.

Many wonderful, premier shoemakers specialize in fabulous bridal shoes featuring bows, beads, silk flowers, interesting heels, or silk ribbons to tie at the ankle. For choosing shoes, the busy dress/simple accessory theory is a helpful rule of thumb. For the many bridal gowns that are finished with

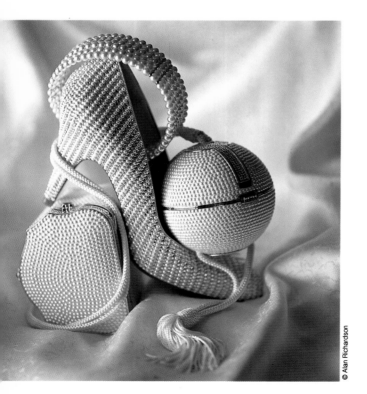

very plain skirts, a wonderfully decorated shoe peeking from under the hem is a beautiful touch. Be sure to break in wedding shoes on clean, dry floors, because you don't want street scuffs or dirt on the toe. Seasoned bridal consultants insist that the bottom of a new shoe be abraded to prevent slipping—marble floors are especially treacherous. Use fine sandpaper to abrade the entire sole, taking care not to damage the fabric. It is not unusual for a bride to stand most of her wedding day, so consider keeping a pair of ballet slippers handy for long receptions.

Since the beginning of time, brides have married with flowers. Ancient brides wore herbal and floral wreaths to protect them from evil spirits and for good luck. Medieval brides always wore garlands of blossoms and myrtle—in their loose, flowing hair. Tudor brides carried gilt rosemary for remembrance. The Victorians coined the language of flowers, using posies to speak their love. The orange blossom, an ancient symbol of beauty and fertility—it is one of the few plants that blossoms and bears fruit at the same time—was the traditional Victorian bridal emblem. Orange blossom often garlanded the bride from head to toe and was immensely popular for over one hundred years, even though it had its detractors. "Custom and romance have raised the chaplet of the orange blossom to unmerited respect. The white of the orange flower is an impure white, and the symbolism of the plant is a reason why some other flower should be adopted," chastised the virtuous-minded author of *Brides and Bridals* in 1872.

Most modern brides opt to carry a bouquet. It is appropriate and wonderful to adorn your body with blossoms, too, as did Victorian and ancient Greek brides. Every season introduces a wonderful new palette of fragrant blooms, and a bride's imagination is her only limitation in using them. In

spring, the gardens are profuse with delicate but colorful blossoms: carry a posy of lily of the valley, a quintessential bridal flower, edged with delicate variegated ivy. Consider holding a clutch of colorful pansies tied with

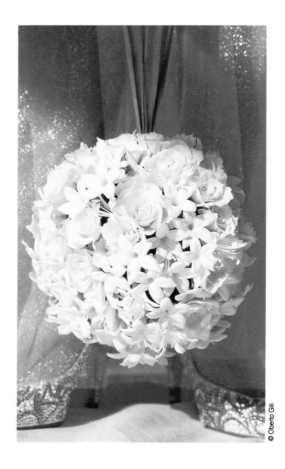

Significant elements of your bridal ensemble— flowers, shoes, jewelry, and headpieces—are all wonderful opportunities to personalize your wedding. **ABOVE:** *A pomander of fragrant buds is a beautiful alternative to a bouquet.* **LEFT:** *An array of pearl-studded extras—a choker, a shoe, and handbags.* **OPPOSITE PAGE:** *Exquisite shoes bedecked with beads, bows, and faux jewels provide the perfect finishing touch.*

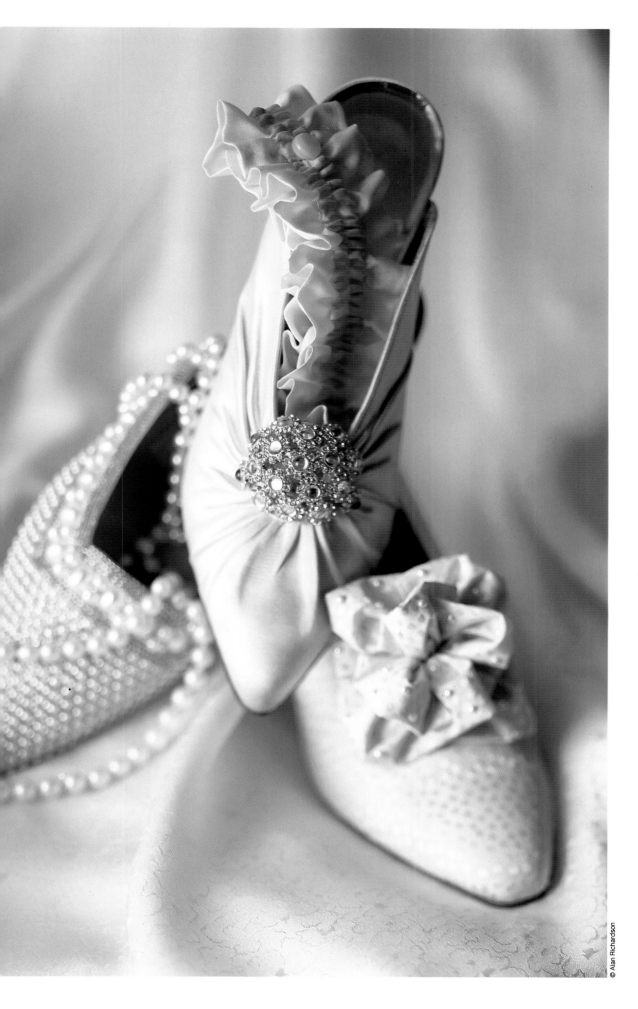

© Alan Richardson

a bright satin ribbon, or wear a necklace of tiny roses, sweet peas, and hyacinth. In summer, wildflowers and hearty cultured roses and lilies proliferate. A perfumy pomander—a round ball of blooms suspended from a satin ribbon—of mixed old-fashioned roses is an unusual but lovely bridal bouquet. A straw hat with flowers brimming over the crown or a rough-hewn basket overflowing with a colorful riot of the freshest larkspurs, zinnias, hydrangea, blue lace, astilbe, and cosmos are perfect for garden weddings. For fall, a lively mix of variegated dianthus—tiny carnations—with a gingham bow keeps summer in mind. Or consider carrying an autumn harvest of fresh wheat and roses or an abundant, airy mass of baby's breath. Adorn the toes of your shoes with bows and tiny serena roses, which are very easy to glue on and dry well for a memorable keepsake. For winter, white stephanotis ringed with gilded ivy and a gilt ribbon is a classic holiday combination or carry red roses tied with a festive red-and-green plaid ribbon. Another idea is to hold a muff covered with red or white carnations.

Whatever the look, bridal bouquets should always be manageable. Round nosegays are a versatile, easy-to-carry shape that looks great with every gown. In addition, virtually any flower looks great in a nosegay. If the bouquet gets very large—Lady Diana's is a good example—you'll struggle to make it down the aisle with a smile. The bouquet, like jewelry, gloves, and veil, is an accessory and should balance and coordinate with your overall look. It should not overpower nor should it be overwhelming to hold; instead, it should be a glorious offering of nature, beautiful yet understated. Generally, bigger gowns can be complemented by lusher, more profuse nosegays, while sheaths and short dresses look best with nosegays of a smaller scale.

THE WEDDING DAY

After months and months of hectic planning it is time to finally say "I do." The benefit of thorough planning is the freedom to indulge in the significance and pleasure of your wedding day without worrying about mundane details. The prelude to your wedding consists of an inordinate focus on its mechanics and style, all for a single purpose: to create a happy memory. On this delightful day, an ancient and lovely ceremony, a simple exchange of words, which is also a profound promise, is reenacted. The triumphant beauty of a couple in love is a wonderfully concrete manifestation of the magic of life. A warm reunion of friends and family to honor and witness this solemn pledge between two people is a celebration of the most precious bonds of humanity. Despite all your efforts to design the perfect wedding, the emotional elements are what you'll savor most; these truly important moments should never be overpowered by last-minute fussing or obscured by the haze of exhaustion. The best way to ensure that you have the luxurious peace of mind to truly enjoy yourself is to let your planning and practice work for you, have confidence in your choices, and keep everything as simple as possible.

The last few weeks before your wedding should be well used. This is the time to hone in on the finishing details, so there will be nothing to do but get dressed on your wedding day. By your final fitting you'll have a dress you love that fits perfectly and flatters every curve. You will also have a finished

headpiece and have had an opportunity to take it to your hair salon for practice sessions. Many salons offer bridal packages that include a cut and styling, a headpiece consultation, and a visit with your hair stylist on your wedding day. Your hair should be cut two weeks to one month before your wedding—you'll want to give your hair a chance to settle, to feel natural rather than newly shorn. Consult with your hair stylist about your wedding style now to avoid surprises

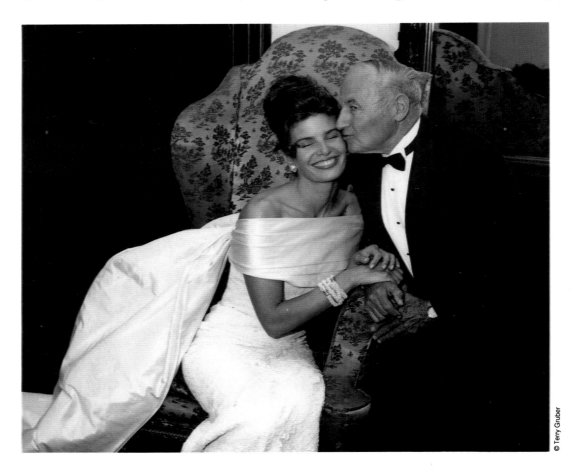

on the wedding day. Treat your hair to deep-conditioning treatments the week before your wedding, because stress affects your hair, too. By your final fitting you should also have a good idea of your makeup plans. If you're nervous about doing it yourself, hire a makeup artist who will do a practice session with you before the wedding, and come in on your wedding day—this is a wonderful splurge that pays off with picture-perfect makeup. By your final fitting you should have

decided on the jewelry you'll wear and have selected your bridal shoes and your lingerie. Unless your bridal salon is out of town, there's no need to pick up your bridal gown more than a week before your wedding. All final plans for your reception and honeymoon should be resolved by the last week.

Many brides (and their mothers) are working women with little time available for making major wedding plans, but even the simplest wedding is a lot of work. Wedding

The grand event of a lifetime, your wedding day is a momentous occasion that requires an outfit you love. **ABOVE:** *A lacy sheath and luxurious taffeta stole by Badgley-Mischka.* **OPPOSITE PAGE:** *A pearl-studded bodice atop a floating organza skirt by Ulla-Maija.*

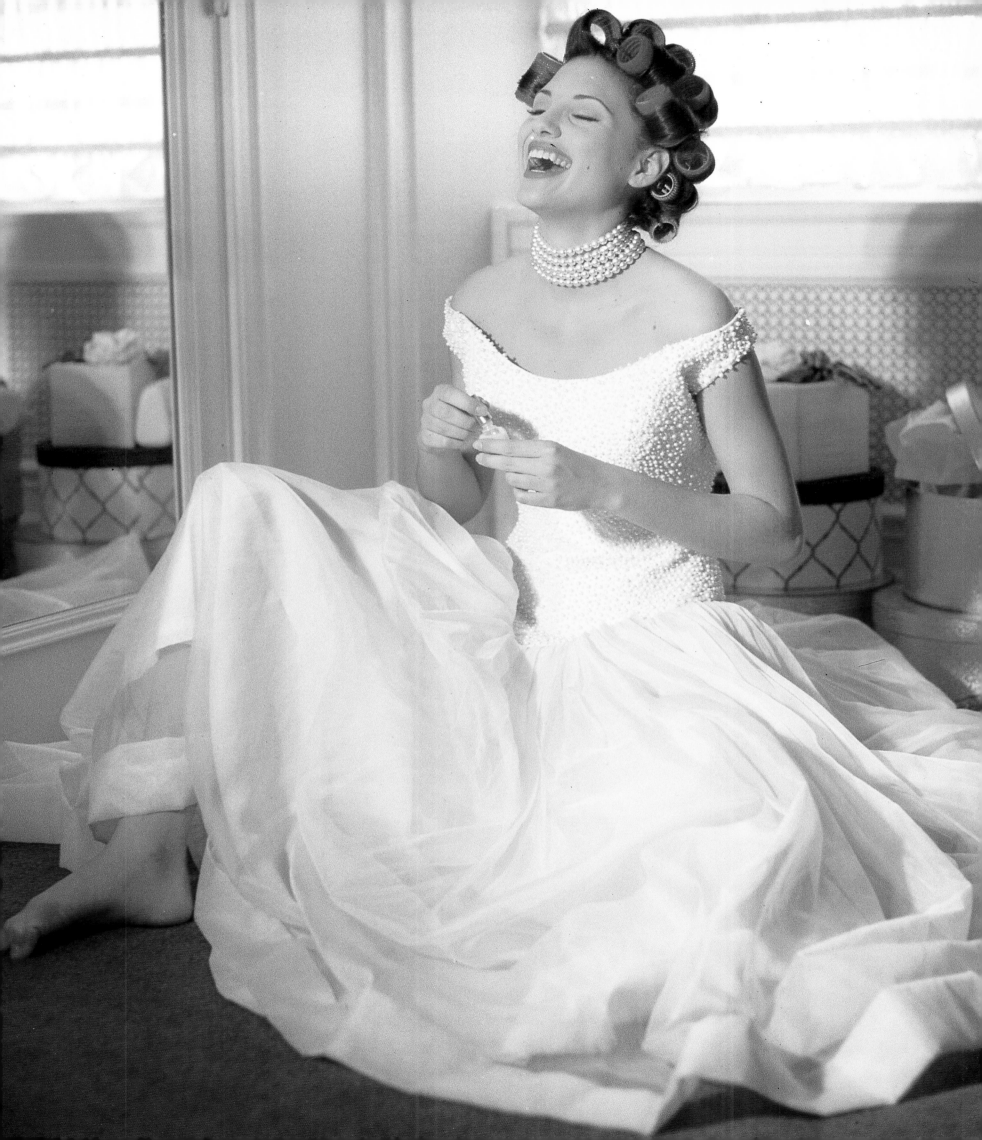

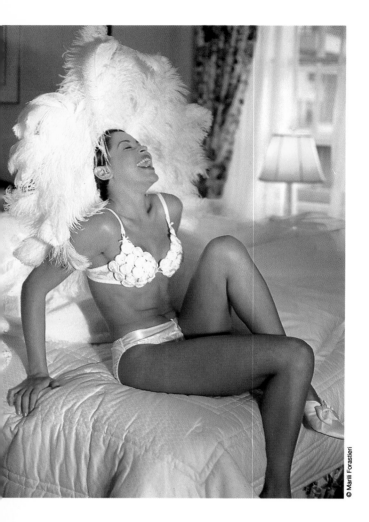

stocked with emergency supplies for you and your guests.

The day before your wedding, you should inspect your gown. If you're dressing at home, you should have already removed the gown from its bag according to your salon's instructions. If you're dressing in a different location, try to take your gown, as early as possible, to the wedding site and remove the gown from the bag to hang free. For protection, always place a clean sheet under the skirt. The skirt won't be bustled when the salon packs it; rather, it will be hung over a separate hanger and stuffed with tissue. Never crush the garment bag while you carry it; instead, hold it aloft by the handle of the hanger. Don't stuff it in a trunk, and do treat it gently to minimize wrinkling. If there are any wrinkles, when the dress is hung out properly the weight of the fabric should pull them out. At your last fitting you should ask for emergency instructions in case you do need to press the gown. Usually it is the skirt, if anything, that needs a touch-up. If you gown is silk, always use a dry iron, because any water drops will spot the dress. Gently iron the wrinkled spots only, either with a pressing mitt while your gown hangs or on an ironing board set up in the middle of the room over a clean sheet. It is best to leave your dress on the hanger and have someone help: one person can iron gently while the other person holds and rotates the gown. Take your time, use a moderate heat and quick, gentle pressing movements. Never rest the iron near the gown, as it may fall and scorch your skirt. If your veil needs a bit of pressing, remove it from the headpiece and hang it in a steamy bathroom. Don't worry too much about tiny pressing imperfections, because once you have the dress on you probably won't even notice them. Check any bows on the dress, if they've flattened, restuff the tissue in the bows. Flowers may need a

little pouffing, too—ask your salon for tips—but in general, gentle fiddling with the petals should do the trick.

The day before your wedding you should pack for your honeymoon and make sure everything is ready for your wedding day: do you have enough stockings, white bobby pins, tissues, waterproof mascara, and powder? Take time to indulge yourself; it will help you relax. Schedule a manicure—opt for classic, sheer pink or beige enamel; no distracting, garish colors for your hands, please—and a pedicure. Treat yourself to a massage, take a nap, enjoy a stroll through your old neighborhood, soak in a tub before bed. You can never be too relaxed on your wedding day, so plan ahead to feel relaxed and rested.

On your wedding day, be sure to eat, make it light and healthy, nothing too heavy but something that gives you energy for hours—

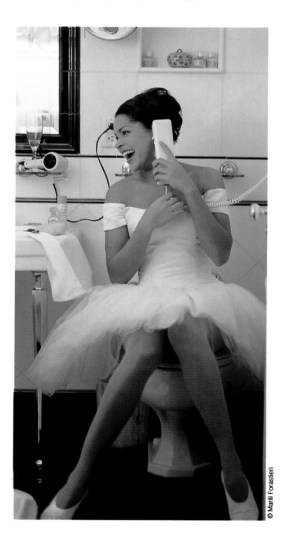

or bridal consulting is a long-standing business with a tradition of assisting the affluent and social-minded for decades. Today, however, a wedding consultant is no longer exclusively for the rich and famous, but a viable option for every busy woman. Advice abounds for engagement stress management, but the best solution may be to hire a consultant. A good consultant has the experience to foresee any problems—this is a professional, who sees the reality and is not blinded by the glamour—and will manage every detail according to your specifications, from making appointments for you with the best fitter at a respected bridal salon to ordering invitations, selecting a menu, finding the right location, attending your last fitting so that she knows exactly how everything fits and works, and above all, keeping you untroubled on your wedding day. She will even put together valuable bathroom baskets you don't want to pass out with your first sip of champagne. Before you dress, have your hair and makeup done. Stick to your plans. Unless you have very fine, straight hair or a short geometric cut, wear your hair up or back; sweeping back your hair will expose your face and keep you picture perfect. Not only will the finished result look special and elegant, but it is trouble free, whereas hair worn down needs frequent rebrushing to keep it looking good. Pin up your hair securely and use hair spray.

After your hair is finished—you should wait to attach your headpiece until you're dressed—apply your makeup. Use a foundation that is perfectly blended to your skin tone. Always use powder to set your makeup and eliminate shine. Powdering will also help keep makeup from smudging. If you're wearing a dress that exposes your neckline and chest, use a perfectly matched dual-finish (available in compacts, they go on wet and dry) foundation powder. This will give a natural, barely covered finish that's just right and not too heavy for this delicate chest and neck area. Avoid bright eye shadow and lipstick colors, as they will date quickly and years from your wedding day you'll regret the mistake. Stick to flattering soft tones—well-blended browns and taupes are universally flattering and classic. Darker skins can manager a more colorful palette around the eye, but be sure to opt for smoky, not garish, shades. Consider wearing waterproof mascara on your wedding day. If not, apply mascara only to the upper lashes to avoid smudges and streaks later.

If you can, apply your lip color after you dress. For more lasting lip color, start with a lip pencil. Choose a color that perfectly matches your own lip tone. Use the pencil not just to outline but to completely cover your lips. If your pencil and lips are dry, dip the pencil in a clear lip balm so it moves eas-

ily. Cover the pencil with a coat of lipstick, blot, dust with very sheer powder and apply a final coat. Use matte lipstick, because glossy tends to slide off the lips. If you're marrying during the day, apply your makeup in natural, not fluorescent light, so you can see how you'll really look. If you're marrying at night, go a shade darker with eye shadows to create drama and check your makeup under low lights. Never go too dark with your makeup, because photographs never lie—they'll capture your raccoon eyes and blush racing-stripes forever.

When it is finally time to don your wedding gown—garters and shoes should already be on—make dressing a delicate procedure. Always dress in a clean room and in an open space, with plenty of room for your full skirt. If necessary, place another sheet on the floor where you will dress. Most wedding gowns are easy to put on and can be gotten into with only a little help. Every salon consultant has a favorite method for getting dressed, but the fashion editors of *Brides & Your New Home* magazine, who have dressed more picture-perfect brides over the years than anyone else, recommend stepping into your gown. The dress will wrinkle less and you won't smudge your makeup on your dress or muss your hair. Unzip your wedding gown all the way (it should have a very long zipper to make it easy to slide your hips inside). Before you step into the dress, insert your petticoat into and under the dress. Make sure the back of the skirt and the petticoat are properly aligned. Have someone hold up the front of the wedding gown at the waistline, letting the bodice fall forward, and clasp the petticoat and gown in the same handful. Hold on to someone's arm and gingerly step into the gown, one leg at a time. Don't play beat the clock, the wedding won't go on without you. Find the floor with your first foot before you swing in your other leg.

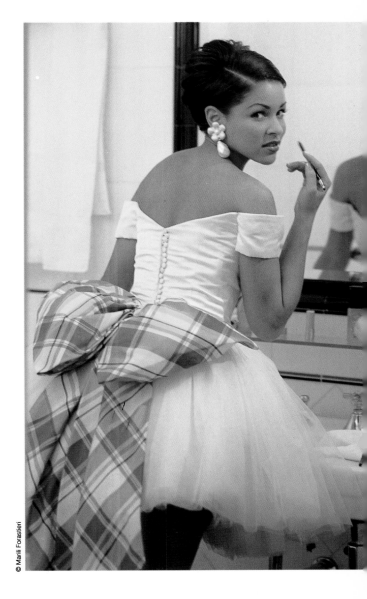

© Marili Forastieri

OPPOSITE PAGE, LEFT: *Silk roses make for whimsical yet sensual lingerie, worn with an ostrich-feather picture hat.* **OPPOSITE PAGE, RIGHT** *and* **THIS PAGE, ABOVE:** *A jaunty satin minidress with a multihued taffeta bow, by Vera Wang.*

Hold up the wedding gown at the waistline while someone fastens your petticoat, then pull on your bodice. Since your dress is so perfectly fitted, it often helps to cinch your waist with your hands while the dress is being zipped through your waistline. If necessary, get another friend to help cinch. Fasten every button and close every snap. Make sure that your neckline fits smoothly, that your bodice is well aligned, that every button is buttoned into its own loop, and your petticoats are fluffed out. If you opt to pull your wedding gown over your head, use a scarf to cover your face while you are dressing to avoid getting any makeup on your gown.

Once your dress is secure, it is time to don the headpiece. Either stand or sit on a stool (but not on your skirt, pull your gown over the stool, concealing it). An extra pair of hands is especially important now. A supply of white bobby pins will come in handy as you anchor the headpiece in your hair. You may need to use a handful of pins, and if they are white you won't notice them on the headpiece. Insert the pins through the tiny loops that are usually found near the comb. Always slide the hair combs against the grain of your hair for a more secure fit. Once you are dressed, many photographers ask to snap a photo of the bride and groom together before the hectic moments of the wedding. If you are a sentimental woman at heart, it is better to wait—preserve that great moment when your groom sees you for the very first time at the end of the aisle as his bride. Even if there are a thousand guests, time will stop, and this shared moment will be only yours to remember forever.

An ounce of prevention is the best remedy for anything. A thoughtful bridesmaid or professional consultant should always prepare an emergency kit to keep on hand, just in case. It is not unusual for a bride to put a hole in her tulle skirt while dressing or for the train to catch on something and tear. Buttons, snaps, beads, and even flowers or bows can come loose. Your emergency kit should include plenty of thread to match your gown and those of everyone in the bridal party, small and large safety pins, scissors (to snip loose threads), clear nail polish for runs, white or off-white chalk to cover smudges, cleaning fluid, extra loose flowers to match your dress (to cover a spot or tear), extra panty hose, nail glue, bandages, painkillers, mouthwash, smelling salts, hand lotion, deodorant, and hair spray. If you don't need any of these things, fine, but if you do, you'll thank God and whoever was smart enough to remember just what you needed.

Before your ceremony, remember to move carefully, get in and out of the car slowly, and try not to sit on the back of your gown—pull

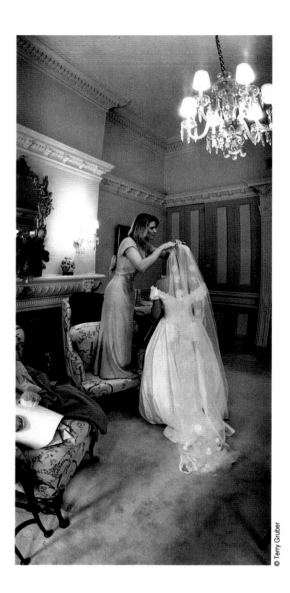

Enlist the services of loved ones, make sure every button is fastened and your headpiece is secure. **LEFT AND ABOVE:** *Richard Glasgow's lace-embroidered shantung silk gown with an off-the-shoulder neckline.* **OPPOSITE PAGE:** *A simple but full taffeta skirt contrasts elegantly with a shirred bodice by Robert Legere for The Diamond Collection.*

it up behind you in the car and sit forward. Don't crunch your gown when you lift it, you can avoid unnecessary wrinkles by holding the skirt softly—no clenched fists full of fabric. If you get a grease or mud spot, conceal it with a smudge of chalk. If your gown tears, sew it up, trying to conceal the stitches near a seam or in the lace. Alternatively, cover a tear with silk flowers. If in the unlikely event you incur a major tear in your train, wear it bustled or remove it completely. Tiny tears in a tulle skirt are often unnoticeable or easily hidden with small stitches. If you use safety pins, hide them under the skirt or bodice— don't let them show. Avoid beverages that stain, like red wine and coffee—drink champagne instead. If necessary, sprinkle salt immediately on a red-wine spot to neutralize it, then blot. Small spots may be concealed with chalk or flowers, but there's no recourse for major spills but camouflage. If it is on the bodice, use your veil as a stole, if it is on your skirt, fashion an apron of tulle or cleverly pick up half your skirt into a swag. Try to keep smiling—things happen and this is not the end of the world.

As you stand at the top of the aisle after spending a day dressing and months preparing, remember a bit of advice your mother always offered: Stand up straight. Your dress will look better, your figure will look better, and your pictures will look better if you pay attention to your posture. Hold your shoulders back, your stomach in, and your back straight. Assign someone to fluff your train just before you walk down the aisle using a secure but gentle up-and-down motion at the base of the train, which will guide enough air underneath to fluff it perfectly. Of course, you'll smile all day long, but don't forget to relax your face muscles from time to time, so you won't end the day with a jawache, and remember to breathe normally. Have a great, great time.

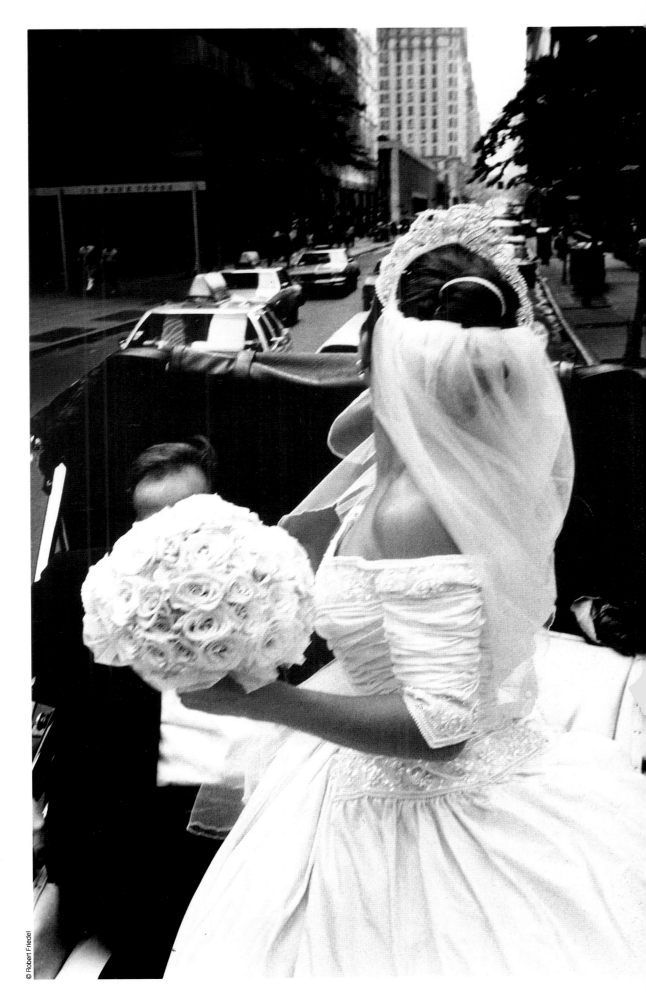

© Robert Friedel

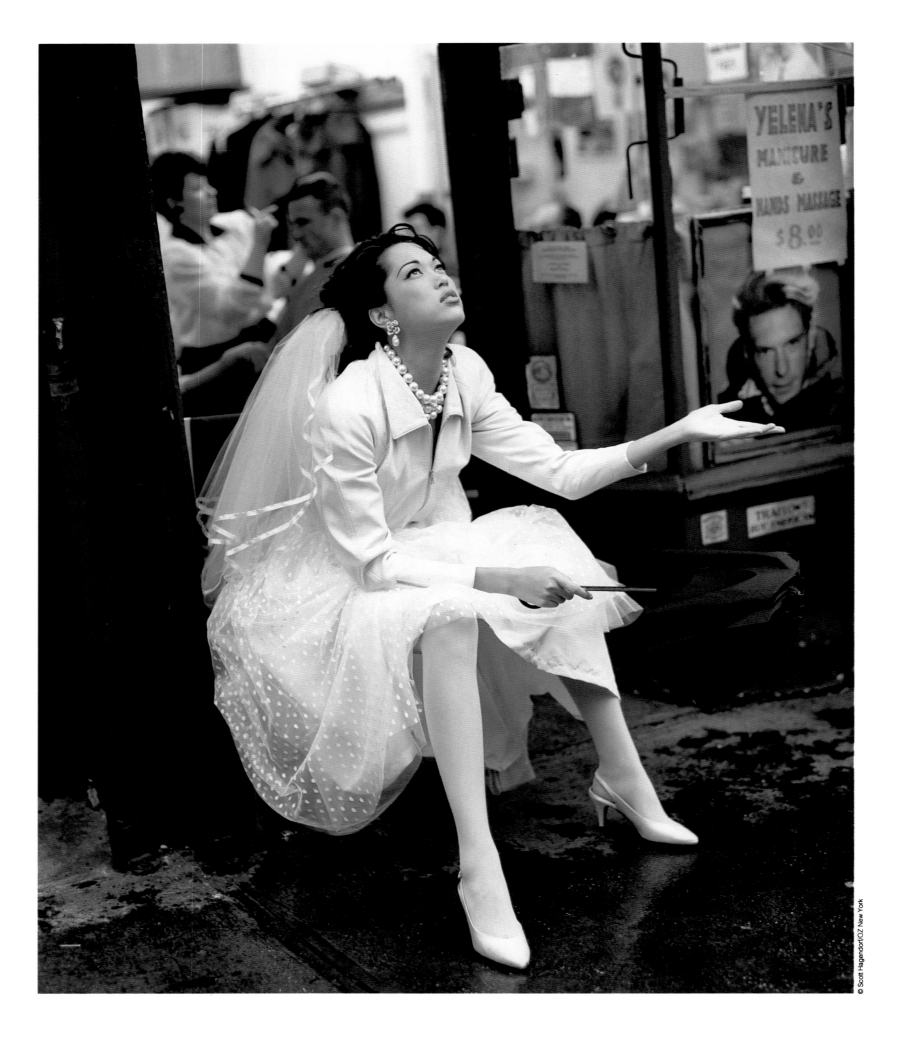

YOUR HEIRLOOM

With the rice and confetti swept away and the honeymoon pictures already returned from the photo lab, what's a newlywed bride to do with a wedding gown now? Whether you decide to rework your gown or save it as an heirloom, you must first have it cleaned. Line up a reputable cleaner before your wedding, because you'll want to send your gown to the cleaners as soon after your wedding as possible. The longer stains sit, the tougher they are to remove. Your dress may look clean, but even a little perspiration is very destructive to fine fabrics, and some stains don't become visible until they age. Your bridal salon should be able to refer you to a reputable cleaner. The local dry cleaners' association and better dress boutiques or restoration specialists should also be able to provide you with the name of a good cleaner. Before you choose a cleaner, inquire about their cleaning and storage procedures. The best cleaners will use clean fluids and launder your gown individually. If your gown is very ornate, choose a hand-laundry specialist to get the best care of the gown you love. If your gown is stained, get a second opinion from a cleaner because some stains are best wet-cleaned rather than dry-cleaned. Do not have your gown stored in an airtight box, especially one with a plastic window, even though this has been a popular practice for over thirty years. Plastic windows deteriorate as they age, depositing acidic residues on the dress. If the box is sealed on a humid day, and it seems as though every day is a humid one at the dry cleaners, moisture can be trapped inside the box. The mildew that will eventually develop will attack the fibers of the gown. Some stains take months to develop, and if your gown is sealed away you'll never notice the destruction at work. Also, natural fibers need to breathe, and sealing the box is counterproductive. One sad bride shares a precautionary horror story: Her cleaner hermetically sealed the gown in a box with no window. Two years later, when

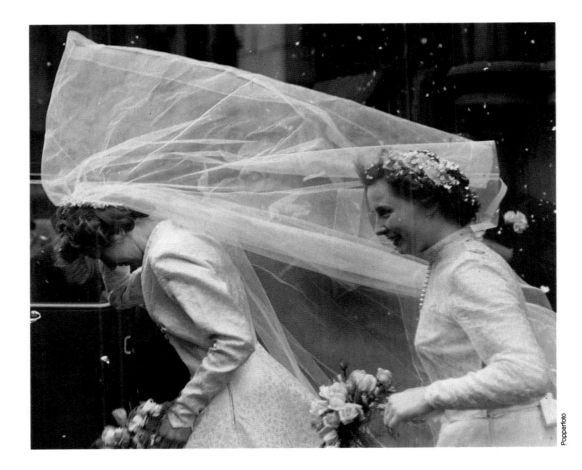

she opened the box, she found it was the wrong dress.

Textile specialists agree, the best protection for any gown is to store it unsealed in a dry, dark, temperate environment, and to periodically remove, shake out, and examine it. Some suggest storing the gown in an acid-free box lined with acid-free tissue—use the tissue to stuff the dress and soften any folds—then simply slide it under the bed. Others recommend hanging the gown—this method allows the dress to oxidize or age evenly. Use a wood hanger and hang the dress by its straps, which can absorb the weight of the dress better than the delicate shoulder fabric. Proponents of hermetically sealed boxes suggest that sealing prevents oxidization, but this is simply not true. Cover the dress with a cotton muslin bag—you can make it yourself with four yards of muslin, washed first to shrink—to keep the dust off the gown, and store it in a dry closet. Dust is

OPPOSITE PAGE *and* **ABOVE:** *Exuberant guests or miserable weather can damage the fine fabrics of your wedding dress, like this jacket from North Beach Leather and Cross & Spellan skirt. Plan ahead: leave instructions for your gown to be delivered to a reliable cleaner.*

not as inert as it looks, and it is microscopically destructive to natural fibers. If your dress is cotton or linen—very sturdy fibers—you can even store it in a cotton pillowcase. Just let the dress gently collapse into a soft pile before placing it in the case. Soft folds, rather than sharp creases, are better for the life of the gown.

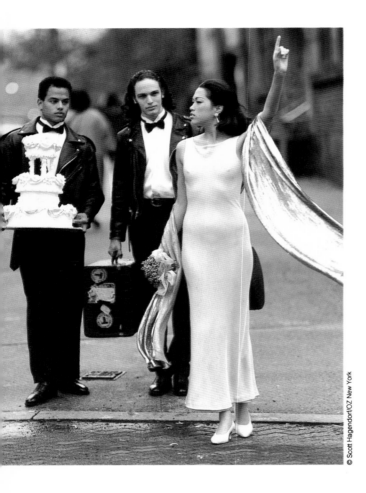

Consider rewearing your wedding gown if it has modern lines and is minimally adorned. **ABOVE:** *Normal Kamali's slinky jersey sheath with a stole of platinum sequins.* **RIGHT:** *Badgley Mischka's lace sheath could be shortened for future wear.* **OPPOSITE PAGE:** *Simply remove the flowers and veil from Richard Glasgow's striped organza pouff.*

If you are more interested in the possibilities of rewearing your gown, it is wise to choose your gown with its future in mind. Unless you choose to marry in a modern, fashionable gown—a lace sheath, a strapless piqué minidress, a big satin skirt with a soft chiffon blouse, or a jersey chemise—it may be impossible to take the bridal out of the gown. Simple, unadorned gowns make the transition best. If you rewear your gown, you'll want it to look just as fabulous in its reincarnation as it did on your wedding day—you don't want to seem like a Miss Havisham who doesn't realize the wedding is over. Many wedding dresses will always look like wedding dresses—your dress may just look like a different wedding gown after a reworking. If you're serious about reworking the gown, take it to a reliable seamstress. Consider shortening the gown, removing the sleeves, opening the neckline, making it strapless, and adding a bright or plaid sash. The best reworking will require that a pair of shears attack the gown somewhere. Dyeing the gown is not recommended, as your bridal gown is probably made from more than one fabric, plus it is sewn and it may be beaded—every thread, every bead, and every seam will take the dye differently, it will never dye evenly.

Consider reusing your gown, as generations of women have, to dress a child's bassinet. The skirt of a wedding gown becomes the skirt for the bassinet and the veil is its drape. Using your gown in this way makes your real life part of the sentimental tradition of a wedding dress, which is lovingly reused, not hidden and forgotten. Or really enjoy your gown on a daily basis as one bride did: she had an oak showcase built as a permanent display case for her gown, and now it stands in her living room.

After all the "I dos" and celebrations are complete, don't feel compelled to find

another use for your wedding gown. The point of all the painstaking planning, all the rigorous fittings, and the exacting fashion coordination was to be married in a beautiful, personally significant, memorable wedding gown. Your gown has already fulfilled its purpose—it really doesn't need another.

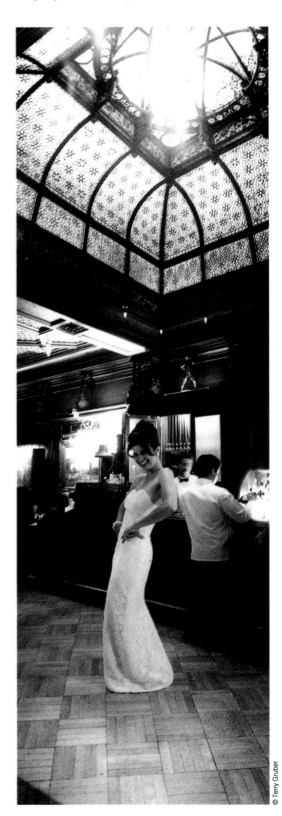

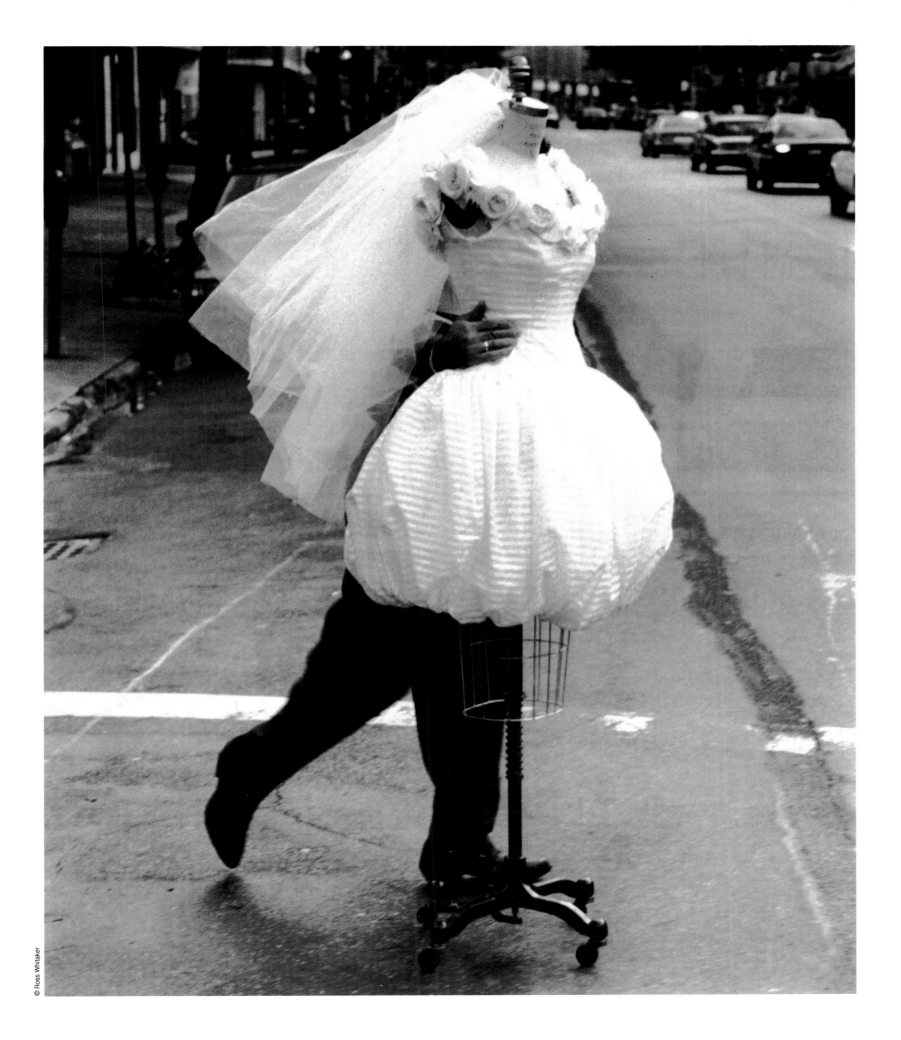

GLOSSARY OF STYLES

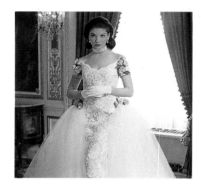

SILHOUETTES

A-line Originated by Christian Dior, skirt flares away from body from under arms to hem; fitted through shoulders. Similar to **princess-line.**

Ball gown Narrow-waisted shape with a full, bell-shaped skirt supported by petticoats or hoops.

Empire High-waisted, with the skirt falling from directly under the bustline.

Princess-line Fitted through shoulders and bodice, skirt flares gently outward; no waistline.

Sheath Svelte, narrow-fitting shape that contours the body; no waistline.

Suit Modern shape finished with a jacket or coat.

LENGTHS

Ballerina Falls to or slightly below the center of the calf.

Floor Most traditional length, rests about an inch from the floor.

Knee Nontraditional length

Mini Above the knee; often chosen by second-time brides.

WAISTLINES

Basque Sits at the natural waistline in the back and dips lower to form a V-shape in the front.

Dropped Falls below the natural waistline in classic flapper style.

Natural Sits at the waist.

NECKLINES

Bateau Shallow curve cut the same in front and back.

Illusion High collar made of a sheer fabric such as net, point d'esprit, or chiffon; appears almost invisible.

Jewel High, rounded neckline with no collar or binding.

Off-the-shoulder Falls just below the shoulder, with a collar or sleeve on the arm.

Portrait Open neckline with a high back, gathered in front above the bustline.

Queen Anne High at nape of neck; sweeps low in front.

Scoop Low, curved sweep extending to the shoulders; may be cut deep in front, back, or both.

Sweetheart Low-cut, resembling the rounded curves of a heart.

V Shaped like a V; cut deep or shallow in front, back, or both.

Wedding band collar High, fitted collar, popular in the 1890s.

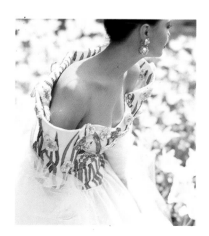

SLEEVES

Bishop Full sleeve gathered into a band at the wrist.

Cap Short sleeve that just covers the top of the arm.

Gigot See **leg o' mutton.**

Juliet Long, fitted sleeve with short puff at the shoulder.

Leg-o'-mutton Wide and rounded at shoulder, fitting snugly on the lower arm; also called **gigot.**

Puff Short, rounded sleeve; gathered at armhole or cuff.

Three-quarter Ends just below the elbow; often finished with small cuff or band.

Wedding point V-shaped extension of a long, fitted sleeve that comes to a point over the bride's hand.

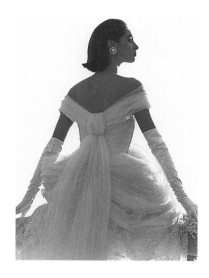

TRAINS

Cathedral Longer than one yard; reserved for the most formal weddings.

Chapel Formal; extends about one yard.

Court Separate piece of fabric that falls from the shoulders.

Detachable Normally attached at back of waist, but may attach to the shoulders or wrap around the waist.

Sweep Just brushes the floor.

Watteau Cascades from the shoulders.

Shapely highlights: **FAR LEFT,** *glamorous sheath under a tulle train skirt;* **CENTER LEFT,** *dazzling off-the-shoulder neckline;* **NEAR LEFT,** *elegant watteau train;* **BELOW,** *regal tiara and veil.*

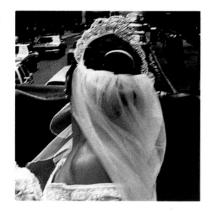

VEILS

Ballet Comes to just an inch above the floor; also called **waltz.**

Bird cage Stiff; covers the face, falls just below the chin.

Blusher Loose, worn forward over the bride's face or lifted back over the headpiece.

Cathedral Falls 3½ yards from the headpiece; ultraformal.

Chapel Falls 2½ yards from the headpiece; formal.

Fingertip Most popular style, reaches to the fingertips; suitable for all but ultraformal gowns.

Flyaway Multiple layers that just brush the shoulders.

Waltz See **ballet.**

HEADPIECES

Floral wreath Worn over the forehead or nestled in the hair.

Juliet cap Fits tightly to crown of head; may be made entirely of pearls or jewels.

Mantilla Lace veil worn surrounding face.

Profile Decorative comb worn on one side of head silhouetting the face.

Tiara Crown that rests on top of the head.

GLOSSARY OF FABRICS

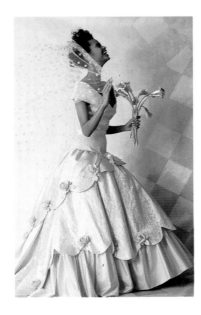

Alençon lace Delicate lace with a pattern of neatly arranged flowers and swags outlined with cord.

Batiste Soft, sheer, lightweight fabric woven in cotton, wool, silk, and rayon.

Battenberg lace Type of lace made by applying Battenberg tape to a design and linking it with decorative stitching.

Bengaline Heavyweight ribbed fabric; may be wool, cotton, rayon, or silk.

Brocade Heavyweight fabric with raised design woven on a Jacquard loom; may be silk, cotton, or synthetic.

Carrickmacross A **guipure lace** made in Scotland with fine needlepoint stitches or appliqué.

Chantilly lace Delicate bobbin lace with hexagonal mesh background and floral designs.

Charmeuse Lightweight, smooth fabric woven from silk, cotton, or rayon, with slight luster.

Chiffon Light, transparent fabric of silk, cotton, rayon, or synthetics.

Crepe charmeuse Pebbly-textured; lays flat and clings.

Crushed velvet **Velvet** with an irregular surface.

Damask Originally silk woven on a Jacquard loom, with high-luster designs on a flat background; now made of cotton, linen, or synthetics.

Dotted Swiss See **point d'esprit.**

Duchesse satin Lightweight, glossy satin-weave fabric; may be silk or rayon.

Dupioni A thicker, coarse, slubby silk weave.

Eyelet Cotton or linen fabric with openwork pattern "punched" out and embroidery worked around each hole.

Faille Thick, ribbed, crisp fabric of silk or silk-rayon. See also **bengaline, gros de Londres.**

Georgette Very sheer, lightweight silk, cotton, or synthetic.

Gros de Londres Fine, flat ribbed silk or rayon; see also **bengaline, faille.**

Guipure lace Heavy tape lace characterized by large motifs with few connecting bars. See also **Carrickmacross.**

Illusion Fine **tulle, maline,** or **net.**

Jacquard Wide variety of patterned dress-weight cloth made on a Jacquard loom; may be silk, rayon, or synthetic.

Lamé Fabric woven with metallic threads; often blended with silk or rayon to appear to be molten silver or gold.

Linen Crisp, lightweight fabric woven from fibers of flax plants.

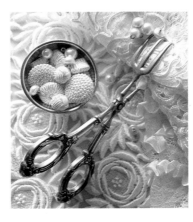

Maline Very fine **net.**

Marquisette Soft, transparent net; virtually weightless.

Matelassé Originally, silk quilted to create a puckered appearance; now made of silk, cotton, rayon, wool, or synthetic fibers.

Moiré Stiff, heavy, ribbed fabric with a pattern that resembles melting jagged stripes; may be silk, rayon, or synthetic.

Net Heavyweight meshlike weave.

Organdy Crisp, sheer, lightweight cloth; can be woven from silk or cotton.

Organza A transparent fabric that is heavier, stiffer, and more formal than chiffon; commonly woven from rayon.

Ottoman Heavy, luxurious, ribbed weave of silk, rayon, cotton, wool, or synthetic fibers.

Paper taffeta Very crisp **taffeta.**

Peau de soie Heavy **satin** woven with fine ribbing, giving it a distinctive dull luster; its name means "skin of silk."

Piqué Honeycomb weave, usually cotton; often used for cuffs and collars.

Point d'esprit Sheer, almost transparent cotton flecked with white dots; also called **dotted Swiss.**

Ribbon lace Modern derivation of Battenberg and Renaissance lace.

Satin Densely woven silk with one lustrous and one matte side. Also made from rayon and synthetics.

Schiffli Allover embroidery design with running stitches instead of knots.

Shantung Plain-weave silk or synthetic fabric with rough, randomly nubby texture, produced by weaving uneven fibers together.

Silk-faced satin See **duchesse satin.**

Taffeta Crisp, lightweight fabric with a smooth finish, made in silk, cotton, rayon, and synthetics.

Tissue taffeta Thin, almost transparent taffeta.

Tulle Sheer meshlike weave with hexagonal holes; made of silk, nylon, or rayon. Also called **illusion, maline,** or **net.**

Velvet Originally silk, now also of rayon or cotton, double-woven with a short, thick pile; plush and soft to the touch.

Velveteen Cotton or rayon velvet; single woven.

Venise lace Needlepoint lace of floral motifs connected with irregularly spaced bridges.

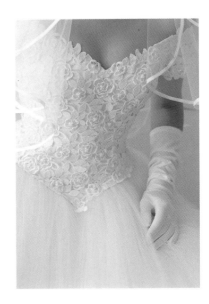

Sensual selections: **FAR LEFT,** *a luxurious golden brocade ball gown;* **CENTER,** *majestic guipure laces;* **ABOVE,** *a romantic lace and tulle ball gown.*

SOURCES

DESIGNERS

Ada Athanassiou
New York, NY
212-689-4771

Amsale
New York, NY
212-971-0170

Anneliese Sharp
London, England
71-584-6942

Atelier Rosalba
Milano, Italy
39-02-795064

Badgley Mischka
New York, NY
212-921-1585

Balenciaga
Paris, France
47-230-600
New York, NY
212-935-3399

Bob Mackie
New York, NY
212-391-8697

Candace Solomon
New York, NY
212-966-8678

Carmela Sutera
New York, NY
212-921-4808

Carolina Herrera
New York, NY
212-944-5757

Cashmere Cashmere
New York, NY
212-988-5252

Catherine Rayner
London, England
71-731-7506

Chanel
New York, NY
212-688-5055
Paris, France
42-617-539

Christian Dior
Paris, France
40-735-444

Christian Lacroix
Paris, France
42-657-908

Christine & Company
West Vancouver, BC
604-922-0350

Christos
New York, NY
212-921-0025

Cynthia Rowley
New York, NY
212-465-9020

David Fielden
London, England
71-351-0002

Diamond Collection
New York, NY
212-302-0201

Dionisi Laura
Milano, Italy
02-807-128

Dior
Willowgrove, PA
215-659-8700

Emanuel Ungaro
Paris, France
47-236-194

Endrius/Andrew Kova
New York, NY
212-838-5880

Eva Chun
New York, NY
212-398-1717

Eva Haynal Forsyth
New York, NY
212-302-7710

Flyte Ostell
London, England
71-284-2273

Galina
New York, NY
212-564-1020

Givenchy
New York, NY
212-772-1322
Paris, France
47-238-136

Guy Laroche
Paris, France
40-696-800

Hanae Mori
New York, NY
212-472-2352
Paris, France
47-427-878

Karl Lagerfeld
Paris, France
43-595-750

Laura Ashley
New York, NY
212-752-7300
London, England
800-866-100

Lori
Bergamo, Italy
35-799-441

Mary McFadden
New York, NY
212-736-4078

Milady
New York, NY
212-736-5696

Norma Kamali
New York, NY
212-957-9797

Norma LeNain
Los Angeles, CA
213-653-7354

North Beach Leather
New York, NY
212-772-0707

Oscar de la Renta
New York, NY
212-354-6777

Pat Kerr
Memphis, TN
901-525-5223

Phillipa Lepley
London, England
71-386-0927

Priscilla of Boston
Charlestown, MA
617-242-2677

Raffaella
Rome, Italy
6-679-0971

Richard Glasgow
New York, NY
212-683-1379

Ritva Westenius
London, England
71-581-3878

Riva Lorenzo
Milan, Italy
2-877-872

Ron LoVece
New York, NY
212-840-3172

Scaasi
New York, NY
212-302-7710

St. Pucci
Dallas, TX
214-631-8738

Sylvia Heisel
New York, NY
212-226-4916

Ulla-Maija
New York, NY
212-570-6085

Valentino
Rome, Italy
6-673-91

Van Lear
New York, NY
212-764-7500

Vera Wang
New York, NY
212-879-1700

Victor Edelstein
London, England
071-244-7481

Victoria Royal
New York, NY
212-944-6844

Yumi Katsura
New York, NY
212-398-9322

Yves Saint Laurent
Paris, France
47-237-271

PRIVATE DESIGNERS

Cathy Nixon
New York, NY
212-979-8699

Lee-Ann Belter
Toronto, ON
416-921-9569

Ondyn Herschelle
San Francisco, CA
415-982-0112

Suzanne Spellan
Brooklyn, NY
718-789-4476

Tricia Cochran
Toronto, ON
416-964-9220

VINTAGE SPECIALISTS

The following specialists collect and refit their own vintage wedding gowns. Those highlighted by an asterisk have retail shops.

Ann Lawrence
New York, NY
212-302-6100

Jean Hoffman*
New York, NY
212-535-6930

Opal White*
New York, NY
212-677-8215

BRIDAL SALONS

Alan Cherry Bridals
Toronto, ON
416-967-1115

Anne Barge for Brides
Atlanta, GA
404-237-0898

Bergdorf Goodman
New York, NY
212-753-7300

Boutique Cassar
Montreal, PQ
514-276-1081

Bridal & Formal
Cincinnati, OH
513-821-6622

The Bridal Gallery
Vancouver, BC
604-434-8715

The Bridal Salon
North Brunswick, NJ
908-940-1944

Bridals by Roma
Paramus, NJ
201-445-3377

The Bride
Newport Beach, CA
714-760-1800

Claire Dratch
Bethesda, MD
301-656-8000

Dayton's
Minneapolis, MN
612-375-2162

El Imperio Salon
Plaza Las Americas,
Puerto Rico
809-724-0221

Exclusives for the Bride
Chicago, IL
312-664-8870

Harrods
London, England
71-730-1234

Hudson's
Southfield, MI
313-442-6375

I. Magnin
San Diego, CA
619-297-2100
Phoenix, AZ
602-955-7200
Seattle, WA
206-682-6111

Jacobson's
Indianapolis, IN
315-574-0088

John Wanamaker
Philadelphia, PA
215-422-2000

Joy Cherry
Toronto, ON
416-489-7973

Kleinfeld
Brooklyn, NY
718-833-1100

L & J Boutique
Brampton, ON
416-459-9370

Lina's Boutique
Weston, ON
416-241-8087

Louise Blum
Houston, TX
713-622-5571

Margies
Oak Lawn, IL
708-966-7000

Marina Morrison
San Francisco, CA
415-781-7920

Marshall Field
Chicago, IL
312-781-3544

Maryann Maxwell
Houston, TX
713-529-3939

Neiman Marcus
St. Louis, MO
314-567-9811
Dallas, TX
214-741-6911

Once Upon a Time
Berkshire, England
62-871-799

One of a Kind Bride
New York, NY
212-966-8678

Priscilla of Boston
Boston, MA
617-242-2677

Saks Fifth Avenue
New York, NY
212-940-4405

Stanley Korshak
Dallas, TX
800-972-5959

Suky Rosan
Ardmore, PA
215-649-3686

Tatters
London, England
71-584-1532

Valencienne
Toronto, ON
416-962-8558

Vera Wang Bridal House
New York, NY
212-628-3400

The Wedding Centre
Bucks, England
62-847-8888

The Wedding Wardrobe
London, England
81-747-3636

Woodward & Lothrop
Washington, D.C.
202-347-7275

**RESTORATION
SPECIALISTS**

Debora Jackson
Brooklyn, NY
718-596-9143

Heirloom Labs
Preservation only
New Haven, CT
203-795-0565

Linens Limited
Milwaukee, WI
414-332-4434

Marguerite Morgan
Rutherford, NJ
201-939-7222

Museum Quality
Storage Box Company
and Preservation Service
Pleasantville, NY
800-937-2693

Sewtique
Groton, CT
203-445-7320

**BRIDAL
CONSULTANTS**

Association of Bridal
Consultants
New Milford, CT
203-355-0464

Connie Kerns
San Francisco, CA
510-339-3370

Marcy Blum
New York, NY
212-644-6687

ACCESSORIES
Items provided
by the following
manufacturers and
services are included
in this book. Retail
stores are highlighted
by an asterisk.

Angel Threads
Custom-made garters,
linens, chuppas
New York, NY
212-673-4592

B & J Fabrics*
Bridal fabrics and laces
New York, NY
212-354-8150

Bell'occhio*
Ribbons, antique
veiling, silk flowers,
cards
San Francisco, CA
415-864-4048

Blue Meadow
Flowers*
Floral design
New York, NY
212-979-8618

Carolina Amato
Decorated gloves
New York, NY
212-532-8413

Ciner
Costume jewelry
New York, NY
212-947-3770

Colette Malouf
Table accessories
New York, NY
212-941-9588

Cultured Pearl
Association of
America
New York, NY
212-688-5580

David Salvatore
Costume jewelry
New York, NY
516-548-8656

Dyeables
Shoes, handbags
to dye
Mount Kisco, NY
800-431-2000

Elizabeth Edema*
Bridal millinery,
accessories, jewelry
London, England
71-229-2564

Emma Hope*
Bridal shoes, mail
order available
London, England
71-833-2367

Fownes Brothers
Gloves
New York, NY
212-683-0150

Gaetano Fazio
Costume jewelry
New York, NY
212-477-3917

Gail Watson Custom
Cakes
New York, NY
212-982-3345

Hat Stop*
London, England
71-253-3643

Jean Hoffman/
Jana Starr Antiques
Antique, collectible
personal accessories
New York, NY
212-535-6930

Jezebel
Bridal lingerie
New York, NY
212-889-9255

Jimmy Choo*
Shoe salon
London, England
71-833-2367

Judith Leiber
Jeweled handbags
New York, NY
212-736-4244

Karl Lagerfeld Bijoux
Costume jewelry
New York, NY
212-725-0600

Kenneth Jay Lane*
Costume jewelry
New York, NY
212-751-6166

Kersen*
Ribbons, trimmings
London, England
71-580-4698

L. Becker Flowers*
New York, NY
212-439-6001

La Sposa Veils*
Custom bridal
millinery, accessories,
fabrics, and notions
New York, NY
212-354-4729

Leslie Kyle Ferrar
Floral design
Watsontown, PA
717-437-2446

Lisa Marinucci
Collection
Costume jewelry
Bala Cynwyd, PA
215-878-8555

Lola's Millinery*
Custom millinery
New York, NY
212-366-5708

Lord West
Formalwear
Woodside, NY
718-204-6640

M & J Trimming*
Ribbons, cording,
bridal millinery
New York, NY
212-391-9072

Maison Moderne*
Collectible
accessories, custom
work available.
New York, NY
212-691-9603

Midori
Organza ribbons
Seattle, WA
206-547-9553

Miho Kofuda*
Florist
New York, NY
212-922-9122

Mish
Precious jewelry
designer
New York, NY
212-575-0700

Only Hearts
Lingerie
New York, NY
212-689-7808

Paloma Picasso
Designer of handbags,
personal accessories
New York, NY
212-421-2260

Patricia Underwood
Designer of millinery
New York, NY
212-368-3774

Peter Fox*
Bridal shoe salon
New York, NY
212-431-7426
Vancouver, BC
604-662-3040
Santa Monica, CA
213-393-9669

Roxanne Assoulin
Costume jewelry
New York, NY
212-869-5090

Shalimar
Leather gloves
New York, NY
212-685-8087

Shaneen Huxham
Designer of decorated
gloves, represented by
wholesale distributor
Metropolitan Design
Group
New York, NY
212-944-6110

Silk
Bridal millinery
and veils
Berkshire, England
75-355-0300

Stuart Weitzman
Bridal shoes
New York, NY
212-582-9500

Susan Bennis/
Warren Edwards*
Shoe salon
New York, NY
212-755-4197

Tom Thomas
Gift specialist
New York, NY
212-627-9046

Valorie Hart
Floral design
New York, NY
212-967-0695

Vanessa Noel*
Bridal shoe salon
New York, NY
212-737-0115

**WEDDING
PHOTOGRAPHERS**
Photographers
represented in
this book:

Denis Reggie
Atlanta, GA
404-237-6440

John Dolan
New York, NY
212-777-1309

Robert Friedel
New York, NY
212-477-3452

Susan Bloch
Atlanta, GA
404-873-5670

Terry Gruber
New York, NY
212-749-2840

LOCATIONS
Locations featured in
this book:

The Pierre Hotel
New York, NY
212-838-8000

The Plaza Hotel
New York, NY
212-546-5485

Nick & Eddie
New York, NY
212-219-9090

INDEX

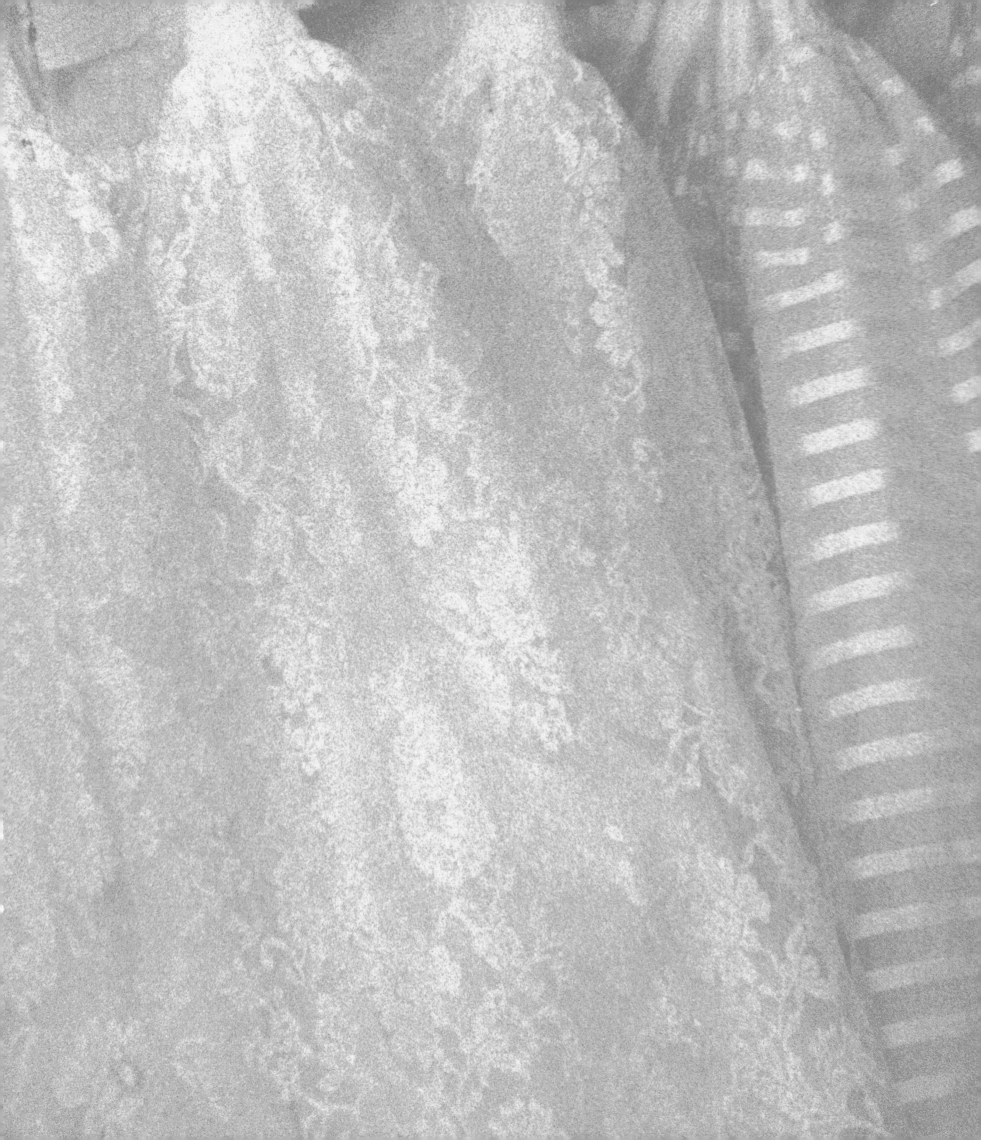